James Cook

A Collection of Voyages Round the World

Performed by royal authrity. Containing a complete historical account of Captain Cook's first, second, third and last voyages. Vol. 6

James Cook

A Collection of Voyages Round the World
Performed by royal authrity. Containing a complete historical account of Captain Cook's first, second, third and last voyages. Vol. 6

ISBN/EAN: 9783337192235

Printed in Europe, USA, Canada, Australia, Japan

Cover: Foto ©Andreas Hilbeck / pixelio.de

More available books at **www.hansebooks.com**

COOK's

Third and Last

VOYAGE to the Pacific Ocean.

CHAP. XIV.

WE had not long been settled at the observatory, before we discovered the habitations of a society of priests, who had excited our curiosity by their regular attendance at the morai. Their huts were erected round a pond, inclosed with a group of cocoa-nut trees, by which they were separated from the beach and the village, and gave the situation an air of religious retirement. Captain Cook being made acquainted with this discovery, he resolved to visit them; and, expecting the manner of his reception would be singular, he took Mr. Webber with him, to enable him to represent the ceremony in a drawing. When arrived at the beach, the commodore was conducted to Harreno-Orono, or the house of Orono. On his approaching this sacred place, he was seated at the foot of a wooden idol, resembling that we had seen at the morai. Here Mr. King again supported one of his arms. He was then arrayed in red cloth, and Kaireekeea, assisted by 12 priests, presented a pig with the usual ceremonies. After this solemnity, the pig was strangled, and thrown into the embers of a fire, prepared for that purpose. When the hair was singed off, a second offering was made, and the chanting repeated as before: after which the dead pig was held some time under Captain Cook's nose, and then laid with a cocoa-nut at his feet. This part of the ceremony being concluded, the performers sat down; and the ava was brewed and handed about; a baked hog was likewise brought in, and we were fed in the same manner as before related on a similar occasion. While we continued in the Bay, whenever the commodore visited the observatory, Kaireekeea and his assistants presented themselves before him, making an offering of hogs, bread-fruit, cocoa-nuts, &c. with the accustomed solemnities. Upon these occasions, some of the inferior chiefs intreated permission to make an offering to the Orono. If their request was complied with, they presented the hog themselves; in the performance of which, their countenance displayed that they were greatly impressed with awe and terror. Kaireekeea and the priests assisted, performing their accustomed orations and hymns. But their civilities extended beyond parade and ceremony: our party on shore were supplied daily by them with hogs and vegetables, sufficient for their subsistence, and to spare; and canoes laden with provisions, were regularly sent off to the ships. Nothing was demanded in return; not even the most distant hint was ever given, that they expected the least compensation. Their manner of conferring favours, appeared more like the discharge of a religious duty, than the result of mere liberality. On our asking to whom we were indebted for all this munificence, we were informed that it was at the expence of Kaoo, the chief priest, and grandfather to Kaireekeea, who was at this time in the suit of the sovereign of the island. But we had less reason to be satisfied with the behaviour of the earees, or warrior chiefs, than with that of the priests. In our intercourse with the former, they were always sufficiently attentive to their own interests; and, besides their propensity to stealing, which may admit of palliation from its universality in these seas,

they

they had other artifices equally dishonourable. The following is one instance, in which we discovered, with regret, that our good friend Koah was a party principally concerned. The chiefs who made us presents of hogs, were always generously rewarded; in consequence of which, we were supplied with more than we could consume. On these occasions, Koah, who attended us constantly, petitioned usually for those that we did not absolutely want, and they were given him of course. A pig was one day presented to us by a man, whom Koah introduced as a chief. The pig we knew to be one of those that had a short time before been given to Koah. Suspecting an imposition, we found upon enquiry, that the pretended chief was one of the common people; and from other concurrent circumstances, we were perfectly convinced, that this was not the first time of our having been made the dupes of Koah's low cunning.

Sunday, the 24th, we were not a little surprized to find, that not any canoes were permitted to put off, and that the natives were confined to their houses. At length we were informed, that the bay was tabooed, and that intercourse with us was interdicted, on account of the arrival of Terreeoboo, their king. On the 25th, we endeavoured by threats and promises, to induce the inhabitants to revisit the ships. Some of them were venturing to put off, when we perceived a chief very active in driving them away: to make him desist, a musquet was fired over his head, which produced the desired effect; for refreshments were soon after to be had as usual. In the afternoon, the ships were privately visited by Terreeoboo, attended only by one canoe, containing his wife and family. When he entered the ship, he fell on his face, as a mark of submission to the commodore, as did all his attendants; and after having made an oration, which none of us understood, he presented the captain with three

barbicued

barbicued hogs, who, in return, put a necklace, composed of several strings of various coloured beads, round his neck, and gave him two looking-glasses, a large glass bowl, with some nails, and other trifles, which he received with much seeming satisfaction, and dispatched immediately a messenger on shore, who soon returned with several large hogs, cocoa-nuts, plantains, and sugar-canes, as much as our small cutter could carry. Having remained on deck about an hour, admiring the construction of the ship, he was conducted into the great cabin, where wine was offered him, which he refused: neither was there any thing he would taste, except a head of bread-fruit; but he appeared delighted with every thing he saw; and before he departed in the evening, gave us to understand that he had 6000 fighting men, always in readiness to war against his enemies. On the 26th, at noon, the king came in great state from the village of Kowrowa, and, in a large canoe, with some of his attendants in two others, paddled slowly towards the ships. Their appearance was really most superb. Terreeoboo, and his chiefs were in the first vessel, arrayed in feathered cloaks, and helmets, and armed with spears and daggers. In the second came Kaoo, the chief priest, having their idols displayed on red cloth. They were figures of an enormous size, made of thick wicker-work, and curiously ornamented with mantles of feathers of various colours. Their eyes were large pearl oysters, with a black nut placed in the middle. A double row of the fangs of dogs was fixed in each of their mouths, which, as well as the rest of their features, appeared strangely distorted. The third canoe was laden with hogs and vegetables. Their images they call E-ah-tu-a, signifying their warrior gods, without which they never engage in battle. As they advanced, the priests chanted their hymns with great solemnity. After paddling round the vessels, they

did

TERREOBOO, KING of OWHYHEE, bringing PRESENTS to CAPT.ⁿ COOK.

did not come on board as we expected, but made immediately towards the shore, at the beach where our tents were fixed. When landed, they hauled up all their canoes on the beach, drew up in martial order, and, led by the king, marched in ranks to their place of worship, distant from our tents about 50 yards; but, seeing the ground tabooed by small green boughs and wands, that marked the boundary, they all made a circuit with their images in procession, till they arrived at their morai, where they placed their idols, and deposited their arms. Captain Cook, when he saw the king's intention of going on shore, went thither also, and landed with Mr. King and others, almost at the same instant. We ushered the chiefs into our tent, and the king had hardly been seated, when he rose up, and threw gracefully over the captain's shoulders the rich feathered cloak that he himself wore, placed a helmet on his head, and presented him with a curious fan. Five or six other cloaks, of great beauty and value, were spread at the commodore's feet. Four hogs were now brought forward by the king's attendants, together with bread-fruit, &c. Then followed the ceremony of Terrecoboo's changing names with Captain Cook; the strongest pledge of friendship among all the islanders of the Pacific Ocean. A solemn procession now advanced, consisting of priests, preceded by a venerable old personage, followed by a train of people leading large hogs; others being laden with potatoes, plantains, &c. We could perceive easily, by the countenance and the gestures of Kaireekeea, that the old man who headed the procession, was the chief priest, on whose bounty we were told we had so long subsisted. He wrapped a piece of red cloth round the shoulders of Captain Cook, and in the usual form, presented him with a pig. He was then seated next the king, and Kaireekeea and their attendants began their vocal ceremonies, Kaeo and the chiefs assisting in the

the responses. In the person of this king, we were surprized to recognize the same emaciated old man, who came on board the Resolution, from the N. E. side of the island of Mowee; and we perceived that several of his attendants were the same persons, who at that time continued with us the whole night. Among these were the king's two youngest sons, the elder about the age of sixteen; and Maiha-Maiha, his nephew, whom we could not immediately recollect, having had his hair plastered over with a dirty paste and powder, which was no small improvement to the most savage countenance we had ever seen. The formalities of this meeting being ended, Captain Cook conducted Terreeoboo and several of his chiefs on board our ship, where they were received with every possible mark of attention and respect; and the commodore, as a compensation for the feathered cloak, put a linen shirt upon the sovereign, and girt his own hanger round him. Kaoo, and about half a dozen other ancient chiefs, remained on shore. All this time not a canoe was permitted to remain in the Bay, and those natives who did not confine themselves to their huts, lay prostrate on the ground. Before the king quitted the Resolution, he granted leave for the natives to trade with us as usual; but the women, we know not on what account, were still interdicted by the taboo; that is, to remain at home, and not have any kind of intercourse with us. At this time the behaviour of the inhabitants was so civil and inoffensive, that all apprehensions of danger were totally vanished. We trusted ourselves among them at all times, and upon all occasions, without the least reserve. Our officers ventured frequently up the country, either singly, or in small parties, and sometimes continued out the whole night. In all places the people flocked about us, anxious to afford every assistance in their power, and appeared highly gratified if we condescended to accept of

their

their services. Variety of innocent arts were practised to attract our notice, or to delay our departure. The boys and girls ran through their villages, stopping us at every opening where there was a convenient spot for dancing. At one time we were solicited to take a draught of milk from cocoanuts, or to accept of such other refreshment as their huts afforded; at another we were encircled by a company of young women, who exerted their skill and ingenuity in amusing us with songs and dances: but though the instances of their generosity and civility were pleasing to us, we could not but dislike that propensity to thieving, which at times they discovered, and to which they were addicted, like all the other islanders in these seas: this was a perplexing circumstance, and obliged us sometimes to exercise a severity, which we should have been happy to have avoided, if it had not been essentially necessary. Some expert swimmers were one day detected under the ships, drawing out the filling nails from the sheathing. This they performed very ingeniously with a flint stone, fastened to the end of a stick. This new art of stealing was a practice so injurious to our vessels, that we fired small shot at the offenders; but that they avoided easily, by diving under the ships bottoms: it therefore became highly necessary to make an example of one of them, which was done by giving him a good flogging on board our consort, the Discovery, where his talent for thieving had been chiefly exercised. About this time, Mr. Nelson, and four other gentlemen, set out on an excursion into the country, in order to examine its natural curiosities and productions, an account of which will be given hereafter. This afforded Kaoo a fresh opportunity of testifying his civility, and exerting his friendly disposition in our favour: for no sooner was he informed of the departure of our party, than he sent after them a large quantity of provisions, with orders that every attention and assistance should be granted them by the inhabitants of those districts through which they should pass. His civility on this occasion was so delicate and disinterested, that even the people he employed were not permitted to accept of the smallest present. At the end of six days the gentlemen returned, without having been able to penetrate farther than twenty miles into the island, owing partly to improper guides, and partly to the nature of the country, which occasioned this expedition to be attended with no small fatigue, and some danger. Mr. Nelson, however, collected a curious assortment of indigenous plants, and some natural curiosities. During their absence, every thing remained quiet at the tents, and the natives supplied the ships with such quantities of provisions, of all kinds, that orders were again given to purchase no more hogs in one day, than could be killed, salted, and stowed away the next day. This order was in consequence of a former one, to purchase all that could be procured for sea stock, by which so many of them were brought on board, that several of them died before they could be properly disposed of.

On Wednesday, the 27th, in the morning, the rudder of our ship was unhung, and sent on shore, in order to undergo a thorough repair. The carpenters at the same time were sent into the country, under the protection and guidance of some of Kaoo's people, to get planks for the head rail work, which was become rotten and decayed. In a visit, on the 28th, from Terreeoboo to Captain Clerke, the latter received a present of 30 large hogs, and such a quantity of vegetables as could not be consumed by his crew in less than a week. This being an unexpected visit, made it the more extraordinary. Not having seen any of the sports or exercises of the natives, at our particular request, they entertained us in the evening with a boxing match. A

vast

vast concourse of people assembled on a level spot of ground, not far distant from our tents. In the centre, a long vacant space was left for them, at the upper end of which the arbitrators presided, under three standards. Slips of cloth of various colours, were pendant from these standards; as were the skins of two wild geese, some small birds, and a few bunches of feathers. The sports being ready to begin, the judges gave the signal, and two combatants appeared in view. They advanced slowly, drawing up their feet very high behind, and rubbing their hands upon the soles. As they came forward, they surveyed each other frequently from head to foot, with an air of contempt, looking archly at the spectators, distorting their features, and practising a variety of unnatural gestures. When they were advanced within the reach of each other, they held both arms straight out before their faces, at which part they always aimed their blows. They struck with a full swing of the arm, which to us had a very awkard appearance. They did not attempt to parry; but endeavoured to elude their adversary's attack, by stooping, or retreating. The battle was decided expeditiously; for if either of them fell, whether by accident, or from a blow, he was deemed vanquished; and the victor expressed his triumph by a variety of strange gestures, which usually excited a loud laugh among the spectators, for which purpose it seemed to be calculated. The successful combatant waited for a second antagonist; and, if again victorious, for a third; and so on, till at last he was defeated. In these combats it was very singular, that, when any two are preparing to attack each other, a third may advance, and make choice of either of them for his antagonist, when the other is under the necessity of withdrawing. If the combat proved long and tedious, or appeared unequal, a chief generally interfered, and concluded it by

putting

putting a stick between the combatants. As this exhibition was at our desire, it was universally expected, that some of us would have engaged with the natives; but, though our people received pressing invitations to bear a part, they did not hearken to the challenges, not having forgot the blows they received at the Friendly Islands.

This day died William Watman, a mariner of the gunner's crew. This event we mention particularly, seeing death had hitherto been uncommon among us. He was a man in years, and much respected by Captain Cook. He had served twenty-one years as a marine, and then entered as a seamen in 1772, on board the Resolution, and served with the commodore in his voyage towards the South Pole. On their return he got admittance into Greenwich Hospital, at the same time with himself; and anxious to follow the fortunes of his benefactor, he also quitted it with him, on the commodore's appointment to the command of the present expedition. Watman had often been subject to slight fevers, in the course of the voyage, and was very infirm when we arrived in the bay; where, having been sent a few days on shore, he thought himself perfectly restored, and requested to return on board. His request was complied with. The day following he had a stroke of the palsy, which in two days afterwards put an end to his life. At the request of Terreeoboo, the remains of this faithful seaman were buried in the morai; the ceremony being performed with great solemnity. Kaoo and his brethren were present at the funeral, who behaved with great decorum, and paid due attention while the service was performing. On our beginning to fill up the grave, they approached it with great awe, and threw in a dead pig, together with some cocoanuts and plantains. For three successive nights they surrounded it, sacrificing hogs, and reciting prayers and hymns till morning. At the head of the grave, we erected a post, and nailed thereto a piece of board, whereon was inscribed the name and age of the deceased, and the day of his departure from this life. These memorials we were assured they would not remove, and, it is probable, they will be permitted to remain, so long as such frail materials can endure.

Being much in want of fuel, Captain Cook desired Mr. King to treat with the priests, for the purchase of the railing belonging to the morai. Mr. King had his doubts respecting the decency of this overture, and apprehended the proposal might be deemed impious; but in this he was much mistaken: for an application being made for the same, they expressed no kind of surprize, and the wood was delivered without the least stipulation. While our people were taking it away, Mr. King saw one of them with a carved image; and, upon enquiry, he was informed, that the whole semicircle (as mentioned in the description of the morai) had been carried to the boats. Though the natives were spectators of this business, they did not seem to resent it; but on the contrary, had even assisted in the removal. Mr. King thought proper to mention the particulars to Kaoo; who seemed exceedingly indifferent about the matter, begging him only to restore the center image; which was immediately done, and it was conveyed to one of the priests houses.

For some time, the king, and his chiefs, had been very importunate to know the time of our departure. From this circumstance, Mr. King's curiosity was excited to know the opinion these people had entertained of us, and what they supposed to be the object of our voyage. He took considerable pains to satisfy himself respecting these points; but the only information he could get was, that they supposed we had left our native country on account of the scantiness of provisions, and that we had visited them

them for the sole purpose of filling our bellies. This conclusion was natural enough, considering the meagre appearance of some of our crew; the voracity with which we devoured their fresh provisions; and our anxiety to purchase as much of it as we were able. It was a matter of entertainment to see the natives patting the bellies of the sailors (who were much improved in sleekness since their arrival at the bay) and telling them, in the best manner they could, that it was time for them to depart; but if they would return the next bread-fruit season, they should be better able to supply them. We had now continued sixteen days in the bay, during which time our consumption of hogs and vegetables, had been so enormous, that we need not be surprized at their wishing to see us take our leave. But Terreeoboo had, perhaps, no other view, in his enquiries, than a desire of having sufficient notice, to prepare suitable presents for us at our departure; for when we informed him of our intention to quit the island in two days, a kind of proclamation was made, requiring the natives to bring in their hogs, and vegetables, for Terreeoboo to present to the Orono.

We were this day much entertained, at the beach, with the buffooneries of one of the natives. He held in his hand an instrument of music, such as we have already described: bits of sea-weed were fastened round his neck; and, round each leg, some strong netting; whereon were fixed rows of dogs teeth, hanging loose. His dancing was accompanied with strange grimaces, and unnatural distortions of the features, which were sometimes highly ridiculous, and, upon the whole, without meaning or expression. But the wrestling and boxing matches afforded us good diversion for the evening; and, in return, we exhibited the few fire-works we had remaining. Nothing could more effectually excite the admiration of these islanders, or strike
them

them with more exalted ideas of our superiority, than such a representation: notwithstanding this was, in every respect, much inferior to that exhibited at Hapaee, yet the astonishment of these people was equally great.

The carpenters who had been sent up the country to cut planks for the head rail-work of our ship, the Resolution, had now been gone three days, and, not having heard from them, we began to be alarmed for their safety. We expressed our apprehensions to Kaoo, who appeared equally concerned with ourselves; but while we were planning measures with him, for sending proper persons after them, they all safely arrived. Our people had gone farther into the country than they expected, before they found any trees suitable for their purpose. This circumstance, together with the badness of the roads, and the difficulty of conveying timber to the ships, had so long detained them. They bestowed high commendations on their guides, who not only supplied them with provisions, but faithfully protected their tools. Having fixed on Thursday, the 4th of February, for our departure, Terreeoboo invited Captain Cook, and Mr. King, to attend him on the 3d, to Kaoo's residence. On our arrival there, we saw large quantities of cloth scattered on the ground; abundance of red and yellow feathers, fastened to the fibres of cocoa-nut husks; and plenty of hatchets and iron ware, which had been received from us in barter. Not far from these was deposited an immense quantity of various kinds of vegetables; and at a little distance, a large herd of hogs. We supposed, at first, that the whole was intended as a present for us; but we were informed by Kaireekeea, that it was a tribute to the king, from the inhabitants of that district. We were no sooner seated than the bundles were brought, and laid severally at Terreeoboo's feet; and the cloth, feathers, and iron, were displayed before him. The king

king was perfectly fatisfied with this mark of duty from his people; and having felected about one third of the iron utenfils, one third of the feathers, and fome pieces of cloth, he ordered thefe to be fet afide by themfelves; and the remainder of the cloth, hogs, vegetables, &c. were afterwards prefented to Captain Cook and Mr. King. The value and magnitude of this prefent, far exceeded any thing that we had before received. The whole was immediately conveyed on board; and the large hogs were fet apart for fea ftores; but the fmaller pigs and vegetables, were divided between the crews. The fame day we quitted the morai, and got our obfervatories on board. The taboo was removed, and, with it vanifhed its magical effects; for as foon as we had quitted the place, the people rufhed in, and vigilantly fearched, in hopes of finding fome valuable articles left behind. Mr. King being the laft on fhore, and waiting for the return of the boat, the inhabitants crowded about him, and having prevailed upon him to fit down among them, expreffed their regret at our feparation. It was even with difficulty that they would fuffer him to depart. Having had, while we lay in the bay, the command of the party on fhore, he became more acquainted with the natives, than thofe who were required to be on board. From the inhabitants in general, he experienced great kindnefs; but the friendfhip fhewn by the priefts was conftant and unbounded. On the other hand, Mr. King was anxious to conciliate their efteem; in which he fo happily fucceeded, that when they were made acquainted with the time of our departure, he was urged to remain behind, and received overtures of the moft flattering kind. When he endeavoured to excufe himfelf, by alledging, that the commodore would not permit it, they propofed to conduct him to the mountains, and there conceal him till the departure of the fhips. On Mr. King's

affuring

assuring them that the ships would not sail without him, the King and Kaoo repaired to Captain Cook, (whom they supposed to be his father) requesting formally, that he might be suffered to remain behind. The commodore, unwilling to give a positive refusal, to a proposal so generously intended, assured them, that he could not part with him at present, but he should return thither the next year, when he would endeavour to oblige them.

On Thursday the 4th of February, early in the morning, having unmoored, the Resolution and Discovery set sail, and cleared the harbour, attended by a vast number of canoes. We proposed to shape our course for Mowee; as we had been informed, that in the island there was a fine harbour, and excellent water, but Captain Cook intended to finish first the survey of Owhyhee, before he went thither, hoping to meet with a road more sheltered than Karakakooa Bay. We had not been long under sail, when the king, who had omitted to take his leave of Captain Clerke, as not expecting our departure to be so sudden, came after the ships, accompanied by the young prince, in a sailing canoe, bringing with them ten large hogs, a great number of fowls, and a small turtle (a great rarity) with bread-fruit in abundance. They also brought with them great quantities of cocoa-nuts, plantains, and sugar-canes. Besides other persons of distinction, who accompanied the king, there was an old priest, who had always shewn a particular attachment to Captain Clerke, and who had not been unrewarded for his civility. It being rather late when they reached the Discovery, they staid on board but a few hours, and then all departed, except the old priest, and some girls, who had the King's permission to remain on board, till they should arrive at some of the neighbouring isles. We were now steering with a fine breeze, but just at the close of the evening, to our great mortification, the wind died away, and a great a great swell succeeding, with a strong current setting right in for shore, we were in the utmost danger, particularly the Discovery, of being driven upon the rocks. At this time the old priest, who had been sent to sleep in the great cabin, leaped over-board unseen with a large piece of Russian silk, Captain Clerke's property, and swam to shore.

On Friday the 5th, we had calm weather, and made but little way. Seeing a large canoe between us and the shore, we hove to for her coming up, and to our great surprize perceived the old king, with several of his chiefs, having with them the priest who had stolen the silk, bound hand and foot, whom the king delivered to Captain Clerke, at the same time requesting that his fault might be forgiven. The king being told his request was granted, unbound him, and set him at liberty; telling the captain that, seeing him with the silk, he judged it was not his own, therefore ordered him to be apprehended; and had taken this method of exposing him, for having injured his friend. This was a singular instance of justice, which we did not expect to see among these people. As soon as they had delivered the silk, which the king refused to accept, they departed. Having a light breeze in the night, we made a little progress to the northward.

On Saturday the 6th, in the morning, we were abreast of a deep bay, called by the natives Toeyah-yah. We flattered ourselves with finding a commodious harbour here; for we saw some fine streams of water to the N. E. and the whole appeared to be well sheltered. These observations seeming to tally with the accounts given by Koah, who was now on board the Resolution, the master was sent in the pinnace, with Koah as his guide, to examine the bay; but, before they set off, Koah altered his name, out of compliment to us, to that of Britannee. In the afternoon, the weather became gloomy, and such violent gusts of wind blew off the land, that we were obliged to take in all the fails, and bring to, under the mizen-ftay-fail. Soon after the gale began, all the canoes left us; and Mr. Bligh, on his return, preferved an old woman and two men from drowning, whofe canoe had been overfet in the ftorm. We had feveral women remaining on board, whom the natives, in their hurry to depart, had left to fhift for themfelves. Mr. Bligh reported, that he had landed at a village on the north fide of the bay, where he was fhewn fome wells of water, that would not, by any means, anfwer our purpofe; that he proceeded farther into the bay; where, inftead of finding good anchorage, he obferved the fhores to be low, and a flat bed of coral rocks extended along the coaft, and upwards of a mile from the land; the depth of water, on the outfide, being twenty fathoms. During this furvey Britannee had contrived to flip away. His information having proved erroneous, he might, perhaps, be afraid of returning. In the evening the weather became more moderate, when we again made fail; but it blew fo violently about midnight, as to fplit the fore and main-top fails.

On Sunday the 7th, in the morning, we bent frefh fails. Being now about four or five leagues from the fhore, and the weather very unfettled, the canoes would not venture off, fo that our female guefts were under the neceffity of remaining with us, though, at this time, much againft their inclination; for they were all exceedingly fea fick, and many of them had left their infants on fhore. The weather continued fqually, yet we ftood in for land, in the afternoon; and being within three leagues of it, we faw two men paddling towards us. We conjectured, that they had been driven off the fhore, by the late boifterous weather; and therefore ftopped the fhip's way, in order to take them in. Thefe poor wretches were fo exhaufted by fatigue, that had not one of the natives on board jumped

jumped into the canoe to their affiftance, they would hardly have been able to fix it to the rope thrown out for that purpofe. It was with great difficulty that we got them up the fhip's fide, together with a child about four years of age, which had been lafhed under the thwarts of the canoe, with only its head above the water. They had left the fhore the morning before, and had been, from that time, without food or water. The ufual precautions were taken in giving them victuals, and the child being committed to the care of the women, they were all perfectly recovered by the next morning. At midnight a gale of wind coming on, we were obliged to double reef the top-fails, and get down the top-gallant yards.

On Monday the 8th, at day-break, we found that the fore-maft had again given way; the fifhes being fprung, and the parts fo very defective, as to make it abfolutely neceffary to unftep the maft. Captain Cook for fome time hefitated, whether he fhould return to Karakakooa, or take the chance of finding a harbour in the iflands to the leeward. The bay was not fo commodious, but that a better might probably be met with, either for repairing the mafts, or procuring **refreshments**; the latter of which, it was imagined, the neighbourhood of Karakakooa had lately been pretty well drained of. It was, on the other hand, confidered, as an imprudent ftep, to leave a tolerable good harbour, which, once loft, could not be regained, for the mere poffibility of meeting with a better; efpecially, as the failure of fuch a contingency, might have deprived us of any refource. We now ftood on towards the land, to give the natives on fhore an opportunity of releafing their friends on board; and, about noon, when we were within a mile of the fhore, feveral canoes came off to us, but fo loaded with people, that no room could be found for any of our guefts; the pinnace was therefore hoifted out to land them;

and

and the master who commanded it, was instructed to examine the south coasts of the bay for water, but returned without success. Variable winds, and a strong current to the northward, retarded their return.

On Tuesday the 9th, at eight o'clock, A. M. it blew very hard from the S. E. which occasioned us to close reef the top-sails.

On Wednesday the 10th, at two o'clock, A. M. in a heavy squall, we found ourselves close in with the breakers, to the northward of the west point of Owhyhee. We had just room to avoid them, and fired several guns to alarm the Discovery, and apprize her of danger. In the forenoon, the weather had been more moderate. A few canoes ventured to come off to us, when we were informed by those belonging to them, that much mischief had been occasioned by the late storms, and that a great many canoes had been lost. We kept beating to windward the remainder of the day; and, in the evening, were within a mile of Karakakooa Bay; but we stood off and on till day-light, the next morning, when we cast anchor in our old station.

On Thursday the 11th, and part of the 12th, all hands were employed in getting out the fore-mast, and conveying it on shore. Besides the damage which the head of the mast had sustained, the heel of it was found by the carpenters, exceeding rotten, having a large hole in the middle. As the necessary repairs were likely to take up several days, Mr. Bayly and Mr. King got the astronomical apparatus on shore, and pitched their tents on the morai, guarded by a corporal and six marines. A friendly intercourse was renewed with the priests, who, for our greater security, tabooed the place with their wands as before. The sail-makers were sent on shore to repair the damages, in their department, sustained by the late heavy gales. They occupied a house adjoining to the morai, that was lent us

by

by the priests. Such were the arrangements on shore. But on coming to anchor in the bay, our reception was so very different from what it had been upon our first arrival, that we were all astonished: no shouts were heard, no bustle or confusion, by the motions of the natives, were perceived; but we found ourselves in a solitary, deserted bay, with hardly a friend appearing, or a canoe stirring. Their curiosity, indeed, might be supposed to be diminished by this time; but the hospitable treatment we had been continually favoured with, and the friendly manner in which we parted, induced us to expect that, on our return, they would have received us with the greatest demonstrations of joy. Various were our conjectures on the cause of this extraordinary appearance, when our anxiety was in part relieved by the return of our boat, the crew of which brought us intelligence, that Terreeoboo was absent, and that the bay was tabooed. This account appeared very satisfactory to many of our company; but some were of opinion, that there was, at this time, somewhat very suspicious in the behaviour of the natives; and that the taboo, or interdiction, on pretence of the king's absence, was contrived artfully, to afford him time to consult his chiefs in what manner we should be treated. Whether those suspicions were well founded, or the account given by the natives was the truth, we were never able to ascertain. For though it is not improbable, that our sudden return, for which they could see no apparent cause, and the necessity of which we afterwards found it very difficult to make them comprehend, might occasion some alarm; yet the unsuspicious conduct of Terreeoboo, who, on his supposed arrival, the next morning, came immediately to visit Captain Cook, and the consequent return of the natives to their former friendly intercourse with us, are strong proofs that they neither meant, nor apprehended,

any

any change of conduct. In support of this opinion, we may add the account of another accident, precisely of the same kind which happened to us, on our first visit, the day before the king's arrival. A native having sold a hog on board our ship, and received the price agreed on, Pareea, who saw the transaction, advised the seller not to part with his hog, without an advanced price. For his interference in this business, he was harshly spoken to, and pushed away; and as the taboo was soon laid on the bay, we, at first, supposed it to be the consequence of the affront offered to the chief. Both these events serve to shew how extremely difficult it is to draw any certain conclusion from the conduct of a people, with whose language and customs we were so imperfectly acquainted. Some idea, however, may be formed of the difficulties those have to encounter, who in their intercourse with these strangers, are obliged to steer their course in the midst of uncertainties, when the most serious consequences may be expected by only imaginary offences. However true or false our conjectures may be, it is certain this day, the 12th, things went on in their usual quiet course.

On Saturday the 13th, at the approach of evening, the officer who commanded the watering party of the Discovery, came to inform Mr. King, that several chiefs were assembled near the beach, and were driving away the natives, who assisted the sailors in rolling the casks to the shore; declaring, at the same time, that their behaviour seemed to be very suspicious, and he imagined they would give him some farther disturbance. Mr. King, agreeable to his request, sent a marine with him, but permitted him to take only his side arms. The officer, in a short time, returned, and informed Mr. King, that the inhabitants had armed themselves with stones, and were become very tumultuous. Mr. King therefore went himself to the watering place, attended by a

marine

marine with his musquet. Seeing them approach, the islanders threw away their stones, and, on Mr. King's application to some of the chiefs, the mob was dispersed. Every thing being now quiet, Mr. King went to meet Captain Cook, who was coming on shore in the pinnace. He related to the commodore all that had recently happened, and received orders to fire ball at the offenders, should they again behave insolently, and in case of their beginning to throw stones. In consequence of these orders Mr. King commanded the corporal to give directions, that the sentinels pieces should be loaded with ball, instead of shot. On our return to the tents, we heard a continued fire of the musquets from the Discovery, which we observed to be directed at a canoe, that we saw paddling towards the shore, in great haste, and pursued by one of our small boats. We immediately concluded, that the firing was in consequence of some theft, and Captain Cook ordered Mr. King to follow him with a marine armed, and to endeavour to seize the people as they came on shore. Accordingly, we ran towards the place where we imagined the canoe would land, but were too late; the people having quitted it, and made their escape into the country before our arrival. We were at this time ignorant, that the goods had been already restored; and thinking it probable, from the circumstances we had at first observed, that they might be of importance, for this reason, we were unwilling to relinquish our hopes of recovering them. Having therefore enquired of the natives which way the fugitves had gone, we followed them, till it was near dark, when judging ourselves to be three miles from the tents, and suspecting that the natives, who frequently encouraged us in the pursuit, were amusing us with false information, we thought it in vain to continue our search any longer, and therefore returned to the beach. During our absence a difference of a

more

more serious nature had happened. The officer who had been dispatched in the small boat after the thieves, and who was returning on board with the goods that had been restored, seeing Captain Cook and Mr. King engaged in the pursuit of the offenders, seized a canoe which was drawn upon the shore. This canoe belonged to Pareea, our friend, who at that instant, arriving from on board the Discovery, claimed his property, and protested his innocence. However, the officer persisted in detaining it, in which he was encouraged by the crew of the pinnace, then waiting for the commodore. The consequence of this imprudent conduct was, what might have been expected: a scuffle ensued; and Pareea unfortunately was knocked down, by a violent blow on the head with an oar. Several of the natives, who had hitherto been unconcerned spectators, began now to attack our people with such a shower of stones, that they were compelled to make a precipitate retreat, and swam off to a rock, at a considerable distance from the shore. The pinace was plundered immediately by the natives, and would have been entirely demolished, had not Pareea interposed, who had not only recovered from his blow, but had also forgot it at the same instant. He ordered the crowd to disperse, and beckoned to our people to come and take possession of the pinnace; and afterwards assured them, that he would use his influence to get the things restored which had been taken out of it. After their departure, he followed them in his canoe, carrying them a midshipman's cap, and some other articles; and expressing much concern at what had happened, begged to know, if the Orono would kill him? And, whether he might be permitted to go on board the next day? He was assured that he would be well received; upon which he joined noses with the officers (their usual token of amity) and paddled over to Kowrowa. When these particulars were related to Captain Cook, he was exceedingly concerned; and when the captain and Mr. King were returning on board, the former expressed his fears, that these islanders would oblige him, though much against his inclination, to use violent measures with them; adding, they must not be permitted to suppose that they had gained an advantage over us. It was too late to take any steps this evening, the commodore therefore only gave orders, that every native should be immediately turned out of the ships. This order having been executed, Mr. King returned to his station on shore; and the events of the day having much abated our former confidence in the natives, we posted a double guard on the morai, with orders to send to Mr. King and let him know, if any of the natives were seen lurking about the beach. At 11 o'clock, five of the natives were seen creeping round the bottom of the morai: they approached silently with great caution, but, perceiving they were discovered, immediately retired out of sight. At midnight, one of them ventured very near the observatory, when one of the sentinels fired over him; whereupon he, with some others, fled with great precipitation, and we had no farther molestation during the remainder of the night. The temper of these islanders was now totally changed; and for some days past, as may be seen from our journal, they became more and more troublesome. In the course of this day, several parties of them were busy in rolling stones from the edge of the hill, with a view, as was supposed, to annoy the ships; but these were at too great a distance to receive any damage; however, the commodore looking upon this as an insult, ordered some of our great guns to be fired among them, and, in less than ten minutes, not an Indian was to be seen near the place. In the afternoon Terreeoboo came on board, and complained of our having killed two of his people, intimating, at the same time, that

they

they had not the least intention of hurting us. He continued on board near two hours, amusing himself with seeing our armourers work, and requested that they might be permitted to make him a pahooa (an instrument used in battle, when they come to close quarters) which was immediately done.

Sunday, the 14th of February, 1779. This is that memorable day, in which are comprized the affecting incidents, and melancholy particulars, that concluded with the assassination of our beloved and honoured commodore. Very early in the morning, a party of the islanders were perceived, who made a great lamentation, and moved slowly along to the beating of a drum, that gave scarcely a stroke in a minute. From this circumstance our people supposed, they were burying the dead who had been killed the preceding day. At day-break Mr. King repaired on board the Resolution, in order to examine the time-keeper. In his way thither, he was hailed by the Discovery, and received the alarming information, that their cutter had been stolen, in some time of the night, from the buoy, where it was moored. The boat's painter had been cut two fathoms from the bouy, and the remainder of the rope was gone with the boat. This gave cause sufficient to suspect that some villainy was hatching by the islanders, and that ill consequences would follow such a daring theft. With these thoughts Mr. King hastened on board the Resolution, whose whole company were by this time in motion. On his arrival, he found the marines arming, the crew preparing to warp the ship nearer to the shore, and Captain Cook loading his double barrel gun. He began with a relation of what had happened in the night at the morai, when the commodore interrupted him with some eagerness, and informed him of the loss of the Discovery's cutter, and of the preparations he was making to recover it; adding, that he was resolved to seize Terreeoboo, and to confine him on board till the boat should be returned. It had been Captain Cook's usual practice, in all the islands of the Pacific Ocean he had visited, whenever any thing of consequence had been stolen by the natives, to get their king, or some of the principal earees on board, where he detained them as prisoners, till the property that had been lost was restored; and this method having hitherto proved successful, he meant to pursue it on the present occasion. In consequence of this hasty determination, the commodore gave orders to stop every canoe that should attempt to leave the bay; having resolved to seize, and destroy them, if the cutter could not be recovered by lenient measures. To this end the boats of both ships, properly manned and armed, were stationed across the bay. The islanders observing our motions, and seeing the ships warping towards the towns, of which there were two, one on each side of the harbour, they concluded that our design was to seize their boats. In consequence of which conjecture, most of their large war canoes took the alarm, and were making off, when our guns, loaded with grape and canister shot, drove them back.

Between the hours of seven and eight o'clock, Captain Cook and Mr King quitted the ship together; the former in the pinnace, having Mr. Phillips, and nine marines with him; and the latter in a small boat. The last orders Captain Cook gave Mr. King, were, to quiet the minds of the people on his side of the bay, by the strongest assurances that they should not be injured; to keep his people together, and to be continually on his guard. Captain Cook and Mr. King then parted; the former intending to proceed to Kowrowa, where Terreeoboo resided, and the latter to the beach. When Mr. King had landed, he perceived many of the warriors of Owhyhee were cloathed in their military

tary mats, though without arms; that they were gathering together in a body from every direction; and that they assumed a very different countenance to what they usually wore upon all former occasions; he therefore, when arrived at his station on shore, issued strict orders to the marines, to continue within the tent, to charge their musquets with ball, and not, on any consideration, to quit their arms. This done, he waited upon old Kaoo, and the priests, at their respective huts, and explained to them, as well as he was able, the reason of the hostile preparations, which had so exceedingly alarmed them. He found they were no strangers to our loss of the cutter, and assured them, that though the commodore was resolved not only to recover it, but to punish, in the most exemplary manner, the perpetrators of the theft; yet they, and all the inhabitants of the village, on our side, need not be alarmed, nor apprehend the least danger from us. He desired the priests to communicate the motives by which we were actuated in our present conduct, to the people, and to intreat them not to entertain groundless fears, but, confiding in our declarations, to remain peaceable and quiet. Mr. King having thus made known our real intention, Kaoo asked, with great emotion, if Terreeoboo, the king, was to be hurt? Mr. King declared he was not; upon which both Kaoo and the rest of the priests seemed much satisfied with this assurance.

In the interval of these transactions, Captain Cook having called off the launch from the N. part of the Bay, and taken it with him, landed, regardless of appearances, at Kowrowa, with Mr. Phillips, lieutenant of the marines, a serjeant, and nine privates. He proceeded immediately into the village, where he was received respectfully; the people, as usual, prostrating themselves before him, and making their accustomed offerings of small hogs; but it was observed, that the chiefs were in some consternation on seeing the captain and his guard, and that they soon disappeared one after another. The commodore perceiving that his main design was not suspected, the next step he took was, to enquire for the king, and the two boys, his sons, who had been his constant guests on board the Resolution. In a short time the boys returned, with some of the natives who had been sent in search of them; and conducted Captain Cook to the habitation where Terreeoboo had slept. The old king had just awoke, and the captain addressed him in the mildest terms; assuring him, that no violence was intended against his person, or any of his people; but only against those who had been guilty of a most unprecedented act of robbery, by cutting from her moorings one of the ship's boats, without which they could neither conveniently water, nor carry on the necessary communication with the shore; requiring of the king, at the same time, to give orders for the cutter to be restored without delay; and requesting his company with him on board, till his orders should be carried into execution. Terreeoboo, in reply, protested his total ignorance of the theft; said he was very ready to assist in discovering the author of it, and should be glad to see him punished; but he shewed great unwillingness to trust his person with those who had lately exercised unusual severities against his people. He was told, that the tumultuous appearance of his people, and their repeated depredations, made some uncommon severities necessary; but that not the least hurt should be done to the meanest inhabitant of his island by any person belonging to the ships; and all that was necessary for the continuance of peace, was, to pledge himself for the honesty of his people. With that view, and that only, he came to request the king to place confidence in him, and to make the Resolution his home, as the most effectual means of putting a stop to the robberies that were daily

daily and hourly committed by his people, both at the tents, and on board the ships, and which were now so daring as to become insufferable. The king upon this remonstrance arose, and accepted the invitation.

In about half an hour Terreeoboo set out with Captain Cook, to attend him on board; and every thing had a prosperous appearance. The two boys were already in the pinnace, and the rest of the party were approaching the water-side; when a woman, named Kanee-kabereea, the mother of the boys, and one of Terreeoboo's favourite wives, followed him, and with many tears and intreaties besought him not to venture on board. At the same time, two warriors who came along with her, laid hold of the king, insisting he should proceed no farther, and obliged him to sit down. A large body of the islanders had by this time got together, who had probably been alarmed by the discharging of the great guns, and the hostile appearances in the the bay. They now began to behave outrageously, and to insult the guard. Thus situated, Mr. Phillips, lieutenant of the marines, perceiving that his men were huddled together in the crowd, consequently unable to use their arms, should there be a necessity for so doing, proposed to the commodore to draw them up along the rocks, close to the edge of the water, upon which the lieutenant received orders to march, and, if any one opposed, to fire upon, or instantly dispatch him; but the natives readily making way for them to pass, Mr. Phillips drew them up in one line, within about thirty yards of the place where Terreeoboo was sitting. The old king continued all this time on the ground. His eyes diffused gloomy discontent; his head drooped, and his whole countenance was impressed with every mark of terror and dejection; as if he was possessed with a foreboding consciousness of the catastrophe, in the bloody tragedy that was now about

about to be acted. Captain Cook, unwilling to abandon the object which occasioned him to come on shore, urged him most earnestly to proceed: but, on the other hand, if the king appeared inclined to attend him, the surrounding chiefs interposed: at first they had recourse to entreaties; but afterwards to force and violence, and even insisted on his remaining on shore; and the word was given, that Tootee was about to carry off their king, and to kill him.

Captain Cook, at length, finding that the alarm had spread too generally, and being sensible that there was not a probability of getting Terreeoboo off without much bloodshed, thought it most prudent to give up the point; observing to Mr. Phillips, that it would be impossible to compel the king to go on board, without running the risk of killing a great number of the inhabitants. Thus the enterprize was abandoned by Captain Cook; nor did it appear, that his person was in the least degree of danger, till an accident happened, the report of which brought forth in an instant a number of warriors from the crowd, and occasioned a fatal turn to the whole affair. The boats stationed across the bay, having fired at some war canoes, for attempting to get out, had unfortunately killed one of their principal chiefs. Intelligence of his death arrived at the spot where the commodore then was, just as he had parted from the king, and was walking slowly towards the shore. The ferment it occasioned was immediately too conspicuous; the women and children were immediately sent away, and the men soon put on their war mats, and armed themselves with spears and stones. One of the natives having provided himself with two of these missive weapons, advanced towards Captain Cook, flourishing a long iron spike, or pahooa, in defiance, and threatening to throw the stone. The captain made signs for him to desist, but the man persisting in

in his infolence, and repeating his menaces with ſtrange grimaces, he was provoked to fire a charge of ſmall ſhot at him; but the warrior being defended by his mat, which the ſhot could not penetrate, this ſerved only to irritate and encourage the iſlanders, whoſe fighting men now puſhed forward, throwing whole vollies of ſtones at the marines. One of the chiefs attempted to ſtab Mr. Phillips with his pahooa, (ſome ſay the very ſame that was made by our armourers, at the requeſt of the king, the day before) but not ſucceeding in this attempt, he received from him a blow with the butt end of his muſquet. A general attack with ſtones ſucceeded, and the quarrel became general. On our ſide, the guns from the ſhips began to pour in their fire upon the multitude of natives, as did likewiſe the marine guard, and thoſe from the boats; neverthelefs, though the ſlaughter among the iſlanders was great, yet, enraged as they were, they ſtood an inceſſant fire with aſtoniſhing intrepidity; and, without giving time for the marines to charge again, they ruſhed in upon them with horrid ſhouts and yells. What followed was a ſcene of horror and confuſion, which can more eaſily be conceived than related. Four of the marines, corporal Thomas, and three privates, namely Hinks, Allen, and Fadget, retreated among the rocks, and fell victims to the fury of the enemy. Three others were dangerouſly wounded; and the lieutenant, who had received a ſtab between the ſhoulders with a pahooa, having fortunately reſerved his fire, ſhot the man who had wounded him, juſt as he was going to repeat his blow. The laſt time our commodore was diſtinctly ſeen, he was ſtanding at the water's edge, ordering the boats to ceaſe firing, and pull in; when a baſe aſſaſſin, coming behind him, and ſtriking him on the head with his club, felled him to the ground, in ſuch a direction, that he lay with his face prone in the water. A general ſhout was set up by the iflanders on feeing the captain fall, and his body was dragged on fhore, where he was furrounded by the enemy, who, fnatching the dagger from each other's hands, difplayed a favage eagernefs to join in his deftruction. It fhould feem that their vengeance was directed chiefly againft our commodore, by whom they fuppofed their king was to be dragged on board, and punifhed at difcretion; for, having fecured his body, they fled without much regarding the reft of the flain, one of whom they threw into the fea.

Thus ended the life of the greateft navigator that this or any other nation could ever boaft of: who led his crews of gallant Britifh feamen twice round the world; reduced to a certainty the non-exiftence of a Southern continent, about which the learned of all nations were in doubt; fettled the boundaries of the earth and fea; and demonftrated the impracticability of a N. W. paffage from the Atlantic to the great Southern Ocean, for which our ableft geographers had contended, and in purfuit of which vaft fums had been fpent in vain, and many valuable mariners had miferably perifhed. His death was doubtlefs premature; yet he lived to accomplifh the great undertaking for which he feemed particularly defigned. How fincerely his lofs was lamented, (we fpeak here in the language of his panegyrift) by thofe who owed their fecurity to his fkill and conduct, and every confolation to his tendernefs and humanity, it is impoffible to defcribe; and the tafk would be equally difficult to reprefent the horror, dejection, and difmay, which followed fo dreadful and unexpected a cataftrophe. Let us therefore turn from fo mournful a fcene, to the pleafing contemplation of his virtues, character, and public fervices, the hiftory of which our readers will find in the fubfequent chapter.

CHAP,

CHAP. XV.

HAVING related the untimely fate of our excellent commander, Captain Cook, we now proceed to give our readers some new and authentic particulars of the life of this great navigator; the whole, we will venture to affirm, making a more correct and complete historical narrative, on so interesting a subject, than has hitherto appeared in any edition whatever of Captain Cook's voyages, under whatever authority published, or however pompously set forth.

The late Captain James Cook, the subject of these memoirs, was born at Marton, in the North Riding of Yorkshire, on February the 3d, 1728. In this particular, we may contradict the ignorant assertions foisted on the public by editors of publications of the like kind with this; but we rest our credibility on the authority of the Rev. Mr. Grenside, whose certificate, taken from the register of births in his parish, is now in the possession of our publisher. The father of Captain Cook was a day labourer to a farmer, and lived in a small village surrounded with mud walls; who afterwards removed to Great Ayton; where he was employed as a peasant by the late Thomas Scuttowe, Esq. with whom he was assisted by young Cook, his son, in the different branches of husbandry. At the age of 13, this youth was put under the tuition of Mr. Pullen, a schoolmaster of Ayton, by whom he was instructed in the arts of writing, common book-keeping, &c. and he is said to have shewn an uncommon genius in his application to the several rules of vulgar arithmetic. In January, 1745, at the age of 17, his father bound him apprentice, to learn the grocery and haberdashery business, at Snaith; but his natural inclination not having been consulted on this occasion, he soon quitted the counter in disgust, after a year and a half's servitude; and having contracted a strong propensity to the sea, his master, willing to indulge him in following the bent of his inclination, gave up readily his indentures. In July, 1746, he was bound apprentice to Mr. Walker, of Whitby, for the term of three years, which time he served to his master's full satisfaction. Under him he first sailed on board the ship Freelove, employed chiefly in the coal trade from Newcastle to London. In the spring of 1750, Mr. Cook shipped himself as a seaman on board the Maria, under the command of Captain Gaskin; in which vessel he continued all that year, in the Baltic trade. In 1753, he entered on board His Majesty's ship the Eagle; "having a mind," as he expressed himself, "to try his fortune that way." Some time after, the Eagle sailed with another frigate on a cruise, in which they were very successful.

In the year 1758, we find this rising mariner, master of the Northumberland, the flag ship of Lord Colville, who had then the command of a squadron stationed on the coast of America. It was here, as he has often been heard to say, that, during a hard winter, he first read Euclid, and applied to the study of the mathematics and astronomy, without any assistance than what a few books, and his own industry afforded. At the same time, that he thus found means to cultivate his understanding, improve his mind, and supply the deficiencies of an early education, he was engaged in most of the busy and active scenes of the war in America. At the siege of Quebec, Sir Charles Saunders committed to his charge the execution of services, of the first importance in the naval department. He piloted the boats to the attack of Montmorency; conducted the embarkation to the heights of Abraham, examined the passage, and laid buoys for the security of the large ships in proceeding up the river.

river. The courage and address with which he acquitted himself in these services, gained him the warm friendship of Sir Charles Saunders and Lord Colville, who continued to patronize him during the rest of their lives, with the greatest zeal and affection.

On the 1st of April 1760, he received a commission as a lieutenant, and soon after a specimen of those abilities, which recommended him to the commands, in the execution whereof he so highly displayed his merit, that his name will be handed down to posterity, as one of the most skilful navigators which this country hath produced. In 1765 he was with Sir William Barnaby, on the Jamaica station; and behaved in such a manner as gained him the approbation of the admiral. At the conclusion of the war, he was appointed, through the recommendation of Lord Colville, and Sir Hugh Pallifer, to survey the Gulph of St. Lawrence, and the coasts of Newfoundland. In this employment he continued till the year 1767, when the Royal Society resolved, that it would be proper to send a navigator into the South Seas, to observe the Transit of the planet Venus over the Sun's disk; and Otaheite being fixed upon, the Endeavour, a ship built for the coal trade, was put into commission, and the command of her given to Lieutenant, the late Captain Cook, who was appointed with Mr. Charles Green to observe the Transit. In this voyage he was accompanied by Joseph Banks, Esq. since Sir Joseph, and Dr. Solander, and other ingenious artists. The Transit of Venus was observed in different parts of the island, and the captain returned, after having being absent almost three years, in which period he had made discoveries equal to all the navigators of his country, from the time of Columbus to the present. From this period, as his services increased in usefulness to the public, so his reputation advanced to a height too great for our encomiums to reach. Perhaps

haps no science ever received greater additions from the labours of a single man, than geography has done from those of Captain Cook; who, in his first voyage to the South Seas discovered the Society Isles; determined the insularity of New Zealand; discovered the straits which separate the two islands, called after his name; and made a complete survey of both. He afterwards explored the eastern coast of New Holland, hitherto unknown; an extent of 27 deg. of lat. or upwards of 2,000 miles.

Soon after the captain's return to England, it was resolved to equip two ships to complete the discovery of the Southern hemisphere. It had long been a prevailing idea, that the unexplored part contained another continent. To ascertain the fact was the principal object of this expedition; and that nothing might be omitted that could tend to facilitate the enterprize, two ships were provided; the one, the Resolution, under the command of Captain Cook; the other, the Adventure, commanded by Captain Furneaux. In this second expedition round the world, Captain Cook resolved the great problem of a southern continent; having so completely traversed that hemisphere, as not to leave a possibility of its existence, unless so near the pole, as to be beyond the reach of navigation. In this voyage New Caledonia, the largest island in the Southern Pacific Ocean, except New Zealand, was discovered; as was also the island of Georgia; and an unknown coast, which the captain named Sandwich land; and having twice visited the tropical seas, he settled the situations of the old discoveries, and made several new ones.

The want of success which attended Captain Cook's attempt to discover a Southern Continent, did not set aside another plan which had been recommended some time before. This was no other than the finding out a N. W. passage, which the fancy of some chimerical projectors had conceived

to

to be a practicable scheme. His services were required for this arduous undertaking, and he offered them without hesitation. This third and last voyage is distinguished by the extent and importance of its discoveries. Not to mention several smaller islands in the Southern Pacific, Captain Cook discovered the group, north of the equinoxial line, called Sandwich Islands; which, on account of their situation and productions, may perhaps become an object of more consequence, than any other discovery in the South Sea. He explored what had remained before unknown of the western coast of America, an extent of 3700 miles; ascertained the proximity of the two continents of Asia and America; sailed through the straits between them, and surveyed the coasts on each side, so far as to be satisfied of the impracticability of a passage in that hemisphere, from the Atlantic into the Pacific Ocean, by an eastern or western coast. In short, he compleated the hydography of the habitable globe, if we except the Japanese Archipelago, and the sea of Amur, which are still known imperfectly by Europeans. Throughout this voyage it must be confessed, that his services as a navigator, are important and meritorious. The methods which he invented, and so successfully put in practice, of preserving the health, (and consequently the lives) of seamen, will transmit his name to future ages, as a friend and benefactor of mankind. It is well known among those who are conversant in naval history, that the advantages which have been sought, through the medium of long sea voyages, have always been purchased at a dear rate. That dreadful disorder which is peculiar to this service, must, without exercising an unwarrantable degree of tyranny over our seamen, have been an insuperable obstacle to our enterprizes. It was reserved for Captain Cook to convince the world, that voyages might be protracted to three, or even four years, in unknown regions, and under every

every change of climate, without affecting the health, in the smallest degree, and even without diminishing the probability of life. A few months after his departure from England, notwithstanding he was then absent, the Royal Society voted him Sir Godfrey Copley's gold medal, as a reward for the account, which he had transmitted to that body, of the method taken to preserve the health of the crew of his ship. Captain Cook was a married man, and left several children behind him. On each of these his Majesty has settled a pension of twenty-five pounds a year, and two hundred pounds per annum on his widow.

The constitution of this great and unparalleled navigator, was robust both by nature and habit; his body having been inured to labour, and rendered capable of undergoing the severest hardships. His stomach bore, without complaining, the most coarse and ungrateful food. Indeed he submitted, with an easy self-denial, to wants of every kind, which he endured with remarkable indifference. The qualities of his mind were of the same hardy vigorous kind with those of his body. His understanding was strong and quick-sighted: his judgment, in whatever related to the services he was engaged in, quick and sure: his designs were bold and daring, yet manly and discreet. His courage was cool and determined, and accompanied with an admirable presence of mind, in the moment of danger. His manners were plain and unaffected.

Some have censured his temper as subject to hastiness and passion; but let it be considered, that these were counteracted, and frequently disarmed, by a disposition benevolent and humane. There are those who have blamed Captain Cook for his severity to the natives of different islands which we visited; but it was not to these alone he was severe in his discipline. He never suffered any fault in his own people, though ever so trivial, to escape unpunished.

punished. If they were charged with insulting a native, or injuring him in his property, if the fact was proved, the offender seldom escaped unpunished. By this impartial distribution of equal justice, the natives themselves conceived so high an idea of his wisdom, and his power too, that they paid him the honours bestowed on their Eatooa, or good spirit.

This is certain, that a most distinguishing feature in Captain Cook's character was, that unremitting perseverance in the pursuit of his object, which was not only superior to the opposition of dangers, and the pressure of hardships, but even exempt from the want of ordinary relaxation. During the three long voyages in which he was engaged, his eagerness and activity were never in the least abated. No incidental temptation could detain him for a moment; even those intervals of recreation, which sometimes occurred unavoidably, and were longed for by us with a longing that persons who have experienced the fatigues of service will readily excuse, were submitted to by him with a certain impatience, whenever they could not be employed in making further provisions for the prosecution of his designs. In the course of this work, we have faithfully enumerated all the particular instances in which these qualities were displayed, during the great and important enterprizes in which he was engaged: and we have likewise stated the result of those services, under the two principal heads to which they may be referred, those of geography and navigation, each of which we have placed in a separate and distinct point of view.

We cannot close these memoirs, without taking a slight retrospect view of the tragical end of this truly great and worthy sea officer. It was imagined by some of those who were present, that the marines, and those who were in the boats, fired without Captain Cook's orders, and that he was anxious to prevent the farther effusion of blood; it is therefore

therefore probable, that, on this occasion, his humanity proved fatal to him; for it was observed, that while he faced the natives, no violence had been offered him; but when he turned about to give directions to the boats, he immediately received the fatal blow. Whether this was mortal or not it is impossible for any one to determine; but we are informed by a gentleman on board the Discovery, whose veracity is unquestionable, that there was time sufficient to have secured the body of our brave commander, had a certain lieutenant, who commanded a boat of the same ship, pulled in, instead of making off. We do not mention the name, but if our information is an undeniable fact, the dastardly officer merits justly that contempt and poverty, to which it is said he is at present reduced. We beg leave further to observe, that the natives had certainly no intention at first of destroying Captain Cook, or any of his party. The cause first originated in the death of the Eree, who was shot by one of our people in the boat: it was this circumstance which alarmed them, and, in consequence of this it was that they armed themselves. At this period Captain Cook might have returned on board with safety; but he was unfortunate in missing the man who behaved insolent to him, and shooting another; he was unfortunate in the firing of the marines; and equally so in the firing of the people in the launch; all which happened in the space of a few minutes. In short, all the causes that brought on the death of this much lamented circumnavigator, were produced by a chain of events which could no more be foreseen than prevented. His memory we leave to the gratitude and admiration of posterity.

We now proceed to relate those particulars, that have come to our knowledge, and which happened subsequent to the death of Captain Cook. We have before observed, that four of the marines, who accompanied

companied the commodore, were killed by the natives; the survivors, with Mr. Phillips, their lieutenant, threw themselves into the sea and made their escape, being protected by a smart fire from the boats. On this occasion, a striking instance of gallant behaviour, and of affection for his men, was displayed by Mr. Phillips; for he had scarcely got into the boat, when, seeing one of the marines, who was not a very expert swimmer, struggling in the water, and in danger of being taken by the islanders, he instantly leaped into the sea to his assistance, though considerably wounded himself; and after receiving a blow on his head from a stone, which had almost sent him to the bottom, he caught the marine by the hair, and brought him off in safety. Our people for some time kept up a constant fire from most of the boats (which, during the whole transaction, were at no greater distance from the land than twenty yards), in order to afford their unfortunate companions, if any of them should still remain alive, an opportunity of effecting their escape. These efforts, seconded by a few guns, that were, at the same time, fired from the Resolution, having at length compelled the enemy to retire, a small boat, manned by five midshipmen, pulled towards the shore, where they perceived the bodies lying on the ground without any signs of life. However, they judged it dangerous to attempt to bring them off with so inconsiderable a force; and their ammunition being nearly consumed, they returned to the ships, leaving the bodies in possession of the natives, together with ten stands of arms.

After the general consternation, which the news of this misfortune had diffused throughout the whole company of both ships, had in some degree subsided, their attention was called to the party at the morai, where the mast and sails were on shore, guarded by only six marines. It is difficult to describe the emotions that agitated the minds of

Mr. King and his attendants, at this station, during the time in which these occurrences had happened, at the other side of the bay. Being at the distance only of a mile from the village of Kowrowa, they could distinctly perceive a vast multitude of people collected on the spot where Captain Cook had just before landed. They heard the firing of the musquets, and observed an uncommon bustle and agitation among the crowd. They afterwards saw the islanders retreating, the boats retiring from the shore, and passing and repassing, with great stillness, between the ships. Mr. King's heart soon misgave him on this occasion. Where so valuable a life was concerned, he could not avoid being alarmed by such new and threatening appearances. Besides this, he knew that Captain Cook, from a long series of success, in his transactions with the natives of this ocean, had acquired a degree of confidence, which might, in some ill-fated moment, put him too much off his guard; and Mr. King now saw all the dangers to which that confidence might lead, without deriving much consolation from the consideration of the experience which had given rise to it. His first care, on hearing the report of the musquets, was to assure the islanders, considerable numbers of whom were assembled round the wall of our consecrated field, and seemed at a loss how to account for what they had heard and seen, that they should meet with no molestation; and that, at all events, he was inclined to continue on peaceable terms with them.

In this situation, Mr. King and his attendants remained till the boats had returned on board, when Captain Clerke perceiving, by means of his telescope, that our party was surrounded by the natives, who, he thought, designed to attack them, ordered two four-pounders to be fired at the islanders. These guns, though well aimed, did no mischief; but they gave the natives a convincing proof of

their

their powerful effects. A cocoa-nut tree, under which some of them were sitting, was broken in the middle by one of the balls; and the other shivered a rock, which stood in an exact line with them. As Mr. King had, just before, given them the strongest assurances of their safety, he was extremely mortified at this act of hostility, and, to prevent its being repeated, instantly dispatched a boat to inform Captain Clerke, that he was, at present, on the most amicable terms with the islanders, and that, if any future occasion should arise for changing his conduct towards them, he would hoist a jack, as a signal for Captain Clerke to afford him his assistance. Mr. King waited the return of the boat with the greatest impatience; and after remaining for the space of a quarter of an hour, under the utmost anxiety and suspence, his fears were at length confirmed, by the arrival of Mr. Bligh, with orders to strike the tents immediately, and to send on board the sails, that were repairing. At the same instant, Kaireekeea having also received information of the death of Captain Cook, from a native who had arrived from the other side of the bay, approached Mr. King, with great dejection and sorrow in his countenance, enquiring whether it was true. At this time the situation of the party was highly critical and important. Not only their own lives, but the issue of the expedition, and the return of at least one of the ships, were involved in the same common danger. They had the mast of the Resolution, and the greater part of the sails, on shore, protected by only half a dozen marines. The loss of these would have been irreparable; and though the islanders had not as yet testified the smallest disposition to molest the party, it was difficult to answer for the alteration, which the intelligence of the transaction at Kowrowa might produce. Mr. King therefore thought proper to dissemble his belief of the death of Captain Cook, and

to

to desire Kaireekeea to discourage the report; apprehending that either the fear of our resentment, or the successful example of their countrymen, might perhaps lead them to seize the favourable opportunity, which at this time presented itself, of giving us a second blow. He, at the same time, advised him to bring old Kaoo, and the other priests, into a large house adjoining to the morai, partly from a regard to their safety, in case it should have been found necessary to have recourse to violent measures; and partly from a desire of having him near our people, in order to make use of his authority with the natives, if it could be instrumental in maintaining peace.

Having stationed the maries on the top of the morai, which formed a strong and advantageous post, he intrusted the command to Mr. Bligh, who received the most positive directions to act solely on the defensive; and he then went on board the Discovery, in order to confer with Captain Clerke, on the dangerous situation of our affairs. He had no sooner left the spot, than the islanders began to annoy our people with stones; and just after he had reached the ship, he heard the firing of the marines. He therefore hastily returned on shore, where he found affairs growing every moment more alarming. The natives were providing arms, and putting on their mats; and their numbers augmented very fast. He also observed several large bodies advancing towards our party along the cliff, by which the village of Kakooa is separated from the north side of the bay, where Kowrowa is situate. At first they attacked our people with stones from behind the walls of their inclosures, and meeting with no resistance, they soon became more daring. A few courageous fellows, having crept along the beach, under cover of the rocks, suddenly presented themselves at the foot of the morai, with an intention of storming it on the side next the sea, which was its only accessible part; and they were

not

not dislodged before they had stood a considerable quantity of shot, and had seen one of their number fall. The amazing courage of one of these assailants deserves to be recorded. Having returned with a view of carrying off his companion, amidst the fire of our whole party, he received a wound, which obliged him to quit the body, and retire; but, a few minutes afterwards, he again made his appearance, and receiving another wound, was under the necessity of retreating a second time. At that moment Mr. King arrived at the morai, and saw this man return a third time, faint from the loss of blood and fatigue. Being informed of what had happened, he forbad the soldiers to fire; and the islander was suffered to carry off his friend, which he was just able to accomplish; and then fell down himself, and breathed his last. About this time a strong reinforcement from both ships having landed, the natives retreated behind their walls; which affording Mr. King access to the priests, he sent one of them to exert his endeavours to bring his countrymen to some terms, and to propose to them, that if they would desist from throwing stones, he would not allow our men to fire. This truce was agreed to, and our people were suffered to launch the mast, and carry off the sails, astronomical instruments, &c. without molestation. As soon as our party had quitted the morai, the islanders took possession of it, and some of them threw a few stones, which, however, did no mischief. Between eleven and twelve o'clock, Mr. King arrived on board the Discovery, where he found that no decisive plan had been adopted for the regulation of our future proceedings. The recovery of Captain Cook's body, and the restitution of the boat, were the objects, which, on all hands, we agreed to insist on; and Mr. King declared it as his opinion, that some vigorous methods should be put in execution, if the demand of them should not be instantly complied

plied with. It may justly be supposed that Mr. King's feelings, on the death of a beloved and respected friend, had some share in this opinion; yet there were doubtless other reasons, and those of the most serious nature, that had some weight with him. The confidence which the success of the natives in killing our commander, and obliging us to leave the shore, must naturally have inspired; and the advantage, however inconsiderable, which they had gained over us the preceding day, would, he had no doubt, excite them to make farther dangerous attempts; and the more particularly, as they had no great reason, from what they had hitherto observed, to dread the effects of our fire-arms. This kind of weapon, indeed, contrary to the expectations of us all, had produced in them no signs of terror. On our side, such was the condition of our vessels, and the state of discipline among us, that, had a vigorous attack been made on us, during the night, the consequences might perhaps have been highly disagreeable. Mr. King was supported, in these apprehensions, by the opinion of the greater part of the officers on board; and nothing seemed to him more likely to encourage the islands to make the attempt, than the appearance of our being inclined to an accommodation, which they could only impute to weakness or fear. On the other hand it was urged, in favour of more conciliatory measures, that the mischief was already done, and was irreparable; that the natives, by reason of their former friendship and kindness had a strong claim to our regard: and the more particularly, as the late calamitous accident did not appear to have taken its rise from any premeditated design; that, on the part of Terreeoboo, his ignorance of the theft, his willingness to accompany Captain Cook on board the Resolution, and his having actually sent his two sons into the pinnace, must rescue his character, in this respect, from the

smallest

smallest degree of suspicion; that the behaviour of his women, and the chiefs, might easily be accounted for, from the apprehensions occasioned in thiir minds by the armed force, with which Captain Cook landed, and the hostile preparations in the bay; appearances so unsuitable to the confidence and friendship, in which both parties had hitherto lived, that the arming of the islanders was manifestly with a design to resist the attempt, which they had some reason to expect would be made, to carry off their sovereign by force, and was naturally to be expected from a people who had a remarkable affection for their chiefs. To these dictates of humanity, other motives of a prudential kind were added; that we were in want of a supply of water, and other refreshments; that the Resolution's foremast would require seven or eight days work, before it could be stepped; that the spring was advancing very fast; and that the speedy prosecution of our next expedition to the northward, ought now to be our sole object; and that, therefore, to engage in a vindictive contest with the natives, might not only subject us to the imputation of needless cruelty, but would require great delay in the equipment of our ships. In this latter opinion Captain Clerke concurred; and though Mr. King was convinced, that an early and vigorous display of our resentment would have more effectually answered every object both of prudence and humanity, he was, upon the whole, not sorry that the measures he had recommended were rejected. For though the contemptuous behaviour of the islanders, and their subsequent opposition to our necessary occupations on shore, arising most probably from a misconstruction of our lenity, obliged us at last to have recourse to violence in our own defence; yet he was not certain that the circumstances of the case would, in the opinion of the generality of people, have justified the use of force, on our part, in the first instance. Cautionary severity is ever invidious, and the rigour of a preventive measure, when it is the most successful, leaves its expediency the least apparent.

During these deliberations, and while we were thus engaged in concerting some plan for our future operations, a very numerous concourse of the natives still kept possession of the shore; and some of them coming off in canoes, approached within pistol-shot of the ships, and insulted us by various marks of defiance and contempt. It was extremely difficult to restrain the seamen from the use of their arms on these occasions; but, as pacific measures had been resolved on, the canoes were allowed to return unmolested. Mr. King was now ordered by Captain Clerke to proceed towards the shore with the boats of both ships, well manned and armed, with a view of bringing the islanders to a parley, and of obtaining, if possible, a conference with some of the erees. If he should succeed in this attempt, he was to demand the dead bodies, and particularly that of Captain Cook: to threaten them, in case of a refusal, with our resentment; but by no means to fire, unless attacked; and not to go ashore on any account whatever. These instructions were delivered to Mr. King before the whole party, in the most positive manner; in consequence of which, he and his detachment left the ships about four o'clock in the afternoon; and as they approached the shore, they perceived every indication of a hostile reception. The natives were all in motion, the women and children retiring; the men arming themselves with long spears and daggers, and putting on their war mats. It also appeared, that since the morning they had thrown up breast-works of stone along the beach, where Captain Cook had landed; in expectation, perhaps, of an attack at that place. When our party were within reach, the islanders began to throw stones at them

them with flings, but without doing any mischief. Mr. King concluded from these appearances, that all attempts to bring them to a parley would be ineffectual, unless he gave them some ground for mutual confidence: he therefore ordered the armed boats to stop, and advanced alone in the small boat, holding in his hand a white flag; the meaning of which, from an universal shout of joy from the natives, he had the satisfaction to find was immediately understood. The women instantly returned from the side of the hill, whither they had retired; the men threw off their mats, and all seated themselves together by the sea-side, extending their arms, and inviting Mr. King to land.

Notwithstanding such behaviour seemed expressive of a friendly disposition, Mr. King could not avoid entertaining suspicions of its sincerity. But when he saw Koah, with extraordinary boldness and assurance, swimming off towards the boat, with a white flag in his hand, he thought proper to return this mark of confidence, and accordingly received him into the boat, though he was armed; a circumstance which did not contribute to lessen Mr. King's suspicions. He had indeed long harboured an unfavourable opinion of Koah. The priests had always represented him as a person of a malicious temper, and no friend to us; and the repeated detections of his fraud and treachery, had convinced us of the truth of their assertions. Besides the melancholy transactions of the morning, in which he was seen performing a principal part, inspired Mr. King with the utmost horror at finding himself so near him; and as he approached him with feigned tears, and embraced him, Mr. King was so distrustful of his intentions, that he took hold of the point of the pahooa, which the chief held in his hand, and turned it from him. He informed the islander that he had come to demand the body of Captain Cook, and to declare war against the natives,

tives, unless it was restored without delay. Koah assured him that this should be done as soon as possible, and that he would go himself for that purpose; and after requesting a piece of iron of Mr. King, with marks of great assurance, he leaped into the water, and swam ashore, calling out to his countrymen, that we were all friends again. Our people waited with great anxiety near an hour for his return. During this interval, the other boats had approached so near the shore, that the men who were in them entered into conversation with a party of the islanders, at a little distance; by whom they were informed, that the captain's body had been cut to pieces, and carried up the country; but of this circumstance Mr. King was not apprized till his return to the ships. He therefore now began to express some degree of impatience at Koah's delay; upon which the chiefs pressed him exceedingly to land, assuring him, that if he would go in person to Terreeoboo, the body would be undoubtedly restored to him. When they found they could not prevail on Mr. King to go ashore, they endeavoured, on pretence of conversing with him with greater ease, to decoy his boat among some rocks, where they might have had it in their power to separate him from the other boats. It was easy to see through these artifices, and he was therefore very desirous of breaking off all communication with them; when a chief approached, who had particularly attached himself to Captain Clerke, and the officers of the Discovery, on board which ship he had sailed, when we last quitted the bay, intending to take his passage to the island of Mowee. He said he came from Terreeoboo, to acquaint our people that the body was carried up the country, but that it should be brought back the following morning. There appeared much sincerity in his manner; and being asked, if he uttered a falshood, he hooked together his two fore-fingers, which is here understood

stood as the sign of veracity, in the use of which these islanders are very scrupulous. Being now at a loss how to proceed, Mr. King sent Mr. Vancover to inform Captain Clerke of all that had passed; that it was his opinion, the natives did not intend to keep their word with us; and, far from being grieved at what had happened, were on the contrary inspired with great confidence on account of their late success, and sought only to gain time, till they could plan some scheme for getting our people into their power. Mr. Vancover came back with orders for Mr. King to return on board, after giving the islanders to understand, that if the body was not restored the next morning, the town should be destroyed. No sooner did they perceive our party retiring, than they endeavoured to provoke them by the most contemptuous and insulting gestures. Several of our people said, they could distinguish some of the natives parading about in the cloaths which had belonged to our unhappy countrymen, and among them, an eree brandishing Captain Cook's hanger, and a woman holding the scabbard. In consequence of Mr. King's report to Captain Clerke, of what he supposed to be the present temper and disposition of the inhabitants, the most effectual methods were taken to guard against any attack they might make during the night. The boats were moored with top-chains; additional sentinels were stationed in each of our ships; and guard-boats were directed to row round them, in order to prevent the islanders from cutting the cables. During the night, we saw a vast number of lights on the hills, which induced some of us to imagine, that they were removing their effects farther up into the country, in consequence of our menaces. But it seems more probable, that they were kindled at the sacrifices that were performing on account of the war, in which they supposed themselves likely to be engaged; and, perhaps the

bodies

bodies of our slain countrymen were at that time burning. We afterwards observed fires of the same kind, as we passed the island of Morotoi; and which, according to the information we received from some of the natives then on board, were made on account of a war they had declared against a neighbouring island. This agrees with what we learned among the Friendly and Society Isles, that, previous to any hostile expedition, the chiefs always endeavoured to animate the courage of the people, by feasts and rejoicings in the night. We passed the night without any disturbance, except from the howlings and lamentations which were heard on shore.

On Monday the 15th, early in the morning, Koah came along-side the Resolution, with a small pig and some cloth, which he desired permission to present to Mr. King. We have already mentioned, that this officer was supposed by the islanders to be the son of Captain Cook; and as the latter had always suffered them to believe it, Mr. King was probably considered as the chief after his death. As soon as he came on deck, he interrogated Koah with regard to the body; and, on his returning evasive answers, refused to accept his presents; and was on the point of dismissing him with expressions of anger and resentment, had not Captain Clerke, with a view of keeping up the appearance of friendship, judged it more proper that he should be treated with the customary respect. This artful priest came frequently to us in the course of the morning, with some trifling present or other; and as we always observed him eyeing every part of the ship with a great degree of attention, we took care he should see we were well prepared for our defence. He was extremely urgent both with Captain Clerke and Mr. King to go on shore, imputing the detention of the bodies to the other chiefs, and assuring those gentlemen, that every thing might be adjusted

justed to their satisfaction, by a personal interview with the king. However, they did not think it prudent to comply with Koah's request; and indeed a fact came afterwards to their knowledge, which proved his want of veracity. For, they were informed, that immediately after the action in which Captain Cook had lost his life, Terreeoboo had retired to a cave in the steep part of the mountain that hangs over the bay, which was accessible only by means of ropes, and where he continued for several days, having his provisions let down to him by cords. After the departure of Koah from the ships, we observed that his countrymen who had assembled by day-break, in vast crowds on the shore, flocked around him with great eagerness on his landing, as if they wished to learn the intelligence he had gained, and what steps were to be taken in consequence of it. It is highly probable, that they expected we should attempt to put our threats in execution; and they appeared fully determined to stand their ground. During the whole morning, we heard conchs blowing in various parts of the coast; large parties were perceived marching over the hills; and, upon the whole, appearances were so alarming, that we carried out a stream anchor, for the purpose of hauling the ship abreast of the town, in case of an attack; and boats were stationed off the northern point of the bay, in order to prevent a surprize from the natives in that quarter. Their warlike posture at present, and the breach of their engagement to restore the bodies of the slain, occasioned fresh debates among us concerning the measures which should now be pursued. It was at length determined, that nothing should be permitted to interfere with the repair of the Resolution's mast, and the preparations for our departure; but that we should nevertheless continue our negociations for the restoration of the bodies of our countrymen. The greater part of this day was employed

ployed in getting the fore-maſt into a proper ſituation on deck, that the carpenters might work upon it; and alſo, in making the requiſite alterations in the commiſſions of the officers. The chief command of the expedition having devolved on Captain Clerke, he removed on board the Reſolution, promoted Lieutenant Gore to the rank of captain of the Diſcovery, appointed Meſſrs. King and Williamſon firſt and ſecond lieutenants of the Reſolution, and nominated Mr. Harvey, a midſhipman, who had accompanied Captain Cook during his two laſt voyages, to fill the vacant lieutenancy. During the whole day, we ſuſtained no interruption from the iſlanders: and in the evening, the launch was moored with a top-chain, and guard-boats ſtationed round each of the ſhips as before. About eight o'clock, it being exceedingly dark, we heard a canoe paddling towards the ſhip; and it was no ſooner perceived, than both the ſentinels on deck fired into it. There were two of the natives in this canoe, who immediately roared out " Tinnee," (which was their method of pronouncing Mr. King's name), and ſaid they were friends, and had ſomething with them which belonged to Captain Cook. When they came on board, they threw themſelves at the feet of our officers, and ſeemed to be extremely terrified. It fortunately happened that neither of them was hurt, notwithſtanding the balls of both pieces had gone through the canoe. One of theſe was the perſon who has been already mentioned under the appellation of the taboo man, who conſtantly attended Captain Cook with the particular ceremonies we have before deſcribed; and who, though a man of diſtinction in the iſland, could ſcarcely be prevented from performing for him the moſt humiliating offices of a menial ſervant. After bewailing, with many tears, the loſs of the Orono, he informed us that he had brought a part of his body. He then gave us a ſmall bundle which he brought

under

under his arm; and it is impossible to describe the horror with which we were seized, upon finding in it a piece of human flesh of the weight of about nine or ten pounds. This, he said, was all that now remained of the body; that the rest had been cut in pieces, and burnt; but that the head, and all the bones, except those which belonged to the trunk, were in the possession of Terreeoboo and the other chiefs; that what we saw had been allotted to Kaoo, the chief of the priests, for the purpose of being used in some religious ceremony; and that he had sent it as a testimony of his innocence, and of his attachment to us. We had now an opportunity of learning whether they were cannibals; and we did not neglect to avail ourselves of it. We first endeavoured, by several indirect questions, put to each of them apart, to gain information respecting the manner in which the other bodies had been treated and disposed of; and finding them very constant in one account, that after the flesh had been cut off, the whole of it was burnt; we at last put the direct question, whether they had not fed on some of it; they immediately testified as much horror at such an idea, as any European would have done; and asked, whether that was the practice among us. They afterwards asked us, with great earnestness, and with an appearance of apprehension, when the Orono would come again? and how he would treat them on his return? the same enquiry was often made in the sequel by others; and this idea is consistent with the general tenour of their conduct towards him, which indicated that they considered him as a being of a superior species. We pressed our two friendly visitants to continue on board till the next morning, but we could not prevail upon them. They informed us, that if this transaction should come to the knowledge of the king, or any of the other erees, it might be attended with the most fatal consequences to their whole society;

to prevent which, they had been under the neceffity of coming to us in the dark; and the fame precaution, they faid, would be requifite in returning on fhore. They further told us, that the chiefs were eager to take revenge on us for the death of their countrymen; and particularly cautioned us againft trufting Koah, who, they affured us, was our implacable enemy; and ardently longed for an opportunity of fighting us, to which the blowing of the conchs that we had heard in the morning, was intended as a challenge. It likewife appeared from the information of thefe men, that feventeen of their countrymen were flain in the firft action, at the village of Kowrowa, five of whom were chiefs; and that Kaneena and his brother, our particular friends, were of that number. Eight, they faid, had loft their lives at the obfervatory; three of whom likewife were perfons of the firft diftinction. At eleven o'clock the two natives left us, and took the precaution to defire that one of our guard-boats might attend them, till they had paffed the Difcovery, left they fhould again be fired upon, which, by alarming their countrymen on fhore, might expofe them to the danger of detection. This requeft was readily complied with, and we had the fatisfaction to find, that they reached the land fafe and undifcovered. During the remainder of this night, we heard the fame loud lamentations, as in the preceeding one. Early the following morning, we received a vifit from Koah. Mr. King was piqued at finding, that notwithftanding the moft glaring marks of treachery in his conduct, and the pofitive declaration of our friends the priefts, he fhould ftill be fuffered to carry on the fame farce, and to make us at leaft appear the dupes of his hypocrify. Our fituation was indeed become extremely aukward and unpromifing; none of the purpofes for which this pacific plan of proceedings had been adopted, having hitherto been in any refpect promoted by it.

No satisfactory answer had been given to our demands; we did not seem to have made any progress towards a reconciliation with the natives; they still remained on the shore in hostile postures, as if determined to oppose any endeavours we might make to go ashore; and yet it was become absolutely necessary to attempt landing, as the completing our stock of water would not admit of any longer delay. However, in justice to the conduct of Captain Clerke, we must remark, that it was highly probable, from the great numbers of the islanders, and from the resolution with which they seemed to expect our approach, that an attack could not have been made without danger; and that the loss of even a very few men might have been severely felt by us, during the remainder of our voyage: whereas the delaying to put our menaces into execution, though, on the one hand, it diminished their opinion of our valour, had the effect of occasioning them to disperse on the other. For this day, about 12 o'clock, upon finding that we persisted in our inactivity, great bodies of them, after blowing their conchs, and using every method of defiance, marched off, over the hills, and never made their appearance afterwards. Those, however, who remained, were not the less daring and presumptuous. One of them had the insolence to come within musquet-shot ahead of the Resolution, and after throwing several stones at us, waved over his head the hat which had belonged to Captain Cook, while his countrymen ashore were exulting and encouraging his audacity. Our people were highly enraged at this insult, and, coming in a body on the quarter-deck, begged they might no longer be obliged to put up with such reiterated provocations, and requested Mr. King to endeavour to obtain permission for them, from Captain Clerke, to take advantage of the first fair occasion of avenging the death of their much lamented commander. On Mr. King's acquainting

quainting the captain with what was passing, he ordered some great guns to be fired at the islanders on shore; and promised the crew, that, if they should be molested at the watering-place, the next day, they should then be permitted to chastise them. Before we could bring our guns to bear, the natives had suspected our intentions, from the bustle and agitation they observed in the ship; and had retired behind their houses and walls. We were consequently obliged to fire, in some degree, at random; notwithstanding which, our shot produced all the effects we could desire: for, in a short time afterwards, we perceived Koah paddling towards us, with the greatest haste; and when he arrived, we learned that some people had lost their lives, and among the rest Maiha-maiha, a principal eree, nearly related to Terreeoboo. Not long after Koah's arrival, two boys swam off from the morai towards our vessels, each armed with a long spear; and after they had approached pretty near, they began in a very solemn manner to chant a song; the subject of which, from their frequently mentioning the word Orono, and pointing to the village where Captain Cook had been slain, we concluded to be the late calamitous occurrence. Having sung for near a quarter of an hour in a plaintive strain, during all which time they continued in the water, they repaired on board the Discovery, and delivered up their spears; and after remaining there a short time, returned on shore. We could never learn who sent them, or what was the object of this ceremony. During the night, we took the usual precautions for the security of the ships; and, as soon as it was dark, the two natives, who had visited us the preceding evening, came off to us again. They assured us, that though the effects of our great guns this afternoon, had greatly alarmed the chiefs, they had by no means relinquished their

hostile

hostile intentions, and they advised us to be on our guard.

On Wednesday, the 17th, the boats of both ships were dispatched ashore to procure water; and the Discovery was warped close to the beach, in order to protect the persons employed in that service. We soon found that the intelligence which had been sent us by the priests, was not destitute of foundation, and that the islanders were determined to neglect no opportunity of annoying us, when it could be done without much hazard. The villages, throughout this whole cluster of islands, are, for the most part, situated near the sea; and the adjacent ground is enclosed with stone walls, of the height of about three feet. These, we at first supposed, were designed for the division of property; but we now discovered that they served for a defence against invasion, for which purpose they were, perhaps, chiefly intended. They consist of loose stones, and the natives are very dexterous in shifting them, with great quickness, to such particular situations, as the direction of the attack may occasionally require. In the sides of the mountain that stands near the bay, they have likewise holes, or caves, of considerable depth, whose entrance is secured by a fence of a similar kind. From behind both these stations, the islanders perpetually harrassed our watering party with stones; nor could the inconsiderable force we had on shore, with the advantage of musquets, compel them to retreat. Thus opposed, our people were so occupied in attending to their own safety, that, during the whole forenoon, they filled only one ton of water. It being therefore impossible for them to perform this service, till their assailants were driven to a greater distance, the Discovery was ordered to dislodge the enemy with her great guns; which being accomplished by means of a few discharges, the men landed without molestation. The natives, however, made their

their appearance again soon afterwards, in their usual method of attack; and it was now deemed absolutely necessary to burn down some straggling huts, near the wall behind which they had sheltered themselves. In executing the orders that were given for that purpose, our people were hurried into acts of unnecessary devastation and cruelty. Some allowance ought certainly to be made for their resentment of the repeated insults, and contemptuous behaviour of the islanders, and for their natural desire of revenging the death of their beloved and respected commander. But, at the same time, their conduct strongly evinced, that the greatest precaution is requisite in trusting, even for a moment, the discretionary use of arms in the hands of private soldiers, or seamen, on such occasions. The strictness of discipline, and the habits of obedience, by which their force is kept directed to suitable objects, lead them to conceive, that whenever they have the power, they have likewise a right to perform. Actual disobedience being almost the only crime for which they expect to receive punishment, they are apt to consider it as the sole measure of right and wrong; and hence they are too ready to conclude, that what they can do with impunity, they may also do consistently with honour and justice; so that the feelings of humanity, and that generosity towards on unresisting enemy, which, at other times, is a striking distinction of brave men, become but feeble restraints to the exercise of violence, when set in opposition to the desire they naturally have of shewing their own power and independence.

We have before observed, that directions had been given to burn only a few straggling houses, which afforded shelter to the islanders. We were therefore greatly surprized on perceiving the whole village in flames; and before a boat, that was sent to stop the progress of the mischief, could reach the land, the habitations of our old and constant friends, the priests,

priests, were all on fire. Mr. King had, therefore, great reason to lament the illness that confined him on board this day. The priests had always been under his protection; and, unfortunately, the officers then on duty having seldom been on shore at the morai, were but little acquainted with the circumstances of the place. Had he been present himself, he might, in all probability, have been the means of preserving their little society from destruction. In escaping from the flames, several of the inhabitants were shot; and our people cut off the heads of two of them, and brought them on board. The fate of one unhappy native was much lamented by all of us. As he was repairing to the well for water, he was shot at by one of the marines. The ball happened to strike his calibash, which he instantly threw from him, and ran off. He was pursued into one of the caves above-mentioned, and no lion could have defended his den with greater bravery and fierceness; till at length, after he had found means to keep two of our people at bay for a considerable time, he expired, covered with wounds. This accident first brought us acquainted with the use to which these caverns are applied. About this time a man, advanced in years, was taken prisoner, bound, and conveyed on board the Resolution, in the same boat, with the heads of his two countrymen. We never observed horror so strongly portrayed, as in the face of this person, nor so violent a transition to immoderate joy, as when he was untied, and given to understand, that he might depart in safety. He shewed us that he was not deficient in gratitude, as he not only often returned afterwards with presents of provisions, but also did us other services.

Soon after the destruction of the village, we saw, coming down the hill, a man, accompanied by fifteen or twenty boys, who held in their hands pieces of white cloth, plantains, green boughs, &c.

It happened that this pacific embassy, as soon as they were within reach, received the fire of a party of our men. This, however, did not deter them from continuing their procession, and the officer on duty came up, in time, to prevent a second discharge. As they made a nearer approach, the principal person proved to be our friend Kaireekeea, who had fled when our people first set fire to the village, and had now returned, and expressed his desire of being sent on board the Resolution. On his arrival we found him extremely thoughtful and grave. We endeavoured to convince him of the necessity there was of setting fire to the village, by which his house, and those of his brethren were unintentionally destroyed. He expostulated with us on our ingratitude and want of friendship; and, indeed, it was not till the present moment, that we knew the whole extent of the injury that had been done them. He informed us, that, confiding in the promises Mr. King had made them, and as well as in the assurances they had received from the men, who had brought us some of Captain Cook's remains, they had not removed their effects back into the country, as the other inhabitants had done, but had put every valuable article of their own, as well as what they had collected from us, into a house adjoining to the morai, where they had the mortification to see it all set on fire by our people. He had, on coming on board, perceived the heads of his two countrymen lying on deck, at which he was greatly shocked, and earnestly desired that they might be thrown over-board. This request, by the directions of Captain Clerke, was immediately complied with. In the evening our watering party returned on board, having sustained no farther interruption. We passed a disagreeable night; the cries and lamentations we heard from the shore being far more dreadful than ever. Our only consolation on this occasion, arose from the hopes that a repetition of such

such severities might not be requisite in future. It is somewhat remarkable, that, amidst all these disturbances, the female natives, who were on board, did not offer to leave us, or discover any apprehensions either for themselves or their friends on shore. They appeared, indeed, so perfectly unconcerned, that some of them, who were on deck when the village was in flames, seemed to admire the spectacle, and frequently exclaimed, that it was maitai, or very fine.

On Thursday, the 18th, in the morning, the treacherous Koah came off to the ships, as usual. There being no longer any necessity for keeping terms with him, Mr. King was allowed to treat him as he thought proper. When he approached the side of the Resolution, singing a song, and offering a hog, and some plantains, to Mr. King, the latter ordered him to keep off, and cautioned him never to make his appearance again without the bones of Captain Cook, lest his life should pay the forfeit of his repeated breach of faith. He did not appear much mortified with this unwelcome reception, but immediately returned on shore, and joined a party of his countrymen, who were throwing stones at our waterers. The body of the young man, who had been killed the preceding day, was found this morning lying at the entrance of the cave; and a mat was thrown over him by some of our people; soon after which they saw several of the natives carrying him off on their shoulders, and could hear them chanting, as they marched, a mournful song. At length the islanders being convinced that it was not the want of ability to chastize them, which had induced us at first to tolerate their provocations, desisted from molesting our people; and, towards the evening, a chief, named Eappo, who had seldom visited us, but whom we knew to be a man of the first distinction, came with presents from Terreeoboo to sue for peace. These presents were accepted, and the chief was dismissed with the following answer: That no peace would be granted, till the remains of Captain Cook should be restored. From Eappo we understood that the flesh of all the bones of our people who had been slain, as well as the bones of the trunks, had been burnt; that the limb-bones of the marines had been distributed among the inferior chiefs; and that the remains of Captain Cook had been disposed of as follows: the head to a great eree, called Kahooopeou; the hair to Maiha-maiha; and the arms, legs, and thighs, to Terreeoboo. After it was dark, many of the natives came off with various sorts of vegetables; and we also received from Kaireekeea two large presents of the same articles.

On the 19th we were principally employed in sending and receiving the messages that passed between Captain Clerke and the old king. Eappo was very urgent, that one of our officers should go on shore; and offered to remain on board, in the mean time, as an hostage. This request, however, was not complied with; and he left us with a promise of bringing the bones the following day. Our watering party, at the beach, did not meet with the least opposition from the islanders; who notwithstanding our cautious behaviour, again ventured themselves among us without any marks of diffidence or apprehension. On Saturday the 20th, early in the morning, we had the satisfaction of getting the fore-mast stepped. This operation was attended with considerable difficulty, and some danger, our ropes being so extremely rotten, that the purchase several times gave way. Between the hours of ten and eleven, we saw a numerous body of the natives descending the hill, which is over the beach, in a sort of procession, each man carrying on his shoulders two or three sugar-canes, and some bread-fruit, plantains, and taro, in his hand. They were preceded by two drummers, who, when they reached

the

the water-side, seated themselves by a white flag, and began beating their drums, while those who had followed them, advanced, one by one, and deposited the presents they had brought with them; after which they retired in the same order. Soon afterwards Eappo appeared in his long feathered cloak, bearing something with great solemnity in his hands; and having stationed himself on a rock, he made signs that a boat should be sent him. Captain Clerke, supposing that the chief had brought the bones of our late commodore (which, indeed, proved to be the case), went himself in the pinnace to receive them, and ordered Mr. King to attend him in the cutter. When they arrived at the beach, Eappoo, entering the pinnace, delivered the bones to Captain Clerke, wrapped up in a great quantity of fine new cloth, and covered with a spotted cloak of black and white feathers. He afterwards attended our gentlemen to the Resolution, but could not be prevailed on to accompany them on board; being, perhaps, from a sense of decency, unwilling to be present at the opening of the parcel. In this we found both the hands of Captain Cook entire, which were well known to us from a scar on one of them, that divided the fore-finger from the thumb, the whole length of the metacarpal bone; the skull, but with the scalp separated from it, and the bones of the face wanting; the scalp, with the ears adhering to it, and the hair upon it cut short; the bones of both the arms, with the skin of the forearms hanging to them; the bones of the thighs and legs joined together, but without the feet. The ligaments of the joints were observed to be entire; and the whole shewed sufficient marks of having been in the fire, except the hands, which had the flesh remaining upon them, and were cut in several places, and crammed with salt, most probably with a view of preserving them. The skull was free from any fracture, but the scalp had a cut in the back

back part of it. The lower jaw and feet, which were wanting, had been seized, as Eappo informed us, by different erees; and he also told us, that Terreeoboo was using every means to recover them.

The next morning, being the 21st of February, Eappo, and the king's son, came on 'board, and brought with them not only the remaining bones of Captain Cook, but likewise the barrels of his gun, his shoes, and some other trifles which had belonged to him. Eappo assured us, that Terreeoboo, Maiha-maiha, and himself were extremely desirous of peace; that they had given us the most convincing proofs of it; and that they had been prevented from giving it sooner by the other chiefs, many of whom were still disaffected to us. He lamented, with the most lively sorrow, the death of six chiefs, who had been killed by our people; some of whom, he said, were among our best friends. He informed us, that the cutter had been taken away by Pareea's people, probably in revenge for the blow that he had received; and that it had been broken up the following day. The arms of the marines, which we had also demanded, had been carried off, he said, by the populace and were irrecoverable.

Nothing now remained, but to perform the last solemn offices to our excellent commander. Eappo was dismissed with orders to taboo all the bay; and, in the afternoon his remains having been deposited in a coffin, the funeral service was read over them, and they were committed to the deep with the usual military honours. Our feelings, on this mournful occasion, are more easy to be conceived than expressed.

CHAP.

CHAP. XVI.

ON the 22nd of February, 1779, during the morning, not a canoe came near the bay, the taboo, which Eappo, at our request, had laid on it the preceding day, having not yet been taken off. At length that chief came on board; when we assured him that we were now perfectly satisfied; and that, as the Orono was buried, all remembrance of the late unhappy transactions was buried with him. We afterwards requested him to take off the taboo, and to make it known, that the islanders might bring provisions to us as usual. The ships were soon surrounded with canoes, and many of the erees came on board, expressing their grief at what had happened, and their satisfaction at our reconciliation. Several of our friends, who did not favour us with a visit, sent presents of large hogs, and other provisions. Among the rest, the old treacherous Koah came off to us, but we refused him admittance. We were now preparing to put to sea, and Captain Clerke imagining, that, if the intelligence of our proceedings should reach the islands to leeward before us, it might have a bad effect, gave orders, that the ships should be unmoored. About eight in the evening, we dismissed all the natives; and Eappo, and the friendly Kaireekeea, took their leave of us in a very affectionate manner. We immediately weighed anchor, and stood out of Karakakooa bay. The islanders were assembled in great numbers on the shore; and, as we passed along, received our last farewels, with every mark of goodwill and affection. About ten o'clock, P. M. having cleared the land, we stood to the northward, with a view of searching for a harbour, which the natives had often mentioned, on the south-east side of Mowee. We found ourselves, the next morning, driven to leeward, by a swell from the N. E.

and

and a fresh gale, from the same quarter, drove us still farther to the westward. At midnight we tacked and stood four hours to the S. to keep clear of the land; and, at day-break, on the 24th, we were standing towards a small barren island, named Tahoorowa, about seven miles S. W. of Mowee. Having now no prospect of making a closer examination of the S. E. parts of Mowee, we bore away, and kept along the S. E. side of Tahoorowa. Steering close round its western extremity, in order to fetch the W. side of Mowee, we suddenly shoaled our water, and saw the sea breaking on some rocks almost right a-head. We then kept away about a league and a half, and again steered to the northward; when we stood for a passage between Mowee, and an island named Ranai. In the afternoon, the weather was calm, with light airs from the W. We stood to the N. N. W. but observing a shoal about sunset, and the weather being unsettled, we stood towards the S. We had passed the S. W. side of this island, without being able to approach the shore. It forms the same distant view as the N. E. as seen when we returned from the N. in November, 1778; the hilly parts, connected by a low flat isthmus, having, at the first view, the appearance of two separate islands. This deceptive appearance continued, till we were within about ten leagues of the coast, which bending a great way inward, formed a capacious bay. The westernmost point, off which the shoal runs that we have just now mentioned, is rendered remarkable by a small hillock; S. of which is a fine sandy bay; and, on the shore, are several huts, with plenty of cocoa-trees about them. In the course of the day, several of the natives visited us, and brought provisions with them. We presently discovered, that they had heard of our unfortunate disaster at Owhyhee. They were extremely anxious to be informed of the particulars, from a woman who had hid herself in the Resolution,

tion, in order to obtain a passage to Atooi; making particular enquiries about Pareea, and some other chiefs; and seeming much agitated at the death of Kaneena, and his brother. But, in whatever light this business might have been represented by the woman, it produced no bad effect in their behaviour, which was civil and obliging to an extreme.

On Thursday, the 25th, in the morning, the wind being at E. we steered along the S. side of Ranai, till almost noon, when we had baffling winds and calms till the evening; after which, we had a light easterly breeze, and steered for the W. of Morotoi. The current, which had set from the N. E. ever since we left Karakakooa bay, changed its direction, in the course of this day, to the S. E. The wind was again variable during the night; but, early in the morning of the 26th, it settled at E. blowing so fresh, as to oblige us to double-reef the top-sails. At seven, we opened a small bay, distant about two leagues, having a fine sandy beach; but not perceiving any appearance of fresh water, we endeavoured to get to the windward of Woahoo, an island which had been seen in January, 1778. We saw the land about two in the afternoon, bearing W. by N. at the distance of about eight leagues. We tacked, as soon as it was dark, and again bore away at day-light on the 27th. Between ten and eleven, we were about a league off the shore, and near the middle of the N. E. side of the island.

The coast to the northward, consists of detached hills, ascending perpendicularly from the sea; the sides being covered with wood, and the vallies, between them, appearing to be fertile, and well cultivated. An extensive bay was observable to the southward, bounded, to the S. E. by a low point of land, covered with cocoa-nut trees; off which, an insulated rock appeared, at the distance of a mile from the shore. The wind continuing to blow fresh, we were unwilling to entangle ourselves with a lee-shore.

shore. Instead of attempting, therefore, to examine the bay, we hauled up, and steered in the direction of the coast. At noon, we were about two leagues from the island, and a-breast of the N. point of it. It is low and flat, having a reef stretching off almost a mile and a half. Between the N. point, and a head-land to the S. W. the land bends inward, and seemed to promise a good road. We therefore steered along the shore, at about a mile distance. At two, we were induced, by the sight of a fine river, to anchor in thirteen fathoms water. In the afternoon, Mr. King attended the two captains on shore, where few of the natives were to be seen, and those principally women. The men, we were informed, were gone to Morotoi, to fight Tahyterree; but their chief, Perrecoranee, remained behind, and would certainly attend us, as soon as he was informed of our arrival. To our great disappointment, the water had a brackish taste, for about two hundred yards up the river; beyond which, however, it was perfectly fresh, and was a delightful stream. Farther up, we came to the conflux of two small rivulets, branching off to the right and left of a steep romantic mountain. The banks of the river, and all that we saw of Woahoo, are in fine cultivation, and full of villages; the face of the country being also, remarkably beautiful and picturesque. It would have been a laborious business to have watered at this place, Mr. King was therefore dispatched to search about the coast to leeward; but, being unable to land, on account of a reef of coral, which extended along the shore, Captain Clerke resolved to proceed immediately to Atooi. In the morning, about eight, we weighed and stood to the north; and, on Sunday, the 28th, at day-light, we bore away for that island, and were in sight of it by noon. We were off its eastern extremity, which is a green flat point, about sun-set. As it was dark, we did not venture to run for the

road

road on the S. W. side, but spent the night in plying on and off, and anchored, at nine the next morning, being Monday the 1st of March, in 25 fathoms water. In running down, from the S. E. point of the island, we saw, in many places, the appearance of shoal water, at some distance from the land. Being anchored in our old station, several canoes came to visit us; but it was very observable, that there was not that appearance of cordiality in their manner, and complacency in their countenances, as when we saw them before. They had no sooner got on board, but one of them informed us, that we had communicated a disorder to the women, which had killed many persons of both sexes. He, at that time, was afflicted with the venereal disease, and minutely described the various symptoms which had attended it. As no appearance of that disorder had been observed amongst them, on our first arrival, we were, it is to be feared, the authors of this irreparable mischief. What we had principally in view, at this place, was to water the ships with as much expedition as possible; and Mr. King was sent on shore in the afternoon, with the launch and pinnace, laden with casks. He was accompanied by the gunner of the Resolution, who was instructed to trade for some provisions; and they were attended by a guard of five marines. Multitudes of people were collected upon the beach, by whom, at first, we were kindly received; but, after we had landed the casks, they began to be exceedingly troublesome. Knowing from experience, how difficult a task it was to repress this disposition, without the interposition of their chiefs, we were sorry to be informed, that they were all at a distant part of the island. Indeed, we both felt and lamented the want of their assistance; for we could hardly form a circle, as our practice usually was, for the safety and convenience of the trading party. No sooner had we taken this step, and posted marines to keep off the populace, than a man took hold of the bayonet belonging to one of the soldiers musquets, and endeavoured to wrench it forcibly from his hand. Mr. King immediately advanced towards them, when the native quitted his hold, and retired; but immediately returned, having a spear in one hand, and a dagger in the other; and it was with difficulty that his countrymen could restrain him from engaging with the soldier. This affray was occasioned by the native's having received, from the soldier, a slight prick with his bayonet, to induce him to keep without the line. At this time, our situation required great management and circumspection; Mr. King accordingly enjoined, that no one should presume to fire, or proceed to any other act of violence, without positive commands. Having given these instructions, he was summoned to the assistance of the watering party, where he found the natives in the same mischievous disposition. They had peremptorily demanded, for every cask of water, a large hatchet; which not being complied with, they would not permit the sailors to roll them to the boats. When Mr. King had joined them, one of the natives approached him, with great insolence, and made the same demand. Mr. King told him, that as a friend, he was welcome to a hatchet, but he certainly would carry off the water, without paying for it; and instantly ordered the pinnace men to proceed; at the same time calling for three marines, from the trading party, to protect them. This becoming spirit so far succeeded, as to prevent any daring attempt to interrupt us; but they still persevered in the most teasing and insulting behaviour. Some of them, under pretence of assisting the sailors, in rolling the casks towards the shore, gave them a different direction; others stole the hats from off our people's heads, pulled them backward by the skirts of their clothes, and tripped up

their

their heels; the populace, during all this time, shouting and laughing, with a mixture of mockery and malice. They afterwards took an opportunity of stealing the cooper's bucket, and forcibly took away his bag. Their principal aim, however, was to possess themselves of the musquets of the marines, who were continually complaining of their attempts to force them from their hands. Though they, in general, preserved a kind of deference and respect for Mr. King, yet they obliged him to contribute his share towards their stock of plunder. One of them approached him, in a familiar manner, and diverted his attention, whilst another seized his hanger, which he held carelessly in his hand, and ran away with it. Such insolence was not to be repelled by force. Prudence dictated that we must patiently submit to it; at the same time, guarding against its effects as well as we were able. Mr. King was, however, somewhat alarmed, on being soon after informed by the serjeant of marines, that, turning suddenly round, he saw a man behind him, armed with a dagger, in the position of striking. Though he might, perhaps, be mistaken, in this particular, our situation was truly critical and alarming; and the smallest error or mistake, on our part, might have been of fatal consequences.

Our people being separated into three small parties; one filling casks at the lake; another rolling them to the shore; and a third purchasing provisions; Mr. King had some intentions of collecting them together, in order to protect the performance of one duty at a time. But, on due reflection, he thought it more adviseable to let them proceed as they had begun. If a real attack had been made, even our whole force could have made but a poor resistance. He thought, on the other hand, that such a step might operate to our disadvantage, as being an evident token of our fears. Besides, in the present case, the crowd was kept divided, and many of them wholly occupied in bartering. Perhaps the principal cause of their not attacking us was, their dread of the effects of our arms; and, as we appeared to place so much confidence in this advantage, as to oppose only five marines to such a multitude of people, their ideas of our superiority must have been greatly exalted. It was our business to cherish this opinion; and, it must ever be acknowledged, to the honour of the whole party, that it was impossible for any men to behave better, in order to strengthen these impressions. Whatever could be considered as a jest, they received with patience and good-nature; but, if they were interrupted by any serious attempt, they opposed it with resolute looks and menaces. At length, we so far succeeded, as to get all our casks to the seaside, without any accident of consequence: but, while our people were getting the casks into the launch, the inhabitants, thinking they should have no farther opportunity of plundering, grew more daring and insolent. The serjeant of marines luckily suggested to Mr. King, the advantage of sending off his party first into the boats, by which means the musquets would be taken out of their reach; which, as above related, were the grand objects the islanders had in view: and, if they should happen to attack us, the marines could more effectually defend us, than if they were on shore. Every thing was now in the boats, and only Mr. King, Mr. Anderson, the gunner, and a seaman of the boat's crew, remained on shore. The pinnace laying beyond the surf, which we were under a necessity of swimming through, Mr. King ordered the other two to make the best of their way to it, and told them he would follow them. They both refused to comply with this order, and it became a matter of contest, who should be the last on shore. Some hasty expression, it seems, Mr. King had just before made use of to the sailor, which he considered as a re-

flection

flection on his courage, and excited his resentment; and the old gunner, as a point of honour was now started, conceived it to be his duty to take a part in it. In this whimsical situation, they, perhaps, might have long remained, had not the dispute been settled by the stones, which began to fly plentifully about us, and by the exclamations of the people from the boats, begging us to be expeditious, as the natives were armed with clubs and spears, and pursuing us into the water. Mr. King arrived first at the pinnace, and, perceiving Mr. Anderson was so far behind, as not to be entirely out of danger, he ordered one musquet to be fired; but, in the hurry of executing his orders, the marines fired two. The natives immediately ran away, leaving only one man and woman on the beach. The man attempted to rise several times, but was not able, having been wounded in the groin. The islanders, in a short time, returned; and, surrounding the wounded man, brandished their spears at us, with an air of defiance; but, by the time we reached the ships, some persons arrived which we supposed to be the chiefs, by whom they were all driven from the shore. During our absence Captain Clerke had been under terrible apprehensions for our safety; which had been considerably increased by his misunderstanding some of the natives, with whom he had conversed on board. The name of Captain Cook being frequently mentioned, accompanied with circumstantial descriptions of his death and destruction, he concluded, that they had received intelligence of the unfortunate events at Owhyhee, to which they alluded. But they were only endeavouring to make him understand, what wars had arisen on account of the goats, which Captain Cook had left at Oneeheow, and that the poor goats had been slaughtered, during the contest for the property of them. Captain Clerke, applying these shocking representations to our misfortunes at

Owhyhee,

Owhyhee, and to an indication of revenge, fixed his telescope upon us the whole time; and, as soon as he saw the smoke of the musquets, ordered the boats to be put off to our assistance.

On Tuesday, the 2nd of March, in the morning, Mr. King was again ordered on shore, with the watering party. As we had so narrowly escaped the preceding day, Captain Clerke augmented our force from both ships, and we had a guard of forty men under arms. This precaution, however, was found to be unnecessary; for the beach was left entirely to ourselves, and the ground, extending from the landing-place to the lake, tabooed. Hence we concluded, that some of the chiefs had visited this quarter; who, being unable to stay, had considerately taken this step, that we might be accommodated with safety. Several men appeared with spears and daggers, on the other side of the river, but never attempted to molest us. Their women came over, and seated themselves close by us, on the banks; and about the middle of the day, some of the men were prevailed on to bring us hogs and roots, and also to dress them for us. When we had left the beach, they came down to the sea-side, and one of them had the audacity to throw a stone at us; but, as his conduct was highly censured by the rest, we did not express any kind of resentment. On the 3d, we completed our watering, without much difficulty; and, on returning to the ships, we were informed, that several chiefs had been on board, and had apologized for the conduct of their countrymen, attributing their riotous behaviour to the quarrels then subsisting among the principal people of the island, and which had destroyed all order and subordination. At this time the government of Atooi was disputed between Toneoneo, who had the supreme power when we were there the preceding year, and a youth named Teavee. By different fathers, they are both the grandsons
of

of Pereeorannee, king of Woahoo; who gave Atooi to the former, and Oneeheow to the latter. The quarrel originated about the goats which we had left at Oneeheow the year before; they being claimed by Toneoneo, as that island was a dependency of his. The adherents of Teavee insisting on the right of possession, both parties prepared to support their pretensions, and a battle ensued just before our arrival, wherein Toneoneo had been defeated. Toneoneo was likely to become more affected by the consequence of this victory, than by the loss of the objects in dispute; for the mother of Teavee having married a second husband, who was not only a chief at Atooi, but also at the head of a powerful faction there, he thought of embracing the present opportunity of driving Toneoneo out of the island, that his son-in-law might succeed to the government. The goats, which had increased to six, and would probably have stocked these islands in a few years, were destroyed in this contest. Thursday, the 4th, we were visited, on board the Resolution, by the father-in-law, the mother, and the sister of the young prince, who made several curious presents to Captain Clerke. Among the rest, were some fishhooks, which were made from the bones of Terreeoboo's father, who had been killed in an unsuccessful descent upon Woahoo. Also a fly-flap, from the hands of the prince's sister, which had a human bone for its handle, and had been given to her by her father-in-law, as a trophy. They were not accompanied by young Teavee, he being then engaged in the performance of some religious rites, on account of the victory he had obtained. The 5th and 6th, were employed in completing the Discovery's water. The carpenters were engaged in caulking the ships, and preparing for our next cruise. We no longer received any molestation from the natives, who supplied us plentifully with pork and vegetables.

This

This day we were visited by an Indian, who brought a piece of iron on board, to be formed into the shape of a pahooa. It was the bolt of some large ship timbers, but neither the officers nor men could discover to what nation it belonged; though from the shape of the bolt, and the paleness of the iron, they were convinced it was not English. They enquired strictly of the native how he came possessed of it, when he informed them, that it was taken out of a large piece of timber, which had been driven upon their island, since we were there in January, 1778.

On Sunday, the 7th, we received a visit from Toneoneo, at which we were surprized. Hearing the dowager princess was on board, he could hardly be prevailed on to enter the ship. When they met, they cast an angry lowering look at each other. He did not stay long, and appeared much dejected. We remarked, however, with some degree of surprize, that the women prostrated themselves before him, both at his coming and going away; and all the natives on board treated him with that respect which is usually paid to persons of his rank. It was somewhat remarkable, that a man, who was then in a state of actual hostility with Teavee's party, should venture alone within the power of his enemies. Indeed, the civil dissensions, which are frequent in all the south sea islands, seem to be conducted without much acrimony; the deposed governor still enjoying the rank of an eree, and may put in practice such means as may arise, to regain the consequence which he has lost.

On the 8th, at nine in the morning, we weighed, and proceeded towards Oneeheow, and came to anchor in 20 fathoms water, at about three in the afternoon, nearly on the spot where we anchored in 1778. With the other anchor, we moored in 26 fathoms water. We had a strong gale from the eastward in the night, and, the next morning, the

ship

ship had driven a whole cable's length, both anchors being almost brought a-head; in which situation we were obliged to continue, this and the two following days.

On Friday, the 12th, the weather being more moderate, the master was dispatched to the N. W. side of the island, in search of a more commodious place for anchoring. In the evening he returned, having found a fine bay, with good anchorage, in 18 fathoms water. The points of the bay were in the direction of N. by E. and S. by W. A small village was situated on the N. side of the bay, to the eastward of which were four wells of good water. Mr. Bligh went far enough to the N. to convince himself that Oreehoua, and Oneeheow, were two separate islands. Being now on the point of taking our final leave of the Sandwich Islands, it may be proper to give here a general and correct account of their situation, and natural history, as well as of the customs and manners of the natives; which will serve as a kind of supplement to a former description, the result of our first visit to these islands.

This group is composed of 11 islands, extending in long. from 199 deg. 36 min. to 205 deg. 6 min. E. and in lat. from 18 deg. 54 min. to 22 deg. 15 min. N. Their names, according to the natives, are, 1. Owhyhee, 2. Atooi, Atowi, or Towi; which is also sometimes called Kowi. 3. Woahoo, or Oahoo. 4. Mowee. 5. Morotoi, or Morokoi. 6. Oreehoua, or Reehoua. 7. Morotinnee, or Morokinnee. 8. Tahoora. 9. Ranai, or Oranai. 10. Oneeheow, or Neheeow. 11. Kahowrowee, or Tahoorowa. These are all inhabited, except Tahoora and Morotinnee. Besides those we have enumerated, we heard of another island named Modoopapapa, or Komodoo-papapa, situated to the W. S. W. of Tahoora; it is low and sandy, and is visited solely for the purpose of catching turtle and waterfowl. As we could never learn that the natives had knowledge of any other islands, it is most probable that no others exist in their neighbourhood. Captain Cook had distinguished this cluster of islands by the name of the Sandwich Islands, in honour of the Earl of Sandwich, then first Lord of the Admiralty, under whose administration he had enriched geography with so many valuable discoveries; a tribute justly due to that nobleman, for the encouragement and support which these voyages derived from his power, and for the zealous eagerness with which he seconded the views of our illustrious navigator.

The most easterly of these islands, called Owhyhee, and by far the largest of them all, is of a triangular figure, and nearly equilateral. The angular points constitute the northern, southern, and eastern extremities. The lat. of the northern extreme is 20 deg. 17 min. N. and its long. 204 deg. 2 min. E. the southern end stands in the long. 204 deg. 15 min. E. and in the lat. of 18 deg. 54 min. N. and the eastern extremity is in the lat. of 19 deg. 34 min. N. and in the long. of 205 deg. 6 min. E. The circumference of the whole island is about 255 geographical miles, or 293 English ones. Its breadth is 24 leagues; and its greatest length, which lies nearly in a N. and S. direction, is 28 leagues and a half. It is divided into six extensive districts, namely, Akona and Koaarra, which are on the W. side; Kaoo and Opoona, on the S. E. and Aheedoo and Amakooa, on the N. E. A mountain, named Mouna Kaah, (or the mountain Kaah) which rises in three peaks, continually covered with snow, and may be discerned at the distance of 40 leagues, separates the district of Amakooa from that of Aheedoo. The coast, to the northward of this mountain, is composed of high and abrupt cliffs, down which fall many beautiful cascades of water. We once flattered ourselves with the hopes of finding a harbour round a bluff head, on a part of this coast, in the lat. of 20 deg. 10 min. N. and the long. of 204 deg.

204 deg. 26 min. E. but after we had doubled the point, and were standing close in, we found that it was connected, by a low valley, with another elevated head to the northweftward. The country rifes inland with a gradual afcent, and is interfected by narrow deep glens, or rather chafms: it feemed to be well cultivated, and to have many villages fcattered about it. The fnowy mountain abovementioned is very fteep, and its loweft part abounds with wood. The coaft of Aheedoo is of a moderate elevation; and the interior parts have the appearance of being more even than the country towards the N. W. We cruifed off thefe two diftricts for near a month; and whenever our diftance from the fhore would permit, were furrounded by canoes laden with refrefhments of every kind. On this fide of the ifland, we often met with a very heavy fea, and a great fwell; and, as there was much foul ground off the fhore, we feldom made a nearer approach to the land than two or three leagues. Towards the N. E. of Apoona, the coaft, which conftitutes the eaftern extreme of the ifland, is rather low and flat. In the inland parts the acclivity is very gradual; and the country abounds with bread-fruit, and cocoa-nut trees. This appeared to us to be the fineft part of the whole ifland; and we were afterwards informed, that the king occafionally refided here. The hills, at the fouth-weftern extremity, rife with fome abruptnefs from the fea-fide, leaving only a narrow border of low land towards the beach. The fides of thefe hills were covered with verdure; but the adjacent country feemed thinly inhabited. When our fhips doubled the E. point of the ifland, we had fight of another fnowy mountain, called by the natives, Mouna Roa (or the extenfive mountain) which, during the whole time we were failing along the fouth-eaftern fide, continued to be a very confpicuous object. It was flat at the fummit, which was perpetually involved

involved in snow; and we once observed its sides also slightly covered with it for a considerable way down. According to the tropical line of snow, as determined by Monsieur Condamine, from observations made on the Cordilleras in America, the height of this mountain must be, at least, 16,020 feet. It therefore exceeds the height of the Pico de Teyde, or Peak of Teneriffe, by 3680 feet, according to the computation of the Chevalier de Borda, or 724, according to that of Dr. Heberden. The peaks of Mouna Kaah seemed to be of the height of about half a mile: and, as they are wholly covered with snow, the altitude of their summits must at least be 18,400 feet.

The district of Kaoo exhibits a most horrid and dismal prospect; the whole country having, to appearance, undergone an entire change from the consequences of some dreadful convulsion. The ground is, in all parts, covered with cinders; and, in many places, intersected with blackish streaks, which seem to mark the progress of a lava that has flowed, not many centuries ago, from Mouna Roa to the shore. The south promontory appears like the mere dregs of a volcano. The head-land consists of broken and craggy rocks, terminating in acute points, and irregularly piled on each other. Notwithstanding the dreary aspect of this part of the island, it contains many villages, and is far more populous than the verdant mountains of Apoona. Nor is it difficult to account for this circumstance. These islanders not being possessed of any cattle, have no occasion for pasturage; and are therefore inclined to prefer such ground as is either more conveniently situated for fishing, or best adapted to the cultivation of plantains and yams. Now amidst these ruins, there are many spots of rich soil, which are with great care laid out in plantations; and the neighbouring sea abounds with excellent fish of various kinds. Off this part of the coast,

coast, at less than a cable's length from the shore, we did not strike ground with 160 fathoms of line, except in a small bight to the E. of the southern point, where we found from 50 to 58 fathoms of water, over a sandy bottom. It may be proper to observe, before we proceed to give an account of the western districts, that the whole coast we have described, from the northern to the southern extreme, affords not a single harbour, nor the least shelter for shipping. The south-western parts of Akona are in a condition similar to that of the adjoining district of Kaoo; but the country further towards the N. has been carefully cultivated, and is exceedingly populous. In this division of the island lies Karakakooa Bay, of which we have already given a description. Scarce any thing is seen along the coast, but the fragments of black scorched rocks; behind which, the ground, for the space of about two miles and a half, rises gradually, and seems to have been once covered with loose burnt stones. These have been cleared away by the inhabitants, frequently to the depth of three feet and upwards; and the fertility of the soil has amply repaid their labour. Here they cultivate in a rich ashy mould, the cloth-plant and sweet potatoes. Groves of cocoa-nut-trees are scattered among the fields, which are enclosed with stone fences. On the rising ground beyond these, they plant bread-fruit-trees, which flourish with surprising luxuriance. The district of Koaarra extends from the most westerly point to the northern extreme of the island. The whole coast between them forms a spacious bay, which is called by the natives Toeyah-yah, and is bounded to the northward by two conspicuous hills. Towards the bottom of this bay, there is foul, corally ground, that extends to the distance of upwards of a mile from the shore, without which there is good anchorage. The country, as far as the eye could discern, appeared to be fruitful and populous;

populous; but no fresh water was to be found. The soil seemed to be of the same kind with that of the district of Kaoo.

Having thus described the coasts of the island of Owhyhee, and the adjacent country, we shall now relate some particulars respecting the interior parts, from the information we obtained from a party, who set out on the 26th of January, on an expedition up the country, principally with an intention of reaching the snowy mountains. Having previously procured two of the islanders to serve them as guides, they quitted the village about four o'clock in the afternoon. Their course was easterly, inclining a little to the south. Within three or four miles from the bay, they found the country as already described; but the hills afterwards rose with a less gradual ascent, which brought them to some extensive plantations, consisting of the taro or eddy root, and sweet potatoes, with plants of the cloth-tree. Both the taro and the sweet potatoes are here planted at the distance of four feet from each other. The potatoes are earthed up almost to the top of the stalk, with a proper quantity of light mould. The taro is left bare to the root, and the mould round it is put in the form of a bason, for the purpose of holding the rain-water; this root requiring a certain degree of moisture. At the Friendly and Society Isles, the taro was constantly planted in low and moist situations, and generally in those places where there was the conveniency of a rivulet to flood it. This mode of culture was considered as absolutely necessary; but we now found that this root, with the precaution before-mentioned, succeeds equally well in a more dry situation. It was, indeed, remarked by all of us, that the taro of the Sandwich Islands was the best we had ever tasted. The walls, by which these plantations are separated from each other, are composed of the loose burnt stones, which are met with in clearing the ground;

and,

and, being totally concealed by sugar-canes, that are planted close on each side, form the most beautiful fences that can be imagined. Our party stopped for the night at the second hut they observed among the plantations, where they supposed themselves to be six or seven miles distant from our ships. The prospect from this spot was described by them as very delightful: they had a view of our vessels in the bay before them; to the left they saw a continued range of villages, interspersed with groves of cocoa-nut-trees, spreading along the shore; a thick wood extending itself behind them; and, to the right, a very considerable extent of ground, laid out with great regularity in well-cultivated plantations, displayed itself to their view. Near this spot the natives ponted out to them, at a distance from every other dwelling, the residence of a hermit, who, they said, had, in the former part of his life, been a great chief and warrior, but had long ago retired from the sea-coast of the island, and now never quitted the environs of his cottage. As they approached him, they prostrated themselves, and afterwards presented him with some provisions. His behaviour was easy, frank, and chearful. He testified little astonishment at the sight of our people, and though pressed to accept of some European curiosities, he thought proper to decline the offer, and soon retired to his cottage. Our party represented him as by far the most aged person they had ever seen; judging him to be, at a moderate computation, upwards of a hundred years of age. As they had supposed that the mountain was not more than ten or a dozen miles distant from the bay, and consequently expected to reach it with ease early the following morning, they were now greatly surprized to find the distance scarce perceivably diminished. This circumstance, with the uninhabited state of the country which they were on the point of entering, rendering it necessary to provide a sup-

ply

ply of provisions, they dispatched one of their conductors back to the village for that purpose. Whilst they waited his return, they were joined by several of Kaoo's servants, whom that generous old man had sent after them, loaded with refreshments, and fully authorized, as their rout lay through his grounds, to demand, and take away with them whatever they might want. Our travellers were surprized on finding the cold here so intense. But, as they had no thermometer with them, they could only form their judgment of it from their feelings; which, from the warm atmosphere they had quitted, must have been a very fallacious method of judging. They found it, however, so cold, that they could scarce get any sleep, and the islanders could not sleep at all; both parties being disturbed, during the whole night, by continual coughing. As they, at this time, could not be at any very great height, their distance from the sea being no more than six or seven miles, and part of the road on a very moderate ascent, this uncommon degree of cold must be attributed to the easterly wind blowing fresh over the snowy mountains. Early the next morning, they proceeded on their journey, and filled their calibashes at a well of excellent water, situate about half a mile from their hut. After they had passed the plantations, they arrived at a thick wood, which they entered by a path that had been made for the convenience of the islanders, who frequently repair thither for the purpose of catching birds, as well as procuring the wild or horse-plantain. Their progress now became extremely slow, and was attended with great labour; for the ground was either swampy, or covered with large stones; the path narrow, and often interrupted by trees lying across it, which they were obliged to climb over, as the thickness of the underwood, on each side, rendered it impracticable to pass round them. They saw, in these woods, pieces

of

of white cloth fixed on poles, at small distances, which they imagined were land marks for the division of property, as they only observed them where the wild plantains grew. The trees were of the same kind with the spice tree of New Holland; they were straight and lofty, and their circumference was from two to four feet. Having advanced nine or ten miles in the wood, they had the mortification of finding themselves, suddenly, within sight of the sea, and not very far from it; the path having turned off imperceptibly to the S. and carried them to the right of the mountain, which it was their intention to reach. Their disappointment was considerably heightened by the uncertainty under which they now were with respect to its true bearings, as they could not at present gain a view of it from the top of the highest trees. They, therefore, thought proper to walk back six or seven miles to an unoccupied hut, where they had left two of their own people, and three of the natives, with the small remnant of their provisions. Here they passed the second night, during which the air was so extremely sharp, that, by the morning, their guides were all gone off, except one.

Being at this time in want of provisions, which laid them under a necessity of returning to some of the cultivated parts of the island, they left the wood by the same path by which they had entered it. When they arrived at the plantations, they were surrounded by the islanders, from whom they purchased a fresh supply of necessaries; and prevailed upon two of them to accompany them as guides, in the room of those who had gone away. Having procured the best information they could possibly obtain with regard to the direction of their road, the party, who were now nine in number, marched for about half a dozen miles along the skirts of the wood, and then entered it again by a path leading towards the E. They passed, for the first three miles,

miles, through a forest of lofty spice-trees, which grew on a rich loam. At the back of these trees they met with an equal extent of low shrubby trees, together with a considerable quantity of thick underwood, upon a bottom of loose burnt stones. This led them to another forest of spice-trees, and the same rich brownish soil, which was again succeeded by a barren ridge of a similar kind with the former. These ridges, as far as they could be seen, appeared to run parallel with the sea shore, and to have Mouna Roa for their centre. In passing through the woods they found many unfinished canoes, and huts in several places; but they saw none of the inhabitants. After they had penetrated almost three miles into the second wood, they arrived at two huts, where they stopped, being greatly fatigued with the day's journey, in the course of which they had walked, according to their own computation, at least twenty miles. Having found no springs from the time they quitted the plantations, they had greatly suffered from the violence of their thirst; in consequence of which they were obliged, before the evening came on, to separate into small parties, and go in quest of water. They, at last, met with some that had been left by rain in the bottom of a half-finished canoe; which, though of a reddish colour, was by no means unwelcome to them. Throughout the night, the cold was more intense than before; and though they had taken care to wrap themselves up in mats and clothes of the country, and to keep a large fire between the two huts, they could get but very little sleep, and were under the necessity of walking about for the greatest part of the night. Their elevation was now, in all probability, pretty considerable, as the ground, over which their journey lay, had been generally on the ascent. On the next morning, which was the 29th, they set out early, with an intention of making their last and greatest effort to

reach

reach the snowy mountain; but their spirits were considerably depressed, on finding that the miserable pittance of water, which they had discovered the preceding night, was expended. The path, which reached no farther than where canoes had been built, being now terminated, they were obliged to make their way as well as they could; frequently climbing up into the most lofty trees, to explore the surrounding country. They arrived, about eleven o'clock, at a ridge of burnt stones, from the top of which they had a prospect of the Mouna Roa, which then appeared to be at the distance of between twelve and fourteen miles from them. They now entered into a consultation, whether they should proceed any further, or rest contented with the view before them of the snowy mountain. Since the path had ceased, their road had become highly fatiguing, and was growing still more so, every step they advanced. The ground was almost every where broken into deep fissures, which, being slightly covered with moss, made them stumble almost continually; and the intervening space consisted of a surface of loose burnt stones, which broke under their feet. Into some of these fissures they threw stones, which seemed from the noise they made, to fall to a considerable depth; and the ground founded hollow as they walked upon it. Besides these circumstances, which discouraged them from proceeding, they found their conductors so averse to going on, that they had reason to think they would not be prevailed on to remain out another night. They, therefore, at length came to a determination of returning to the ships, after taking a survey of the country from the highest trees they could find. From this elevation, they perceived themselves surrounded with wood towards the sea; they were unable to distinguish, in the horizon, the sky from the water; and betwixt them and the snowy mountain, was a valley of about eight miles in breadth. They passed this night at a hut in the second forest; and the following day, before noon, they had passed the first wood, and found themselves nine or ten miles to the N. E. of the ships, towards which they marched through the plantations. As they walked along, they did not observe a spot of ground, that was susceptible of improvement, left unplanted; and, indeed, the country, from their account, could scarcely be cultivated to greater advantage for the purposes of the natives. They were surprised at seeing several fields of hay; and, upon their enquiry, to what particular use it was applied, they were informed, that it was intended to cover the grounds where the young taro grew, in order to preserve them from being scorched by the rays of the sun. They observed, among the plantations, a few huts scattered about, which afforded occasional shelter to the labourers: but they did not see any villages at a greater distance from the sea than four or five miles. Near one of them, which was situated about four miles from the bay, they discovered a cave, forty fathoms in length, three in breadth, and of the same height. It was open at each end; its sides were fluted, as if wrought with a chissel; and the surface was glazed over, perhaps by the action of fire. Having thus related the principal circumstances that occurred in the expedition to the snowy mountain at Owhyhee, we shall now proceed to describe the other islands of this groupe.

That which is next in size, and nearest in situation to Owhyhee, is Mowee. It stands at the distance of eight leagues N. N. W. from Owhyhee, and is 140 geographical miles in circuit. It is divided by a low isthmus into two circular peninsulas, of which that to the eastward is named Whamadooa, and is twice as large as that to the W. called Owhyrookoo. The mountains in both rise to a very great height, as we were able to see them at the distance of about 30 leagues. The northern shores,

like

like those of the isle of Owhyhee, afford no soundings; and the country bears the same aspect of fertility and verdure. The E. point of Mowee is in the latitude of 20 deg. 50 min. N. and in the longitude of 204 deg. 4 min. E. To the southward, between Mowee and the adjacent islands, we found regular depths with 150 fathoms, over a bottom of sand. From the western point, which is rather low, runs a shoal, extending towards the island of Ranai, to a considerable distance; and to the S. of this, is an extensive bay, with a sandy beach, shaded with cocoa-trees. It is not improbable that good anchorage might be met with here, with shelter from the prevailing winds; and that the beach affords a commodious landing-place. The country further back is very romantic in its appearance. The hills rise almost perpendicularly, exhibiting a variety of peaked forms; and their steep sides, as well as the deep chasms between them, are covered with trees, among which those of the bread-fruit principally abound. The summits of these hills are perfectly bare, and of a reddish brown hue. The natives informed us, that there was a harbour to the S. of the eastern point, which they asserted was superior to that of Karakakooa; and we also heard that there was another harbour, named Keepookeepoo, on the north-western side.

Ranai is about nine miles distant from Mowee and Morotoi, and is situate to the S. W. of the passage between those two isles. The country, towards the S. is elevated and craggy; but the other parts of the island had a better appearance, and seemed to be well inhabited. It abounds in roots, such as sweet potatoes, taro, and yams; but produces very few plantains, and bread-fruit trees. The S. point of Ranai is in the latitude of 20 deg. 46 min. N. and in the longitude of 203 deg. 8 min. E.

Morotoi lies at the distance of two leagues and a half to the W. N. W. of Mowee. Its south-western coast,

coast, which was the only part of it we approached, is very low; but the land behind rises to a considerable elevation; and, at the distance from which we had a view of it, appeared to be destitute of wood. Yams are its principal produce; and it may probably contain fresh water. The coast, on the southern and western sides of the island, forms several bays, that promise a tolerable shelter from the trade winds. The W. point of Morotoi is in the longitude of 202 deg. 46 min. E. and in the latitude of 21 deg. 10 min. N.

Tahoorowa is a small island situated off the southwestern part of Mowee, from which it is nine miles distant. It is destitute of wood, and its soil seems to be sandy and unfertile. Its latitude is 20 deg. 38 min. N. and its longitude 203 deg. 27 min. E. Between it and Mowee stands the little island of Morrotinnee, which has no inhabitants.

Woahoo lies about seven leagues to the N. W. of Morotoi. As far as we were enabled to judge, from the appearance of the north-western and north-eastern parts (for we had not an opportunity of seeing the southern side) it is by far the finest of all the Sandwich Islands. The verdure of the hills, the variety of wood and lawn, and fertile well cultivated valleys, which the whole face of the country presented to view, could not be exceeded. Having already described the bay in which we anchored, formed by the northern and western extremes, it remains for us to observe, that, in the bight of the bay, to the southward of our anchoring-place, we met with foul rocky ground, about two miles from the shore. If the ground tackling of a ship should happen to be weak, and the wind blow with violence from the N. to which quarter the road is entirely open, this circumstance might be attended with some degree of danger: but, provided the cables were good, there would be no great hazard, as the ground from the anchoring place, which is

opposite

London: Published as the Act directs, by Alexr. Hogg, at the Kings Arms, No. 16, Paternoster Row.

opposite the valley through which the river runs, to the northern point, consists of a fine sand. The latitude of our anchoring-place is 21 deg. 43 min. N. and the longitude 202 deg. 9 min. E.

The district of Atooi is about 25 leagues to the N. W. of Woahoo. Towards the N. E. and N. W. the face of the country is ragged and broken; but, to the southward, it is more even; the hills rise from the sea-side with a gentle acclivity, and, at a little distance back, are covered with wood. Its produce is the same with that of the other islands of this cluster; but its inhabitants greatly excel the people of all the neighbouring islands in the management of their plantations. In the low grounds, contiguous to the bay wherein we anchored, these plantations were regularly divided by deep ditches; the fences were formed with a neatness approaching to elegance, and the roads through them were finished in such a manner, as would have reflected credit even on an European engineer. The longitude of Wymoa Bay, in this island, is 200 deg. 20 min. E. and its latitude 21 deg. 57 min. N.

Oneeheow is five or six leagues to the westward of Atooi. Its eastern coast is high, and rises with abruptness from the sea; but the other parts of the island consist of low ground, except a round bluff head on the south-eastern point. It produces plenty of yams, and of the sweet root called tee. The anchoring-place at this island lies in the latitude of 21 deg. 50 min. N. and in the longitude of 199 deg. 45 min. E.

Oreehoua and Tahoora are two little islands, situate in the neighbourhood of Oneeheow. The former is an elevated hummock, connected with the northern extreme of Oneeheow, by a reef of coral rocks. Its latitude is 22 deg. 2 min. N. and its longitude 199 deg. 52 min. E. The latter stands to the S. E. and is uninhabited: its longitude is 199 deg. 36 min. E. and its latitude 21 deg. 43 min. N.

The climate of the Sandwich Isles is, perhaps, rather

rather more temperate than that of the West India Islands, which are in the same latitude; but the difference is very inconsiderable. The thermometer, on shore near Karakakooa Bay, never rose to a greater height than 88 deg. and that but one day: its mean height, at twelve o'clock, was 83 deg. Its mean height at noon, in Wymoa Bay, was 76 deg. and, when out at sea, 75 deg. In the island of Jamaica, the mean height of the thermometer, at twelve o'clock, is about 86 deg. at sea, 80 deg. Whether these islands are subject to the same violent winds and hurricanes with the West Indies, we could not ascertain, as we were not here during any of the tempestuous months. However, as no vestiges of their effects were any where to be seen, and as the islanders gave us no positive testimony of the fact, it is probable, that, in this particular, they resemble the Friendly and Society Isles, which are, in a great degree, free from such tremendous visitations. There was a greater quantity of rain, particularly in the interior parts, during the four winter months that we continued among these islanders, than commonly falls in the West Indies in the dry season. We generally observed clouds collecting round the summits of the hills, and producing rain to leeward; but after the wind has separated them from the land, they disperse, and are lost, and others supply their place. This occurred daily at Owhyhee; the mountainous parts being usually enveloped in a cloud; showers successively falling in the inland country; with a clear sky, and fine weather, in the neighbourhood of the shore. The winds were, for the most part, from E. S. E. to N. E. In the harbour of Karakakooa we had every day and night a sea and land breeze. The currents sometimes set to windward, and at other times to leeward, without the least regularity. They did not seem to be directed by the winds, nor by any other cause that we can assign: they often set to windward

ward against a fresh breeze. The tides are exceedingly regular, ebbing and flowing six hours each. The flood-tide comes from the E. and, at the full and change of the moon, it is high-water at three quarters of an hour after three o'clock. Their greatest rise is two feet seven inches.

The quadrupeds of these islands, are confined to three sorts, namely, hogs, dogs, and rats. The dogs are of the same species with those we saw at Otaheite, having pricked ears, long backs, and short crooked legs. We did not observe any variety in them, except in their skins; some being perfectly smooth, and others having long rough hair. They are about as large as a common turnspit, and seem to be extremely sluggish in their nature; though this may, probably, be more owing to the manner in which they are treated, than to their natural disposition. They are generally fed with the hogs, and left to herd with those animals; and we do not recollect a single instance of a dog being made a companion here, as is the custom in Europe. Indeed, the practice of eating them seems to be an insuperable bar to their being admitted into society; and as there are no beasts of prey, nor objects of chace, in these islands, the social qualities of the dog, its attachment, fidelity, and sagacity, will, in all probability, remain unknown to the natives. In our observations it did not appear that the dogs in the Sandwich Islands were near so numerous, in proportion, as at Otaheite. But, on the other hand, they have a much greater plenty of hogs, and the breed is of a larger kind. We procured from them an amazing supply of provisions of this sort. We were upwards of three months, either cruising off the coast, or in harbour at Owhyhee; during all which time the crews of both ships had constantly a large allowance of fresh pork, insomuch that our consumption of that article was computed at about 60 puncheons of 500 weight each. Besides this quantity, and the extraordinary waste, which, amidst such abundance, could not be entirely prevented, 60 more puncheons were salted for sea store. The greater part of this supply was drawn from the isle of Owhyhee alone; and yet we did not perceive that it was at all exhausted, or even that the plenty had decreased. The birds of these islands are numerous, though the variety is not great. Some of them may vie with those of any country in point of beauty. There are four species that seem to belong to the trochili, or honey-suckers of Linnæus. One of them is somewhat larger than a bullfinch; its colour is a glossy black, and the thighs and rump-vent are of a deep yellow. The natives call it hoohoo. Another is of a very bright scarlet; its wings are black, with a white edge, and its tail is black. It is named eeeeve by the inhabitants. The third is variegated with brown, yellow, and red, and seems to be either a young bird, or a variety of the preceding. The fourth is entirely green, with a yellow tinge, and is called akaiearooa. There is also a small bird of the fly-catcher kind; a species of thrush, with a greyish breast; and a rail, with very short wings, and no tail. Ravens are met with here, but they are extremely scarce; they are of a dark brown colour, inclining to black, and their note is different from that of the European raven. We found two small birds, that were very common, and both of which were of one genus. One of these was red, and was usually observed about the cocoa-trees, from whence it seemed to derive a considerable part of its subsistence. The other was of a green colour. Both had long tongues, which were ciliated, or fringed at the tip. A bird with a yellow head was likewise very common here: from the structure of its beak, our people called it a parroquet: it, however, does not belong to that tribe, but bears a great resemblance to the lexia flavicans, or yellow crofs-bill of Linnæus. Here are alfo owls, curlews, petrels, and gannets; plovers of two fpecies, one nearly the fame as our whiftling plover; a large white pigeon; the common water-hen; and a long-tailed bird, which is of a black colour, and the vent and feathers under the wings yellow.

The vegetable produce of the Sandwich Ifles is not very different from that of the other iflands of the Pacific Ocean. We have already obferved, that the taro root, as here cultivated, was fuperior to any we had before tafted. The bread-fruit trees thrive here, not indeed in fuch abundance as at Otaheite, but they produce twice as much fruit as they do on the rich plains of that ifland. The trees are nearly of the fame height; but the branches fhoot out from the trunk confiderably lower, and with greater luxuriance of vegetation. The fugarcanes of thefe iflands grow to an extraordinary fize. One of them was brought to us at Atooi, whofe circumference was eleven inches and a quarter; and it had fourteen feet eatable. At Onecheow we faw fome large brown roots, from fix to ten pounds in weight, refembling a yam in fhape. The juice, of which they yield a great quantity, is very fweet, and is an excellent fuccedaneum for fugar. The natives are exceedingly fond of it, and make ufe of it as an article of their common diet; and our people likewife found it very palatable and wholefome. Not being able to procure the leaves of this vegetable, we could not afcertain to what fpecies of plant it belonged; but we fuppofed it to be the root of fome kind of fern.

The natives of the Sandwich Ifles are doubtlefs of the fame extraction with the inhabitants of the Friendly and Society Iflands, of New Zealand, the Marquefas, and Eafter Ifland; a race which poffeffes all the known lands between the longitudes of 167 deg. and 260 deg. E. and between the latitudes of 47 deg.

deg. S. and 22 deg. N. This fact, extraordinary as it is, is not only evinced by the general resemblance of their persons, and the great similarity of their manners and customs, but seems to be established, beyond all controversy, by the identity of their language. It may not, perhaps, be very difficult to conjecture, from what continent they originally emigrated, and by what steps they have diffused themselves over so immense a space. They bear strong marks of affinity to some of the Indian tribes, which inhabit the Ladrones and Caroline Isles; and the same affinity and resemblance, may also be traced among the Malays and the Battas. At what particular time these migrations happened is less easy to ascertain; the period, in all probability, was not very late, as they are very populous, and have no tradition respecting their own origin, but what is wholly fabulous; though, on the other hand, the simplicity which is still prevalent in their manners and habits of life, and the unadulterated state of their general language, seem to demonstrate, that it could not have been at any very remote period. The natives of the Sandwich Islands, in general, exceed the middle size, and are well made. They walk in a very graceful manner, run with considerable agility, and are capable of enduring a great degree of fatigue: but, upon the whole, the men are inferior with respect to activity and strength, to the inhabitants of the Friendly Islands, and the women are less delicate in the formation of their limbs than the Otaheitean females. Their complexion is somewhat darker than that of the Otaheiteans; and they are not altogether so handsome in their persons as the natives of the Society Isles. Many of both sexes, however, had fine open countenances; and the women, in particular, had white well-set teeth, good eyes, and an engaging sweetness and sensibility of look. The hair of these people is of a brownish black, neither uniformly curling,

ing, like that of the African Negroes, nor uniformly straight, as among the Indians of America; but varying, in this respect, like the hair of Europeans. There is one striking peculiarity in the features of every part of this great nation; which is, that, even in the most handsome faces, there is always observable, a fulness of the nostril, without any flatness or spreading of the nose, that distinguishes them from the inhabitants of Europe. It is not wholly improbable, that this may be the effect of their customary method of salutation, which is performed by pressing together the extremities of their noses. The same superiority that we generally observed at other islands in the persons of the erees, is likewise found here. Those that were seen by us were perfectly well formed; whereas the lower class of people, besides their general inferiority, are subject to all the variety of figure and make, that is met with in the populace of other parts of the world. But we met with more frequent instances of deformity here, than in any of the other islands we visited. While we were cruising off Owhyhee, two dwarfs came on board; one of whom was an old man, of the height of four feet two inches, but very well proportioned; and the other was a woman, nearly of the same stature. We afterwards saw, among the natives, three who were hump-backed, and a young man who had been destitute of hands and feet, from the very moment of his birth. Squinting is also common among them; and a man, who, they told us, had been born blind, was brought to us for the purpose of being cured. Besides these particular defects, they are, in general, extremely subject to boils and ulcers, which some of us ascribed to the great quantity of salt they usually eat with their fish and flesh. Though the erees are free from these complaints, many of them experience still more dreadful effects from the too frequent use of the ava. Those who were the most affected by it, had

their

their eyes red and inflamed, their limbs emaciated, their bodies covered with a whitish scurf, and their whole frame trembling and paralytic, attended with a disability of raising their heads.

Though it does not appear that this drug universally shortens life, (for Terreeoboo, Kaoo, and several other chiefs, were far advanced in years) yet it invariably brings on a premature and decrepid old age. It is a fortunate circumstance for the people, that the use of it is made a peculiar privilege of the chiefs. The young son of Terreeoboo, who did not exceed 12 or 13 years of age, frequently boasted of his being admitted to drink ava; and shewed us, with marks of exultation, a small spot in his side that was beginning to grow scaly. When Captain Cook first visited the Society Isles, this pernicious drug was very little known among them. In his second voyage, he found it greatly in vogue at Ulietea; but it had still gained little ground at Otaheite. During the last time we were there, the havock it had made was almost incredible, insomuch that Captain Cook scarce recognized many of his former acquaintances. It is also constantly drank by the chiefs of the Friendly Isles, but so much diluted with water, that it scarcely produces any bad consequences. At Atooi, likewise, it is used with great moderation; and the chiefs of that island are, on this account, a much finer set of men, than those of the neighbouring islands. It was remarked by us, that, upon discontinuing the use of this root, its noxious effects quickly wore off. We prevailed upon our friends Kaoo and Kaireekeea, to abstain from it; and they recovered surprisingly during the short time we afterwards remained among them.

It may be thought, that to form any probable conjectures with regard to the population of islands, with many parts of which we have but an imperfect acquaintance, to be a task highly difficult.

There

There are two circumstances, however, which remove much of this objection. One is, that the interior parts of the country are almost entirely uninhabited: if, therefore, the number of those who inhabit the parts adjoining to the coast, be ascertained, the whole will be determined with some degree of accuracy. The other circumstance is, that there are no towns of any considerable extent, the houses of the islanders being pretty equally scattered in small villages round all their coasts. On these grounds we shall venture at a rough calculation of the number of persons in this cluster of islands.

Karakakooa Bay, in Owhyhee, is about three miles in extent, and comprehends four villages of about 80 houses each, upon an average, in all 320; besides many straggling habitations, which may make the whole amount to 350. If we allow six people to each house, the country about the bay will then contain 2,100 persons. To these we may add 50 families, or 300 souls, which we imagine to be nearly the number employed among the plantations in the interior parts of the island; making, in all, 2,400. If this number be applied to the whole coast round the island, a quarter being deducted for the uninhabited parts, it will be found to contain 150,000 persons. The other Sandwich Islands, by the same method of calculation, will appear to contain the following number of inhabitants: Mowee, 65,400; Atooi, 54,000; Morotoi, 36,000; Woahoo, 60,200; Ranai, 20,400; Oneeheou, 10,000; and Orechoua, 4,000. These numbers, including the 150,000 in Owhyhee, will amount to 400,000. In this computation we have by no means exceeded the truth in the total amount.

We must confess, notwithstanding the great loss we sustained from the sudden resentment and violence of these islanders, that they are of a very mild

mild and affectionate disposition, equally remote from the distant gravity and reserve of the natives of the Friendly Isles, and the extreme volatility of the Otaheiteans. They seem to live in the greatest friendship and harmony with each other. Those women who had children, shewed a remarkable affection for them, and paid them a particular and constant attention; and the men, with a willingness that did honour to their feelings, frequently afforded their assistance in those domestic employments. We must, however, remark, that they are greatly inferior to the inhabitants of the other islands, in that best criterion of civilized manners, the respect paid to the female sex. Here the women are not only deprived of the privilege of eating with the men, but are forbidden to feed on the best sorts of provisions. Turtle, pork, several kinds of fish, and some species of plantains, are denied them; and we were informed, that a girl received a violent beating, for having eaten, while she was on board one of our ships, a prohibited article of food. With regard to their domestic life, they seem to live almost wholly by themselves, and meet with little attention from the men, though no instances of personal ill-treatment were observed by us. We have already had occasion to mention the great kindness and hospitality, with which they treated us. Whenever we went ashore, there was a continual struggle who should be most forward in offering little presents for our acceptance, bringing provisions and refreshments, or testifying some other mark of respect. The aged persons constantly received us, with tears of joy, appeared to be highly gratified with being permitted to touch us, and were frequently drawing comparisons between us and themselves, with marks of extreme humility. The young women, likewise, were exceedingly kind and engaging, and attached themselves to us, without reserve, till they perceived, notwithstanding all
our

our endeavours to prevent it, that they had cause to repent of our acquaintance. It must, however, be observed, that these females were, in all probability, of the inferior class; for we saw very few women of rank during our continuance here. These people, in point of natural capacity, are, by no means, below the common standard of the human race. The excellence of their manufactures, and their improvements in agriculture, are doubtless adequate to their situation and natural advantages. The eagerness of curiosity, with which they used to attend the armourer's forge, and the various expedients which they had invented, even before our departure from these islands, for working the iron obtained from us, into such forms as were best calculated for their purposes, were strong indications of docility and ingenuity. Our unhappy friend, Kaneena, was endowed with a remarkable quickness of conception, and a great degree of judicious curiosity. He was extremely inquisitive with respect to our manners and customs. He enquired after our sovereign, the form of our government, the mode of constructing our ships, the productions of our country, our numbers, our method of building houses; whether we waged any wars; with whom, on what occasions, and in what particular manner they were carried on; who was our deity; besides many other questions of a similar import, which seemed to indicate a comprehensive understanding. We observed two instances of persons disordered in their senses; the one a woman at Oneeheow, the other a man at Owhyhee. From the extraordinary respect and attention paid to them, it appeared, that the opinion of their being divinely inspired, which prevails among most of the oriental nations, is also countenanced here.

We are inclined to think, that the practice of feeding on the bodies of enemies, was originally prevalent in all the islands of the Pacific Ocean, though it is not known, by positive and decisive evidence, to exist in any of them, except New-Zealand. The offering up human victims, which is manifestly a relique of this barbarous custom, still universally obtains among these islanders; and it is not difficult to conceive why the inhabitants of New-Zealand should retain the repast, which was, perhaps, the concluding part of these horrid rites, for a longer period than the rest of their tribe, who were situated in more fertile regions. As the Sandwich islanders, both in their persons and disposition, bear a nearer resemblance to the New-Zealanders, than to any other people of this very extensive race, Mr. Anderson was strongly inclined to suspect, that, like them, they are still cannibals. The evidence, which induced him to entertain this opinion, has been already laid down; but, as Mr. King had great doubts of the justness of his conclusions, we shall mention the grounds on which he ventured to differ from him. With regard to the intelligence received on this head from the natives themselves, it may not be improper to observe, that most of the officers on board took great pains to enquire into so curious a circumstance; and that, except in the instances above referred to, the islanders invariably denied that any such practice existed among them. Though Mr. Anderson's superior knowledge of the language of those people, ought certainly to give considerable weight to his judgment, yet, when he examined the man who had the little parcel, containing a piece of salted flesh, Mr. King, who was present on that occasion, was strongly of opinion, that the signs made use of by the islander intimated nothing more, than that it was designed to be eaten, and that it was very agreeable or wholesome to the stomach. In this sentiment Mr. King was confirmed, by a circumstance of which he was informed, after the decease of his ingenious friend Mr. Anderson, namely, that most of the inhabitants of these islands carried about with them a small piece of raw pork, well salted, either put in a calibash, or wrapped up in some cloth, and fastened round the waist: this they esteemed a great delicacy, and would frequently taste it. With regard to the confusion the lad was in, (for his age did not exceed 16 or 18 years) no person could have been surprized at it, who had been witness of the earnest and eager manner in which Mr. Anderson interrogated him. Mr. King found it less easy to controvert the argument deduced from the use of the instrument made with shark's teeth, which is of a similar form with that used by the New-Zealanders for cutting up the bodies of their enemies. Though he believed it to be an undoubted fact, that they never make use of this instrument in cutting the flesh of other animals, yet as the practice of sacrificing human victims, and of burning the bodies of the slain, still prevails here, he considered it as not altogether improbable, that the use of this knife (if it may be so denominated) is retained in those ceremonies. He was, upon the whole, inclined to imagine, and particularly from the last-mentioned circumstance, that the horrible custom of devouring human flesh has but lately ceased in these and other islands of the Pacific Ocean. Omiah acknowledged, that his countrymen, instigated by the fury of revenge, would sometimes tear with their teeth the flesh of their slain enemies; but he peremptorily denied that they ever eat it. The denial is a strong indication that the practice has ceased; for in New-Zealand, where it is still prevalent, the natives never scrupled to confess it.

The natives of the Sandwich Islands, almost universally permit their beards to grow. There were, however, a few who cut off their beard entirely, among whom was the aged king; and others wore it only on their upper-lip. The same variety that is found among the other islanders of this ocean, with respect to the mode of wearing the hair, is likewise observable here. They have, besides, a fashion which seems to be peculiar to themselves: they cut it close on each side of their heads, down to their ears, and leave a ridge, of the breadth of a small hand, extending from the forehead to the neck; which, when the hair is pretty thick and curling, resembles, in point of form, the crest of the helmet of an ancient warrior. Some of them wear great quantities of false hair, flowing in long ringlets down their backs; while others tie it into one round bunch on the upper part of their heads, nearly as large as the head itself; and some into six or seven separate bunches. They use, for the purpose of daubing or smearing their hair, a greyish clay, mixed with shells reduced to powder, which they keep in balls, and chew into a sort of paste, whenever they intend to make use of it. This composition preserves the smoothness of the hair, and changes it, in process of time, to a pale yellow. Necklaces, consisting of strings of small variegated shells, are worn both by men and women. They also wear an ornament, about two inches in length, and half an inch in breadth, shaped like the handle of a cap, and made of stone, wood, or ivory, extremely well polished: this is hung round the neck by fine threads of twisted hair, which are sometimes doubled an hundred fold. Some of them, instead of this ornament, wear a small human figure on their breast, formed of bone, and suspended in a similar manner. Both sexes make use of the fan, or fly-flap, by way of use and ornament. The most common sort is composed of cocoa-nut fibres, tied loosely in bunches, to the top of a polished handle. The tail-feathers of the cock, and those of the tropic-bird, are used for the same purpose. Those that are most in esteem, are such as have the handle formed of the leg or arm bones of an enemy killed in battle: these are preserved

with

with extraordinary care, and are handed down, from father to son, as trophies of the highest value. The practice of tatooing, or puncturing the body, prevails among these people; and, of all the islands in this ocean, it is only at New-Zealand, and the Sandwich Isles, that the face is tatooed. There is this difference between these two nations, that the New-Zealanders perform this operation in elegant spiral volutes, and the Sandwich Islanders in straight lines that intersect each other at right angles. Some of the natives have half their body, from head to foot, tatooed, which gives them a most striking appearance. It is generally done with great neatness and regularity. Several of them have only one arm thus marked; others, a leg; some, again, tatoo both an arm and a leg; and others only the hand. The hands and arms of the women are punctured in a very neat manner; and they have a remarkable custom of tatooing the tip of the tongues of some of the females. We had some reason to imagine, that the practice of puncturing is often intended as a sign of mourning, on the decease of a chief, or any other calamitous occurrence: for we were frequently informed, that such a mark was in memory of such a chief; and so of the others. The people of the lowest order are tatooed with a particular mark, which distinguishes them as the property of the chiefs to whom they are respectively subject.

The common dress of the men of all ranks consists, in general, of a piece of thick cloth, called the maro, about a foot in breadth, which passes between the legs, and is fastened round the waist. Their mats, which are of various sizes, but, for the most part, about five feet in length, and four in breadth, are thrown over their shoulders, and brought forward before. These, however, are rarely made use of, except in time of war, for which purpose they appear to be better calculated than for common use, since they are of a thick heavy

heavy texture, and capable of breaking the blow of a stone, or of any blunt weapon. They generally go bare-footed, except when they travel over burnt stones, on which occasion they secure their feet with a kind of sandal, which is made of cords, twisted from cocoa-nut fibres. Besides their ordinary dress, there is another, which is appropriated to their chiefs, and worn only on extraordinary occasions. It consists of a feathered cloak and cap, or helmet, of uncommon beauty and magnificence. This dress having been minutely described, in a former part of our work, we have only to add, that these cloaks are of different lengths, in proportion to the rank of the person who wears them; some trailing on the ground, and others no lower than the middle. The chiefs of inferior rank have likewise a short cloak, which resembles the former, and is made of the long tail-feathers of the cock, the man-of-war bird, and the tropic-bird, having a broad border of small yellow and red feathers, and also a collar of the same. Others are composed of white feathers, with variegated borders. The cap, or helmet, has a strong lining of wicker-work, sufficient to break the blow of any warlike weapon; for which purpose it appears to be intended. These feathered dresses seemed to be very scarce, and to be worn only by the male sex. During our whole continuance in Karakakooa Bay, we never observed them used, except on three occasions; first, in the remarkable ceremony of Terreeoboo's first visit to our ships; secondly, by some chiefs, who appeared among the crowd on shore, when our unfortunate commander was killed; and, thirdly, when his bones were brought to us by Eappo. The striking resemblance of this habit to the cloak and helmet which the Spaniards formerly wore, excited our curiosity to enquire, whether there might not be some reasonable grounds for imagining that it had been borrowed from them. After all our endeavours

vours to gain information on this head, we found, that the natives had no immediate acquaintance with any other people whatever; and that no tradition existed among them of these islands having ever before received a visit from such vessels as ours. However, notwithstanding the result of our enquiries on this subject, the form of this habit seems to be a sufficient indication of its European origin; particularly when we reflect on another circumstance, viz. that it is a remarkable deviation from the general agreement of dress, which is prevalent among the several branches of this great tribe, dispersed over the Pacific Ocean. From this conclusion, we were induced to suppose, that some buccaneer, or Spanish ship, might have been wrecked in the neighbourhood of these islands. When it is considered, that the course of the Spanish trading vessels from Acapulco to Manilla, is not many degrees to the S. of Sandwich Isles, in their passage out, and to the N. on their return, this supposition will not, we think, be deemed improbable.

In the common dress of the men, and that of the women, there is very little difference. The latter wear a piece of cloth wrapped round the waist, which descends half way down their thighs; and sometimes, during the cool of the evening, they throw loose pieces of fine cloth over their shoulders, like the females of Otaheite. They have another kind of dress called the pan, which the younger part of the sex often wear: it consists of the thinnest and finest cloth, wrapped several times about the middle, and reaching down to the leg; so that it has the appearance of a full short petticoat. They cut their hair, and turn it up before, after the custom of the New-Zealanders and Otaheiteans. One woman, indeed, whom we saw in Karakakooa Bay, had her hair arranged in a very singular manner: having turned it up behind, she brought it over her forehead, and doubled it back, so that it

formed

formed a kind of shade to the face, and somewhat resembled a small bonnet. Besides their necklaces, which are composed of shells, or of a shining, hard, red berry, they wear dried flowers of the Indian mallow, formed into wreaths, and likewise another elegant ornament, termed eraie, which is sometimes fastened round the hair in the manner of a garland, but is usually put round the neck; though it is worn occasionally in both these ways at once. It is a kind of ruff, about as thick as a finger, formed with great ingenuity, of very small feathers, woven closely together, insomuch, that the surface may be said to equal the richest velvet in smoothness. The ground is, in general, red, with alternate circles of black, yellow and green. We have already described their bracelets, of which they have a great variety. Some of the women of Atooi wear small figures of the turtle, made very neatly of ivory or wood, fastened on their fingers, in the same manner that rings are worn by us. They have likewise an ornament consisting of shells, tied in rows on a ground of strong net work, so as to strike against each other, while in motion; which both sexes, when they dance, fasten either round the ancles, or just below the knee, or round the arm. They sometimes, instead of shells, use for this purpose, the teeth of dogs, and a hard red berry. Another ornament, if it deserves that name, is a kind of mask, composed of a large gourd, having holes cut in it for the nose and eyes. The top of it is stuck full of green twigs, which appear at some distance, like a waving plume; and the lower part has narrow stripes of cloth hanging from it, somewhat resembling a beard. These masks we never saw worn but on two occasions, and both times by a number of persons assembled in a canoe, who approached the side of the ship, laughing and making droll gesticulations. We could never learn whether they were not also made use of as a defence for the head

against

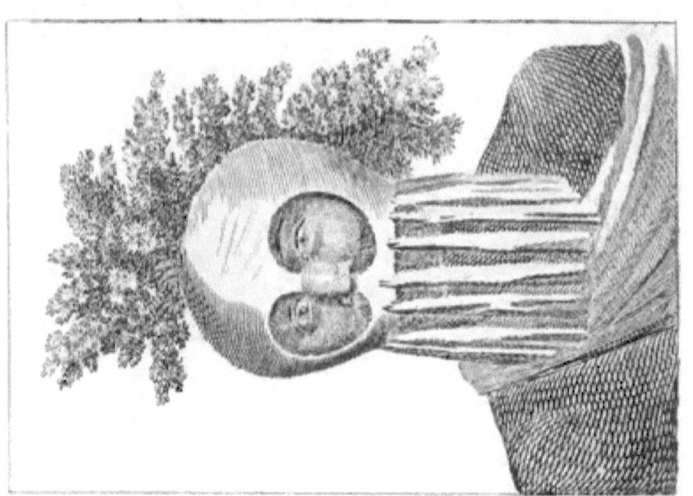

against stones, or in some of their public sports and games, or were disguises merely for the purposes of mummery and sport.

The natives of Sandwich Islands dwell together in small towns or villages, which contain from about 100 to 200 houses, built pretty close to each other, without order or regularity, and having a winding path that leads through them. They are flanked frequently, towards the sea-side, with loose detached walls, which are, in all probability, intended for shelter and defence. Their habitations are of various dimensions, from 45 feet by 24, to 18 by 12. Some are of a larger size, being 50 feet in length, 30 in breadth, and entirely open at one end. These, we were informed, were designed for the accommodation of strangers or travellers, whose stay was likely to be short. Some of the best houses have a court-yard before them, railed in very neatly, with smaller habitations for servants erected round it: in this area the family usually eat and sit in the day time. In the sides of the hills, and among the steep rocks, we saw several holes or caves, which seemed to be inhabited; but the entrace being defended by wicker-work, and, in the only one that we visited, a stone fence being observed running across it within, we supposed that they were chiefly intended as places of retreat, in case of an attack from enemies.

People of an inferior class feed principally on fish, and vegetables, such as plantains, bread-fruit, sweet potatoes, sugar-canes, yams, and taro. To these persons of superior rank add the flesh of dogs and hogs, dressed after the same method that is practised at the Society Isles. They likewise sometimes eat fowls of a domestic kind; but these, however, are neither plentiful, nor in any degree of estimation. On our first arrival at these islands, yams, and breadfruit, seemed scarce; but, on our second visit, we did not find this to be the case: it is therefore probable,

bable, that, as these vegetable articles are commonly planted in the interior parts of the country, the islanders might not have sufficient time for bringing them down to us, during our short continuance in Wymoa Bay. Their fish are salted, and preserved in gourd-shells, not, indeed, with a view of providing against an occasional scarcity, but from the inclination they have for salted provisions; for we found, that the chiefs had frequently pieces of pork pickled in the same manner, which they considered as a great delicacy. Their cookery is much the same as at the Friendly and Society Islands; and though some of our people disliked their taro puddings, on account of their sourness, others were of a different opinion. It is remarkable, that they had not acquired the art of preserving the bread-fruit, and making of it the sour paste, named maihee, as is the practice at the Society Isles; and it afforded us great satisfaction, that we had it in our power to communicate to them this secret, in return for the generous treatment we received from them. At their meals they are very cleanly; and their method of dressing both their vegetable and animal food, was acknowledged universally to be superior to ours. The erees begin constantly their meals with a dose of the extract of pepper root, or ava, prepared in the usual mode. The women eat a part from the other sex, and are prohibited, as before observed, from feeding on pork, turtle, and some particular species of plantains. Notwithstanding this inderdiction, they would eat, privately, pork with us: but we could never prevail on them to taste the two latter articles of food. They generally rise with the sun; and having enjoyed the cool of the evening, retire to their repose a few hours after sun-set. The erees are employed in making canoes, and mats; the towtows are chiefly engaged in their plantations, and in fishing; and the women in the manufacture

of

of cloth. They amuse themselves, in their leisure hours, with various diversions. The youth of both sexes are fond of dancing; and on more solemn occasions, they entertain themselves with wrestling and boxing matches, performed after the manner of the natives of the Friendly Islands; to whom, however, they are greatly inferior in these respects. Their dances, which bear a greater resemblance to those of the New-Zealanders, than of the Friendly or Society Islanders, are introduced with a solemn kind of song, in which the whole number join, at the same time moving slowly their legs, and striking gently their breasts; their attitudes and manner being very easy and graceful. So far they resemble the dancers of the Society Islands. After this has continued about the space of ten minutes, they quicken gradually their motions and the tune, and do not desist till they are oppressed with fatigue. This part of the performance is the counter-part of that of the inhabitants of New-Zealand; and, as among those people, the person whose action is the most violent, and who continues this exercise the longest, is applauded by the spectators as the best dancer. It must be remarked, that, in this dance, the females only engage; and that the dances of the men resemble those we saw of the small parties at the Friendly Isles; and which may, perhaps, more properly, be termed the accompanyment of songs, with the correspondent motions of the whole body. But as we saw some boxing exhibitions, of the same kind with those we had seen at the Friendly Isles, it is not improbable, that they had here likewise their grand dances, wherein both men and women were performers. Their music, on these, and other occasions, is of a rude kind; for the only instruments, we observed among them, were drums of various sizes. Their songs, however, which they are said to sing in parts, and which they accompany with a gentle motion of their arms,

like

like those of the inhabitants of the Friendly Isles, have a very pleasing effect.

These people are greatly addicted to gambling. One of their games resembles our game of draughts; but, from the number of squares, it seems to be much more intricate. The board is of the length of about two feet, and is divided into 238 squares, 14 in a row. In playing they use white and black pebbles, which they move from one square to another. They have a game which consists in concealing a stone under some cloth, spread out by one of the parties, and rumpled in such a manner, that it is difficult to perceive where the stone lies. The antagonist then strikes, with a stick, that part of the cloth where he supposes the stone to be; and the chances being, upon the whole, against his hitting it, odds of all degrees, varying with the opinion of the dexterity of the parties, are laid on the occasion. Their manner of playing at bowls nearly resembles that of ours. They often entertain themselves with races between boys and girls, on which they lay wagers with great spirit. We saw a man beating his breast, and tearing his hair, in the violence of rage, for having lost three hatchets at one of these races, which he had purchased from us with near half his property a very little time before. In swimming, both sexes are very expert; an art that, among these people, is deemed necessary, and is their favourite diversion. One particular method, in which we sometimes saw them amuse themselves, is worthy of notice. The surf, that breaks on the coast round this bay, extends about 150 yards from the shore; and within that space, the surges of the sea are dashed against the beach with extreme violence. Whenever the impetuosity of the surf is augmented to its greatest height, they make choice of that time for this amusement, which they perform in this manner: about 20 or 30 of the natives take each a long narrow board, rounded

at

at both ends; and set out in company with each other from the shore. They plunge under the first wave they meet, and, after they have suffered it to roll over them, rise again beyond it, and swim further out into the sea. They encounter the second wave in the same manner with the first. The principal difficulty consists in seizing a favourable opportunity of diving under it; for, if a person misses the proper moment, he is caught by the surf, and forced back with great violence; and his utmost dexterity is required, to prevent his being dashed against the rocks. When in consequence of these repeated efforts, they have gained the smooth water beyond the surf, they recline themselves at length upon the boards, and prepare for their return to shore. The surf being composed of a number of waves, of which every third is observed to be considerably larger than the rest, and to flow higher upon the shore, while the others break in the intermediate space; their first object is to place themselves on the top of the largest surge, which drives them along with astonishing rapidity towards the land. If, by mistake, they should place themselves on one of the smaller waves, which breaks before they gain the shore, or should find themselves unable to keep their board in a proper direction on the upper part of the swell, they remain exposed to the fury of the next; to avoid which, they are under the necessity of diving again, and recovering the place from whence they set out. Those who succeed in reaching the shore, are still in a very hazardous situation. As the coast is defended by a chain of rocks, with a small opening between them in several places, they are obliged to steer their plank through one of these openings; or, in case of ill success in that respect, to quit it before they reach the rocks, and, diving under the wave, make their way back again as well as they are able. This is considered as highly disgraceful, and is attended with

with the loss of the plank, which we have seen dashed to pieces, at the very instant the native quitted it. The amazing courage and address, with which they perform these dangerous atchievements are almost incredible. The following accident evinces, at how early a period they are so far accustomed to the water, as to lose all apprehensions of its perils, and even set them at defiance. A canoe, in which was a woman and her children, happening to overset, one of the children, an infant of about four years old, appeared to be greatly delighted, swimming about at its ease, and playing a number of tricks, till the canoe was brought to its former position. Among the amusements of the children, we observed one that was frequently played at, and which shewed a considerable share of dexterity. They take a short stick, through one extremity whereof runs a peg sharpened at both ends, extending about an inch on each side, then throwing up a ball, formed of green leaves moulded together, and fastened with twine, they catch it on one of the points of the peg; immediately after which, they throw it up again from the peg, then turn the stick round, and catch the ball on the other point of the peg. Thus, for some time, they continue catching it on each point of the peg alternately, without missing it. They are equally expert at another diversion of a similar nature, throwing up in the air, and catching, in their turns, many of these balls; and we have often seen little children thus keep five balls in motion at once. This latter game is also practised by the young people of the Friendly Isles. The figure and dimensions of the canoes, seen by us at Atooi, have been already described. Those belonging to the other Sandwich Islands were made exactly in the same manner; and the largest we saw was a double one, the property of Terreeoboo, measuring 70 feet in length, 12 in breadth, and between 3 and 4 in depth;

depth; and each was hollowed out of one tree. Their method of navigation, as well as that of agriculture, resemble those of the other islands in the Pacific Ocean. They have made considerable proficiency in the art of sculpture, and in painting or staining cloth. The most curious specimens of their sculpture, that we had an opportunity of observing, were the wooden bowls, in which the erees drink ava. These are, in general, eight or ten inches in diameter, perfectly round, and extremely well polished. They are supported by three or four small human figures, represented in different attitudes. Some of them rest on the shoulders of their supporters; others on the hands, extended over the head; and some on the head and hands. The figures are very neatly finished, and accurately proportioned; even the anatomy of the muscles is well expressed.

Their cloth is manufactured in the same manner as at the Society and Friendly Islands. That which they intend to paint, is of a strong and thick texture, several folds being beaten and incorporated together; after which they cut it in breadths, two or three feet wide, and then paint it in a great variety of patterns, with such regularity and comprehensiveness of design, as shew an extraordinary portion of taste and fancy. The exactness with which the most intricate patterns are continued, is really astonishing, as they have no stamps, and as the whole is performed by the eye, with a piece of bamboo cane dipped in paint; the hand being supported by another piece of the same sort of cane. They extract their colours from the same berries, and other vegetable articles, which are made use of at Otaheite for this purpose. The operation of staining or painting their cloth, is confined to the females, and is denominated kipparee. They always called our writing by this name. The young women would frequently take the pen from our hands,

hands, and shew us that they were as well acquainted with the use of it as we ourselves; telling us, at the same time, that our pens were inferior to theirs. They considered a manuscript sheet of paper as a piece of cloth striped after the mode of our country; and it was with the greatest difficulty that we could make them understand that our figures contained a meaning in them, which theirs was destitute of. Their mats they make of the leaves of the pandanus; and these, as well as their cloths, are beautifully worked in various patterns, and stained with divers colours. Some of them have a ground of straw-colour, embellished with green spots: others are of a pale green, spotted with squares, or rhomboids, of red; and some are ornamented with elegant stripes, either in straight or waved lines of red and brown. In this branch of manufacture, whether we regard the fineness, beauty, or strength, these islanders may be said to excel the whole world. Their fishing hooks are of various sizes and figures; but those that are principally made use of are about two or three inches in length, and are formed in the shape of a small fish, serving as a bait, with a bunch of feathers fastened to the head or tail. They make their hooks of bone, mother-of-pearl, or wood, pointed and barbed with little bones, or tortoise-shell. Those with which they fish for sharks, are very large, being, in general, of the length of six or eight inches. Considering the materials of which these hooks are composed, their neatness and strength are amazing; and, indeed, upon trial, we found them superior to our own. Of the bark of the toota, or cloth-tree, neatly twisted, they form the line which they use for fishing, for making nets, and for some other purposes. It is of different degrees of fineness, and may be continued to any length. They have also a sort, made of the bark of a shrub, named areemah; and the finest is composed of human hair: this last, however,

however, is chiefly made use of in the way of ornament. They likewise make cordage of a stronger kind, from cocoa-nut fibres, for the rigging of their canoes. Some of this, which was purchased by us for our own use, was found to be well calculated for the smaller kinds of running rigging. They also manufacture another sort of cordage, which is flat, and extremely strong, and is principally used for the purpose of lashing the roofs of their houses. This last is not twisted after the manner of the former sorts, but is formed of the fibrous strings of the coat of the cocoa-nut, plaited with the fingers, in the same manner which is practised by our seamen in making their points for the reefing of sails.

Their gourds are applied to various domestic purposes. These grow to such an enormous magnitude, that some of them will contain from ten to a dozen gallons. In order to adapt them the better to their respective uses, they take care to give them different shapes, by fastening bandages round them during their growth. Thus some of them are in the form of a dish, serving to hold their puddings, vegetables, and salted provisions: others are of a long cylindrical form, and serve to contain their fishing tackle; which two sorts are furnished with neat close covers, made also of the gourd. Others are in the shape of a long-necked bottle; and in these water is kept. They score them frequently with a heated instrument, so as to communicate to them the appearance of being painted, in a great variety of elegant designs. Their pans in which they make their salt, are made of earth lined with clay, and are in general six or eight feet square, and about two thirds of a foot in depth. They are elevated on a bank of stones, near the high-water-mark, whence the salt water is conducted to the bottom of them, in trenches, out of which they are filled; and in a short time the sun performs the process of the evaporation. The salt we met with at Oneeheow and Atooi, during our first visit, was brownish, and rather dirty; but that which we afterwards procured in Karakakooa Bay, was white, and of an excellent quality. We obtained an ample supply of it, insomuch that, besides the quantity used by us in salting pork, we filled all our empty casks with it.

The warlike weapons of the inhabitants of these islands are daggers, which they call by the name of pahooa, spears, slings, and clubs. The pahooa is made of a black, heavy wood, that resembles ebony. It is commonly from one to two feet in length, and has a string passing through the handle, by which it is suspended from the arm. The blade is somewhat rounded in the middle: the sides are sharp, and terminate in a point. This offensive weapon is intended for close engagements, and in the hands of the natives is a very destructive one. Their spears are of two kinds, and are formed of hard wood, which, in its appearance, is not unlike mahogany. One sort is from six to eight feet in length, well polished, and increasing gradually in thickness from the extremity till within the distance of six or seven inches from the point, which tapers suddenly, and has five or six rows of barbs. It is probable that these are used in the way of javelins. The other sort, with which the warriors we saw at Atooi and Owhyhee were chiefly armed, are from 12 to 15 feet in length, and instead of being barbed, terminate towards the point, in the manner of the daggers. Their slings are the same with our common ones, except in this respect, that the stone is lodged on matting, instead of leather. Their clubs are formed indifferently of several kinds of wood: they are of various sizes and shapes, and of rude workmanship.

The inhabitants of the Sandwich Islands are divided into three classes. The erees, or chiefs of each district, are the first; and one of these is superior

rior to the rest, who is called, at Owhyhee, eree-taboo, and eree-moee, the first name expressing his authority, and the latter signifying that, in his presence, all must prostrate themselves. Those of the second class appear to enjoy a right of property, but have no authority. Those who compose the third class, are called towtows, or servants, and have neither rank nor property. The superior power and distinction of Terreeoboo, the eree-taboo of Owhyhee, was sufficiently evident from his reception at Karakakooa, on his first arrival. The inhabitants all prostrated themselves at the entrance of their houses, and the canoes were tabooed, till he discharged the interdict. He was then just returned from Mowee, an island he was contending for, in behalf of his son, Teewarro, whose wife was the only child of the king of that place, against Taheeterree, his surviving brother. In this expedition he was attended by many of his warriors; but we could never learn whether they served him as volunteers, or whether they held their rank and property under that tenure. That the subordinate chiefs are tributary to him, is evidently proved in the instance of Kaoo, which has been already related. We have also observed, that the two most powerful chiefs of the Sandwich Islands, are Terreeoboo and Perreeorannee; the former being chief of Owhyhee, and the latter of Woahoo; all the smaller isles being governed by one of these sovereigns: Mowee was, at this time, claimed by Terreeoboo, for his son and intended successor; Atooi and Oneeheow being in the possession of the grandsons of Perreeorannee. Without entering into the genealogy of the kings of Owhyhee and Mowee, it may be necessary to mention, that, when we were first off Mowee, Terreeoboo and his warriors were there, to support the claims made by his wife, his son, and his daughter-in-law; and a battle had then been fought with the opposite party, in which Terreeoboo had been victorious. Matters, however, were afterwards compromised; Taheeterree was to have possession of the three neighbouring islands, during his life; Teewarro to be acknowledged chief of Mowee, and to succeed to Owhyhee, on the death of Terreeoboo, together with the three islands contiguous to Mowee, after the decease of Taheeterree. Should Teewarro, who has lately married his half sister, die, and leave no issue behind him, those islands are to descend to Maiha-maiha, whom we have frequently mentioned, he being the son of Terreeoboo's deceased brother: and should he die without issue, it is doubtful who would be the successor, for Terreeoboo's two younger sons, being born of a mother who had no rank, would be debarred all right of succession. We did not see Queen Rorarora, whom Terreeoboo had left at Mowee; but we had an opportunity of seeing Kanee Kaberaia, the mother of the two youths of whom he was so extremely fond. From what has been already mentioned, it should seem that their government is hereditary; whence it appears probable, that the inferior titles, as well as property, descend in the same channel. Respecting Perreeorannee, we only discovered that he is an eree-taboo; that he was, on some pretence, invading the possession of Taheeterree; and that the islands to the leeward were governed by his grandsons.

The erees appear to have unlimited power over the inferior classes of people; many instances of which occurred daily while we continued among them. On the other hand, the people are implicitly obedient. It is remarkable, however, that we never saw the chiefs exercise any acts of cruelty, injustice, or insolence towards them; though they put in practice their power over each other, in a most tyrannical degree: which the two following instances will fully demonstrate. One of the lower order of chiefs having shewn great civility to the
master

master of our ship, when employed on the survey of Karakakooa Bay; Mr. King, some time afterwards, took him on board, and introduced him to Captain Cook, who engaged him to dine with us. While at table, Pareea entered, whose countenance manifested the highest indignation at seeing our guest so honourably entertained. He seized him by the hair of his head, and would have dragged him out of the cabbin, if the captain had not interfered. After much altercation, we could obtain no other indulgence (without quarreling with Pareea) than, that our guest should be permitted to remain in the cabbin, on condition that he seated himself on the floor, while Pareea occupied his place at the table. An instance somewhat similar happened when Terreeoboo came first on board the Resolution; where Maiha-maiha, who attended the king, seeing Pareea upon deck, turned him most ignominiously out of the ship; even though we knew Pareea to be a man of the first consequence in the island. Whether the lower class of people have their property secured from the rapacity of the great, we cannot possibly say, but it appears to be well protected against theft and depredation. All their plantations, their houses, their hogs, and their cloth, are left unguarded, without fear or apprehension of plunderers. In the plain country, they separate their possessions by walls; and, in the woods, where horse plantains grow, they use white flags to discriminate property, in the same manner as they do bunches of leaves at Otaheite. These circumstances strongly indicate, that, where property is concerned, the power of the erees is not arbitrary, but so far limited, as to afford encouragement to the inferior orders to cultivate the soil, which they occupy distinct from each other.

The information we obtained, respecting the administration of justice is very imperfect. If a quarrel arose among the lower class of people, the matter

ter was referred to some chief for his decision. When an inferior chief had offended one of superior rank, his punishment was dictated by, and the result of, the feelings of the superior at that moment. If the offender should fortunately escape the first transports of the great man's rage, he perhaps found means, through the mediation of friends, to compound for his offence, by all, or a part of his effects. As to the religion of these people, it resembles that of the Society and Friendly Islands. In common with each other, they have all their morais, their whattas, sacred orations, hymns, and sacrifices. These are convincing proofs that their religious rites and tenets are derived from the same source. The ceremonies here are, indeed, longer, and more numerous than in the islands above-mentioned; and though in all these places, the care and performance of their religious rites, is committed to a particular class of people; yet we had never found a regular society of priests, till we arrived at Kakooa, in Karakakooa Bay. Orono was the title given to the principal of this order; a title which seemed to imply something sacred in a high degree, and which almost received adoration in the person of Omeeah. The privilege of holding the principal offices in this order, is doubtless limited to certain families. Omeeah, the orono, was Kaoo's son, and Kaireekeea's nephew. Kaireekeea presided in all religious ceremonies at the morai, in the absence of his grandfather: it was observed, likewise, that the son of Omeeah, an infant of about the age of five years, had always a number of attendants, and such other marks of distinction and esteem were shewn him, as we never observed in any similar instances. Hence we concluded, that his life was an object of much consequence, and that he would eventually succeed to the high dignity of his father. The title of orono, we have already observed, was bestowed on Captain Cook;

and

and it is very certain, that they considered us, as a race of beings superior to themselves; frequently repeating that the great Eatooa lived in our country. The favourite little idol on the morai, before which Captain Cook fell prostrate, is called Koonooraekaiee, and is Terrecoboo's god, which they said resided also among us. An almost infinite variety of these images were to be seen, both on the morais, and about their houses, on which they bestow different names; but they certainly were held in very little estimation, from their contemptuous expressions when speaking of, or to them, and from their exposing them to sale for mere trifles; though they generally had one particular figure in high favour, to which, while it continued a favourite, all their adoration was addressed. They arrayed it in red cloth, beat their drums, and chanted hymns before it; placed bunches of red feathers, and different vegetables at its feet; and frequently exposed a pig or a dog, to rot on the whatta, near which it was placed. In a bay to the southward of Karakakooa, a party of us were conducted to a large house, in which we saw the figure of a black man, resting on his toes and fingers, and his head inclined backward: the limbs were well proportioned, and the whole was beautifully polished. This figure was called maee; round which thirteen others were placed, with shapes rude and distorted. These, we were told, were the eatooas of deceased chiefs, whose names they repeated. Numbers of whatta's were seen within this place, with the remains of offerings on many of them. They also have in their habitations many ludicrous and obscene representations by idols, not unlike the Priapus of the ancients. Former navigators have remarked, that the Society and Friendly Islanders pay adoration to particular birds, and it seems to be a custom prevalent in these islands: ravens may here, perhaps, be objects of worship; for Mr. King saw two of these birds

perfectly

perfectly tame, and was told they were eatooas: that gentlemen offered several articles for them, which were all refused; and he was particularly cautioned not to offend, or hurt them. Among their religious ceremonies may be classed the prayers and offerings made by their priests before their meals. As they always drink ava before they begin a repast, while that is chewing, the superior in rank begins a sort of hymn, in which he is soon after joined by one or more of the company; the bodies of the others are put in motion, and their hands are clapped together in concert with the fingers. The ava being ready, cups of it are presented to those who do not join in the hymn, which are held in their hands till it is concluded; when, with united voice, they make a loud response, and drink their ava. The performers are then served with some of it, which they drink, after the same ceremony has been repeated. And, if any person of a superior rank should be present, a cup is presented to him last of all; who having chanted for a short time, and hearing a response from others, he pours a small quantity on the ground, and drinks the rest. A piece of the flesh, which has been dressed, is then cut off, and together with some of the vegetables, is placed at the foot of the figure of the eatooa; and, after another hymn has been chanted, they begin their meal. A ceremony, in many respects resembling this, is also performed by the chiefs, when they drink ava between their regular meals. According to the accounts given by the natives, human sacrifices are more common here than in any of the islands we have visited. They have recourse to these horrid rites, on the commencement of a war, and previous to a battle, or any signal enterprize. The death of every chief demands an offering of one or more towtows; and we were informed not less than ten were devoted to suffer, on the decease of Terreeoboo, the king. But the unhappy
victims

victims are totally unacquainted with their ordained fate; which is, to be attacked with large clubs, wherever they may happen to be; and after they are dead, are conveyed to the place where the subsequent rites are to be performed. This brings to our remembrance the skulls of those who had been sacrificed on the decease of some principal chief, and were fixed to the morai at Kakooa; at which village we received further information on this subject; for we were shewn a small piece of ground, within a stone fence, which we were told was a heree-eree, or burying place of a chief. The person who gave us this information, pointing to one of the corners, added; and there lie the tangata and waheene-taboo, or the man and woman who became sacrifices at his funeral. The knocking out their fore teeth, may be with propriety classed among their religious customs. Most of the common people, and many of the chiefs, had lost one or more of them; and this, we understood, was considered as a propitiatory sacrifice to the eatooa, to avert his anger; and not like the cutting off part of the finger at the Friendly Islands, to express the violence of their grief at the decease of a friend. Concerning their opinions, respecting a future state, we had very defective information. Enquiring of them, whither the dead were gone? we were told, that the breath, which they seemed to consider as the immortal part, was fled to the Eatooa. They seemed also to give a description of some place, which they suppose to be the abode of the dead; but we could not learn, that they had any idea of rewards and punishments.

Here an explanation of the word taboo may not be improperly introduced. On asking the reasons of the intercourse being interdicted between us and the islanders, the day preceding Terreeoboo's arrival, we were informed, that the bay was tabooed. The same interdiction took place, by our desire,

desire, when we interred the remains of Captain Cook. The most implicit obedience, in these two instances, was rendered by the natives; but whether on religious principles, or in deference to civil authority, we cannot pretend to determine. The ground whereon our observatories were fixed, and the place whereon our masts were deposited, were tabooed, and the operation was equally efficacious. This consecration was performed by the priests only; and yet, at our request, the men ventured on the spot which was tabooed; whence it should seem they entertained no religious apprehensions, their obedience being limited merely to our refusal. No inducements could bring the women near us; on account, it is presumed, of the morai adjoining; which they are, at all times, prohibited from approaching; not only here, but in all the islands of the south seas, women, it has been observed, are always tabooed, or forbidden to eat certain articles of food. We have seen many of them, at their meals, have their meat put into their mouths by others; and, on our requesting to know the reason of it, we were informed, that they were tabooed, and not permitted to feed themselves. This prohibition was always the consequence of assisting at any funeral, touching a dead body, and many other occasions. The word taboo, is indifferently applied, either to persons or things; as the natives are tabooed, the bay is tabooed, &c. This word is also expressive of any thing sacred, devoted, or eminent. The king of Owhyhee is called eree-taboo, and a human victim, tangata-taboo; and, among the Friendly Islanders, Tonga, where the king resides, is called Tonga-taboo.

With respect to their marriages, very little can be said, except that such a compact seems to exist among them. It has already been mentioned, that, when Terreeoboo had left his queen Rora-rora, at Mowee, another woman cohabited with him, by whom

whom he had children, and seemed particularly attached to her; but whether polygamy is allowed, or whether it is mixed with concubinage, either among the principal or inferior orders, we saw too little of, to warrant any conclusions. From what we observed of the domestic concerns of the lower class of people, one man and one woman seemed to have the direction of the house, and the children were subordinate to them, as in civilized countries. The following is the only instance of any thing like jealousy, which we have seen among them, and which shews, that, among married women of rank, not only fidelity, but even a degree of reserve, is required. At one of their boxing matches, Omeah rose two or three times from his place, and approaching his wife, with strong marks of displeasure, commanded her, as we supposed, to withdraw. Whether he thought her beauty engaged too much of our attention, or whatever might be his motives, there certainly existed no real cause of jealousy. She, however, continued in her place, and, at the conclusion of the entertainment, joined our party, and even solicited some trifling presents. She was informed that we had not any about us, but that, if she would accompany us to the tent, she should be welcome to make choice of what she liked. She was, accordingly, proceeding with us; which being observed by Omeah, he followed in a great rage, seized her by the hair, and, with his fists, began to inflict severe corporal punishment. Having been the innocent cause of this extraordinary treatment, we were exceedingly concerned at it; though we understood it would be highly improper for us to interfere between husband and wife of such superior rank. The natives, however, at length interposed, and, the next day, we had the satisfaction of meeting them together, perfectly satisfied with each other; besides, what was extremely singular, the lady would not permit us to rally the husband on his behaviour, which we had an inclination to do; plainly telling us, that he had acted very properly.

We had twice an opportunity, at Karakakooa Bay, of seeing a part of their funeral rites. Hearing of the death of an old chief, not far from our observatories, some of us repaired to the place, where we beheld a number of people assembled. They were seated round an area, fronting the house where the deceased lay; and a man, having on a red feathered cap, came to the door, constantly putting out his head, and making a most lamentable howl, accompanied with horrid grimaces, and violent distortions of the face. A large mat was afterwards spread upon the area, and thirteen women and two men, who came out of the house, sat down upon it in three equal rows; three of the women, and the two men being in front. The women had feathered ruffs on their necks and hands, and their shoulders were decorated with broad green leaves, curiously scolloped. Near a small hut, at one corner of this area, half a dozen boys were placed, waving small white banners, and taboo sticks, who would not permit us to approach them. Hence we imagined, that the dead body was deposited in the hut; but we were afterwards informed that it remained in the house, where the tricks were playing at the door by the man in the red cap. The company seated on the mat, sung a melancholy tune, accompanied with a gentle motion of the arms and body. This having continued some time, they put themselves in a posture between kneeling and sitting, and their arms and bodies into a most rapid motion, keeping pace, at the same time, with the music. These last exertions being too violent to continue, at intervals they had flower motions. An hour having passed in these ceremonies, more mats were spread upon the area, when the dead chief's widow, and three or four other elderly women came out of the house with slow and solemn pace; and, seating themselves

selves before the company, began to moan most bitterly, in which they were joined by the three rows of women behind them; the two men appearing melancholy and pensive. They continued thus, with little variation, till late in the evening, when we left them; and, at day-light, in the morning, the people were dispersed, and every thing appeared perfectly quiet. We were then given to understand, that the body was removed; but we could not learn how it was disposed of. While we were directing our enquiries to this object, we were addressed by three women of rank, who signified to us, that our presence interrupted the performance of some necessary rites. Soon after we had left them, we heard their cries and lamentations; and, when we met them a few hours afterwards, the lower parts of their faces were painted perfectly black. We had also an opportunity of observing the ceremonies at the funeral of one of the ordinary class. Hearing some mournful cries, issuing from a miserable hut, we entered it, and discovered two women, whom we supposed to be mother and daughter, weeping over the body of a man who had that moment expired. They first covered the body with cloth: then lying down by it, they spread the cloth over themselves, beginning a melancholy kind of song, and repeating frequently Aweh medoaah! Aweh tanee! Oh my father! Oh my husband! In one corner of the hut a younger daughter lay prostrate on the ground, having some black cloth spread over her, and repeating the same expressions. On our quitting this melancholy scene, we found many of their neighbours collected together at the door, who were all perfectly silent, and attentive to their lamentations.

 Mr. King was willing to have embraced this opportunity of knowing in what manner the body would be disposed of; and therefore, after being convinced that it was not removed till after he went to bed, he ordered the sentries to walk before the house, and if there were any appearances of removing the body, to acquaint him with it. The sentries, however, were remiss in the performance of their duty, for, before the morning, the body was taken away. On asking, how it had been disposed of, they pointed towards the sea, perhaps thereby indicating, that it had been deposited in the deep, or that it had been conveyed to some burying-ground beyond the bay. The place of interment for the chiefs, is the morai, or heree erees, and those who are sacrificed on the occasion, are buried by the side of them. The morai in which the chief was interred, who, after a spirited resistance, had been killed in the cave, is adorned with a hanging of red cloth round it. Having thus laid before our readers a circumstantial and comprehensive account of the whole group of the Sandwich Islands, we proceed to relate the transactions, incidents and events, during our second expedition to the north, by the way of Kamtschatka, and on our return home, by the way of Canton, and the Cape of Good Hope, from March 1779, to August 1780. But it may not be amiss to close this chapter, with an abstract of the astronomical observations, which were made at the observatory in Karakakooa Bay, for determining its latitude and longitude; to which we shall add the latitude and longitude of the Sandwich Islands, collected into one point of view. The latitude of the observatory, deduced from meridian zenith distances of the sun, and some particular stars, we found to be 19 deg. 28 min. N. and its longitude, deduced from 253 sets of lunar observations, to be 204 deg. E.

The LATITUDE and LONGITUDE of the SANDWICH ISLANDS.

		Latitude		Longitude	
		deg.	min.	deg.	min.
Owhyhee	The North-point	20	17	204	2
	South-point	18	54	204	15
	East-point	19	34	205	6
	Karakakooa Bay	19	28	204	0
Mowee	East-point	20	50	204	4
	South-point	20	34	203	48
	West-point	20	54	203	24
Morokinnee	-	20	39	203	33
Tahoorowa	-	20	38	203	27
Ranai	South-point	20	46	203	8
Morotoi	West-point	21	10	202	46
Woahoo	Anchoring-point	21	43	202	9
Atooi	Wymoa Bay	21	57	200	20
Oneeheow	Anchoring-place	21	50	199	45
Oreehoua	-	22	2	199	52
Tahoora	-	21	43	199	36

CHAP. XVII.

ON Monday, the 15th of March 1779, we weighed anchor, and passing to the N. of Tahoora, stood to the S. W. in expectation of falling in with the island of Modoopapappa; the natives having assured us, that it lay in that direction, within five hours sail of Tahoora. The next day at five o'clock, P. M. we made a signal for the Discovery to come under our stern, having given over all hopes of seeing Modoopapappa. On Wednesday, the 17th, we steered W. Captain Clerke intending to keep in the same parallel of latitude, till we made the longitude of Awatska Bay; and then to steer N. for the harbour of St. Peter and St. Paul,

Paul, which was also fixed on as our rendezvous, if we should happen to separate. This track was chosen, because we supposed it to be yet unexplored, and we might probably meet with some new islands in our passage. On Tuesday, the 30th, the winds and unsettled state of the weather, induced Captain Clerke to alter his plan, and, at six in the evening, we began to steer N. W. which we continued till Tuesday, the 6th of April, at which time we lost the trade wind. The fine weather we met with between the tropics, had not been idly spent. The carpenters found sufficient employment in repairing the boats. The best bower cable had been so much damaged that we were obliged to cut forty fathoms from it. The airing of sails and other stores, which from the leakiness of the decks, and sides of the ship, were perpetually subject to be wet, had now become a troublesome part of duty. For some time past, even the operation of mending the sailors old jackets, had risen into a duty both of difficulty and importance. It may be necessary to inform those who are unacquainted with the habits of seamen, that they are so accustomed, in ships of war, to be directed in the care of themselves by their officers, that they lose the very idea of foresight, and contract the thoughtlessness of infants. Had these people been left to their own discretion alone, the whole crew would have been very thinly clad, before the voyage had been half finished. It was natural to expect, that their experience, during the voyage to the N. last year, would have made them sensible of the necessity of paying some attention to these matters; but if such reflections ever occurred to them, the impression was so transient, that, upon returning to the tropical climates, their fur jackets, and the rest of their clothes, adapted to a cold country, were kicked about the decks as things of no value; though it was known in both ships, that we were to make another voyage towards the pole.

pole. They were, of course, picked up by the officers; and, being put into casks, restored about this time to the owners. In the afternoon of Wednesday, the 7th, we observed some of the sheathing floating by the ship; and, on examination, found that 12 or 14 feet had been washed off from under the larboard-bow, where the leak was supposed to have been; which, ever since leaving the Sandwich Islands, had kept our people almost constantly at the pumps, making 12 inches water in an hour; but, as we had always been able to keep it under with the hand-pumps, it gave us no great uneasiness, till Tuesday, the 13th, when, about six o'clock, P. M. we were greatly alarmed by a sudden inundation, that deluged the whole space between decks. The water which had lodged in the coal-hole, not finding a sufficient vent into the well, had forced up the platforms over it, and in a moment set every thing afloat. Our situation was now exceedingly distressing; nor did we perceive immediately any means of relief. At last we thought of cutting a hole through the bulk-head that separated the coal-hole from the fore-hold, and, by that means, to make a passage for the body of water into the well. As soon as a passage was made, the greatest part of the water emptied itself into the well, and enabled us to get out the rest in buckets: but the leak was now so much increased, that we were obliged to keep one half of our people pumping and baling constantly, till the noon of Thursday, the 15th. Our men bore, with great chearfulness, this excessive fatigue, which was much increased by their having no dry place to sleep in; on which account they had their full allowance of grog. On Thursday, the 22nd, the cold was exceedingly severe; and the ropes were so frozen, that it was with difficulty they could be forced through the blocks. On Friday, the 23d, in latitude 52 deg. 9 min. longitude 160 deg. 7 min. we saw mountains co-vered

vered with snow, and a high conical rock, distant about four leagues; and soon after this imperfect view we were enveloped in a thick fog. According to our maps, we were now but 8 leagues from the entrance of Awatska Bay; therefore when the weather cleared up, we stood in to take a nearer survey of the country. A most dismal and dreary prospect presented itself. The coast is straight, and uniform, without bays or inlets. From the shore, the ground rises in moderate hills, and behind them are ranges of mountains, whose summits penetrate the clouds. The whole was covered with snow, except the sides of some cliffs which rose perpendicularly from the sea. The wind blew strong from the N. E. with hazy weather and sleet, from the 24th to the 28th. The ship resembled a complete mass of ice; the shrouds being so incrusted with it, as to double their dimensions in circumference: in short, the experience of the oldest seaman among us had never met with such continued showers of sleet, and that extreme cold which we had now to encounter. Soon after our departure from Karakakooa Bay, Captain Clerke was taken ill, and during this run, the sea was in general so rough, and the Resolution so leaky, that the sail-makers had no place to repair the sails in, except the captain's apartments, which in his declining state of health, was a serious inconvenience to him. At this time the inclemency of the weather, the difficulty of working our ships, and the incessant duty required at the pumps, rendered the service intolerable to the crew, some of whom were much frost bitten, and others were confined with colds.

Sunday, the 25th, we were favoured with a transient glance of the entrance of Awatska Bay; but, in the present state of the weather, we could not presume to venture into it. For this reason we again stood off, when we lost sight of the Discovery; but this gave us little concern, being now so near
the

the place of rendezvous. Wednesday, the 28th, in the morning, the weather cleared up, and we had a fine day, when our men were employed in taking the ice from the rigging, sails, &c. that in case of a thaw, which was now expected, it might not fall on our heads. At noon, in latitude 52 deg. 44 min. longitude 159 deg. the entrance of Awatska Bay bore N. W. The mouth of it opens in the direction of N. N. W. On the S. side, the land is moderately high, rising to the northward into a bluff head. Three remarkable rocks lie in the channel between them, not far from the N. E. side; and, on the opposite side, a single rock of considerable size. At three o'clock, P. M. we stood into the bay, with a fair wind from the southward, having from 22 to 7 fathoms soundings. There is a look-out house on the north-head, used as a light-house, when any of the Russian ships are expected upon the coast. It had a flag-staff, but we could not perceive any person there. Having passed the mouth of the bay, which extends about four miles in length, a circular bason presented itself of about 25 miles in circumference; in this we anchored about four o'clock; fearing to run foul of a shoal mentioned by Muller to lie in the channel. Great quantities of loose ice drifted with the tide in the middle of the bay, but the shores were blocked up with it. Plenty of wild fowl, of various kinds, were seen; also large flights of Greenland pigeons, together with ravens and eagles. We examined every corner of the bay, with our glasses, in order to discern the town of St. Peter and St. Paul, which, from the accounts we had received at Oonalashka, we supposed to be a place of strength and consequence. At length we discovered, to the N. E. some miserable log-houses, and a few conical huts, amounting, in the whole, to about 30, which, from their situation, notwithstanding all the respect we wished to entertain for a Russian ostrog, or town, we concluded to be Petropaulowſka. In juſtice, however, to the hoſpitable treatment we found here, it may not be amiſs to anticipate the reader's curioſity, by aſſuring him that our diſappointment proved, in the end, a matter of entertainment to us. In this wretched extremity of the earth, beyond conception barbarous and inhoſpitable, out of the reach of civilization, bound and barricaded with ice, and covered with ſummer ſnow, we experienced the tendereſt feelings of humanity, joined to a nobleneſs of mind, and elevation of ſentiment, which would have done honour to any clime and nation.

On Sunday the 29th, in the morning, at daylight, Captain King was ſent with the boats to examine the bay, and to preſent the letters to the Ruſſian commander, which he had brought from Oonalaſhka. Having proceeded as far as we were able with the boats, we got upon the ice, which extended near half a mile from the ſhore. The inhabitants had not yet ſeen either the ſhip, or the boats; for even after we had got upon the ice, we could not perceive any ſigns of a living creature in the town. We ſunk at every ſtep almoſt knee deep in the ſnow, and though we found tolerable footing at the bottom, yet the weak parts of the ice not being diſcoverable, we were conſtantly expoſed to the danger of breaking through it. This accident, at laſt, actually happened to Captain King; who ſtepping on quickly over a ſuſpicious ſpot, in order to preſs with leſs weight upon it, he came upon a ſecond before he could ſtop himſelf, which broke under him, and in he fell. Fortunately he roſe clear of the ice; and a man who was a little way behind with a boat hook, throwing it out, the captain, by that means, was enabled to get upon firm ice again. The nearer we approached the ſhore, we found the ice ſtill more broken. The ſight of a ſledge advancing towards us, however, afforded ſome comfort.

fort. But inftead of coming to our relief, the driver ftopt fhort, and called out to us. Captain King immediately held up Ifmyloff's letters; in confequence of which, the man turned about, and drove full fpeed back again, followed with the execrations of fome of our party. Unable to draw any conclufion from this unaccountable behaviour, we ftill proceeded towards the oftrog, though with the greateft circumfpection; and, when at the diftance of about a quarter of a mile from it, we obferved a body of armed men advancing to meet us. To avoid giving them any alarm, and to preferve the moft peaceable appearance, the captain, and Mr. Webber, marched in front, and the men, who had boat-hooks in their hands, were ftationed in the rear. The armed party confifted of about 30 foldiers, headed by a perfon with a cane in his hand. Within a few paces of us he halted, and drew up his men in martial order. Captain King prefented Ifmyloff's letters to him, but in vain endeavoured to make him underftand that we were Englifh, and had brought thefe difpatches from Oonalafhka. After an attentive examination of our perfons, he conducted us towards the village in folemn filence, halting frequently his men, and ordering them to perform different parts of their manual exercife; with a view, as we fuppofed, to convince us, that if we fhould prefume to offer any violence, we fhould have to deal with thofe who knew how to defend themfelves. During the whole of this time, the captain was in his wet clothes, fhivering with cold; yet he could not avoid being diverted with this military parade, though it was attended by an unfeafonable delay. Arriving, at length, at the habitation of the commanding officer of the party, we were ufhered in; and, after giving orders to the military without doors, our hoft appeared, accompanied by the fecretary of the port. One of the letters from Ifmyloff was now opened,

and

and the other sent express to Bolcheretsk, a town on the west side of Kamtschatka, and the place of residence of the Russian commander of this province.

It appeared to us extraordinary, that the natives had not seen the Resolution the preceding day when we cast anchor, nor this morning, till our boats approached the ice. The first sight of the ship, we understood, had struck them with a considerable panic. The garrison was put instantly under arms; two field-pieces were placed before the commander's house; and powder, shot, and lighted matches, were all in readiness. The officer who had conducted us to his dwelling, was a serjeant, and also the commander of the ostrog. After he had recovered from the alarm which our arrival had produced, the kindness and hospitality of his behaviour was astonishing. His house, indeed, was intolerably hot, but remarkably neat and clean. After Captain King had changed his clothes, by putting on a compleat suit of the serjeant's, at his earnest request, which was doubtless the best he could procure; and, considering our visit was unexpected, was ingeniously conducted. To have made soup and bouillie would have required some time; instead therefore of this, we had some cold beef sliced, with boiling water poured over it. The next course was a large roasted bird, the taste of which was most delicious, though we were unacquainted with its species. Having eaten a part of this, it was removed, and fish was served up, dressed in two different ways. Soon after which, the remainder of the bird appeared again in savoury and sweet pates. Our liquor was what the Russians distinguish by the name of quass, and was the most indifferent part of our entertainment. The serjeant's wife served up several of the dishes, and was not permitted to sit down at table with us. Our repast being finished, during which our conversation

tion was limited to a few bows, and other personal tokens of mutual respect, we strove to explain
to our host the occasion of our visit to this port.
Probably, Ismyloff's letters we had delivered made
him readily comprehend our meaning; but as there
was not a person in the place, who understood any
other languages than those of Russia or Kamtschatka, we found it extremely difficult to comprehend
what he endeavoured to communicate to us. Having spent much time in our attempts to understand
each other, the sum of the intelligence we had received appeared to be, that though we could not be
supplied with provisions or stores at this place, yet
those articles were to be procured in great plenty at
Bolcheretsk. That he doubted not, but the commander would readily supply us with what we
wanted; but that, till he received his orders, neither he, nor any of the natives could even venture
on board the vessel. It being now time for us to
depart, and as Mr. King's clothes were not yet dry,
he had again recourse to the serjeant's benevolence,
for his permission to carry those on board which he
had borrowed of him. This request was chearfully
complied with, and a sledge, with five dogs and a
driver, was instantly provided for each of our party.
This mode of conveyance afforded high entertainment for the sailors; and they were delighted still
more, when they found that the two boat-hooks
had a sledge appropriated solely for their conveyance.
These sledges are so light, and so admirably well
constructed for the purposes intended, that they went
safely and expeditiously over the ice, and over parts
of it which we should have found extremely difficult
to have passed on foot. On our return, the boats
were towing the Resolution towards the village;
and, at seven, we moored close to the ice; the entrance of the bay bearing S. by E. and the ostrog N.
distant one mile and a half. On Friday, the 30th,
the casks and cables were taken to the quarter-deck,

to

to lighten the vessel forward, and the carpenters proceeded to stop the leak which had occasioned us so much trouble. In the middle of the day we had such warm weather, that the ice began to break away very fast, and almost choaked up the entrance of the bay. Several of our officers waited upon the serjeant, who received them with great civility; and Captain Clerke sent him a present of two bottles of rum, thinking he could not send him any thing more acceptable. In return, he received twenty fine trouts, and some excellent fowls of the grouse kind. Though the bay swarmed with ducks and Greenland pigeons, our sportsmen had no success; for, being exceedingly shy, they could not kill any.

On Saturday, the 1st of May, in the morning, we saw our consort, the Discovery, standing into the bay: a boat was immediately dispatched to her assistance, and she was moored in the afternoon close by the Resolution. On the 3d, in the morning, two sledges having been observed to drive into the village, Mr. King was ordered on shore, to learn whether an answer was arrived from the commander of Kamtschatka. The distance from Bolcheretsk to St. Peter and St. Paul's is 135 English miles. The dispatches were sent off in a sledge, drawn by dogs, on the 29th, at noon, and returned with an answer early this morning; so that they performed a journey of 270 miles in little more than three days and a half. For the present, the return of the commander's answer was concealed from us. While Mr. King was on shore, his boat, and another belonging to the Discovery, were bound fast to the ice. In this situation, the Discovery's launch was sent to their assistance, which soon partook of the same fate: but on the 4th, the floating ice was drifted away, by the wind changing, and the boats were set at liberty, without sustaining the smallest damage. At 10 o'clock, A. M. several sledges having

ing arrived at the edge of the ice, a boat was sent from the ship to conduct those who were in them on board. One of them proved to be a Russian merchant from Bolcheretsk, whose name was Fedositsch; and the other a German, named Port, with dispatches from Major Behm, commander of Kamtschatka, to Captain Clerke. Arriving at the edge of the ice, and seeing distinctly the magnitude of the ships, within 200 yards of them, they were exceedingly alarmed; and before they ventured to embark, stipulated that two of our boat's crew should remain on shore, as hostages for their safety. It afterwards appeared, for what reasons we could not conceive, that Ismyloff, in his letter to the commander, had mentioned our ships as two small trading vessels; and that the serjeant, having seen them at a distance only, had not rectified the mistake. When they had arrived on board, we perceived, by their timid behaviour, that they entertained some very extraordinary apprehensions. However, an uncommon degree of satisfaction was visible in their countenances, when the German found a person among us, with whom he could enter into conversation. Mr. Webber spoke that language fluently, and convinced them, though not without difficulty, that we were Englishmen and friends. Mr. Port was introduced to Captain Clerke, to whom he delivered the commander's letter. It was written in the German language, and merely complimental, giving him and his officers an invitation to Bolcheretsk. Mr. Port, at the same time, acquainted him, that the Major had conceived a very strong idea of the size of the ships, and of the service they were engaged in; Ismyloff, in his letter, having represented them as two small pacquet-boats, and cautioned him to be on his guard, insinuating, that he suspected us to be no better than pirates. In consequence of this letter, he said, there had been various conjectures formed about us at Bolcheretſk. We were much diverted with the fears and apprehenſions of theſe people; and eſpecially with an account given by Mr. Port, of the ſerjeant's extreme caution the day before. On ſeeing Mr. King and ſome other gentlemen come on ſhore, he concealed him and the Ruſſian merchant in the kitchen, to give them an opportunity of liſtening to our converſation with each other, in order to diſcover whether we were Engliſhmen or not.

Being now enabled, by the aid of an interpreter, to converſe with the Ruſſians, our firſt enquiries were directed to the means of procuring a ſupply of freſh proviſions and naval ſtores; particularly the latter, for the want of which we had been in great diſtreſs. On enquiry, it appeared, that the whole ſtock of live cattle, which the country about the bay could furniſh, amounted only to two heifers; and theſe the ſerjeant very readily promiſed to ſecure for us. Our next applications were made to the merchant, whoſe terms for ſerving us were ſo exorbitant, that Captain Clerke thought it expedient to ſend an expreſs to the commander, to learn the price of ſtores at Bolcheretſk. This determination being communicated to Mr. Port, he diſpatched a meſſenger to the commander at Bolcheretſk, to acquaint him with our intentions, and to remove the ſuſpicions that had been entertained reſpecting the purpoſes of our voyage. For the above ſervice Mr. King was fixed upon, and ordered to prepare for ſetting out the next day, together with Mr. Webber, who was to accompany him as interpreter. That day, and the next, however, the weather proved too ſtormy for beginning a journey through ſo deſolate and wild a country: but on Friday, the 7th of May, the weather became more favourable, and we ſet out in the ſhip's boats, early in the morning, in order to reach the entrance of the Awatſka at high-water, on account of the

ſhoals

shoals at the mouth of that river. The country boats were to meet us here, to conduct us up the stream. Captain Gore was also added to our party, and we were likewise accompanied by Mr. Port and the Russian merchant, with two Cossacks, having been previously furnished with warm furred cloathing; a very necessary precaution, as it began to snow briskly immediately after our setting out. About eight o'clock, we were stopped by shoal water, within a mile of the mouth of the river; when some Kamtschadales took us and our baggage, in some small canoes, and conveyed us over a bank of sand, which the rapidity of the river had thrown up, and which, we were informed, was continually shifting. Having passed this shoal, the water again deepened, and we were furnished with a commodious boat, resembling a Norway yawl, to convey us up the river, together with canoes for the reception of our baggage. The breadth of the mouth of Awatska is about a quarter of a mile, but it gradually narrowed as we advanced. Having proceeded a few miles, we passed several branches, many of which, we were told, emptied themselves into other parts of the bay; and that some of those on the left ran into the Paratounca river. For the first 10 miles, the general direction of the river from the bay, is to the N. and afterwards it turns to the westward. Except this bend, it chiefly preserves a straight course; and flows through a low flat country, to the distance of 30 miles from the sea, which is subject to frequent inundations. Six men were employed in pushing us on with long poles, three of them being at each end of the boat; and proceeded against the stream, at the rate of about three miles an hour. Our conductors endured this severe labour for 10 hours; stopping only once, and that for a short space of time, to take a little refreshment. Having been informed, at our first setting out, that we could easily reach

Karachin

Karachin that night, we were greatly disappointed to find ourselves 15 miles from that place at sun-set. This was attributed to the delay in passing the shoals, both at the entrance of the river, and in many other places. Our men been exceedingly fatigued, and as the difficulty of navigating the river would have encreased by the darkness of the night, we declined all thoughts of proceeding on our journey that evening: we therefore fixed upon a place that was tolerably well sheltered, and, clearing it of the snow, erected a small marquée, which we had providentially taken with us; and, with the assistance of a good fire, and some excellent punch, passed the night agreeably. Our principal inconvenience was, the being obliged to keep at a considerable distance from the fire; for as soon as it was lighted, it thawed every part round it into an absolute puddle. The Kamtscadales were extremely alert and expeditious in erecting our marquée, and cooking our provisions; but we were much surprized at finding they had brought with them their utensils for making tea, considering it as a most intolerable hardship if they cannot, two or three times a day, regale themselves with drinking tea. When daylight appeared, we proceeded on our journey, and, before we had made much progress, were met by the Toion, or chief of Karachin, who, being apprized of our coming, had provided canoes that were better accommodated for navigating the higher parts of the river. A commodious vessel, (made by lashing two canoes together) furnished with fur cloaks, and lined with bear-skins, was also procured for us. We now proceeded rapidly, the Toion's people being remarkably expert in this kind of business. At ten we arrived at the ostrog, named Karachin, and the seat of his command, where we were received by the Kamtscadale men and women, and some Russian servants belonging to the merchant, Fedositsch. They were all attired in their

best

best habiliments; those of the women being gay and pleasing, and consisting of a loose robe of white nankeen, gathered close round the neck, and fastened with a silk collar. A short jacket, without sleeves, was worn over this, consisting of different coloured nankeens; and they had petticoats made of a slight Chinese silk. Their shifts, which were also made of silk, had sleeves extending to the wrists; and their heads were bound with coloured silk handkerchiefs, which entirely concealed the hair of the married women; but the unmarried ones placed the handkerchief under the hair, permitting it to flow loosely down the shoulders.

The ostrog of Karachin is pleasantly situated on the side of the river, and composed of three log-houses, nineteen balagans, or summer habitations, and three jourts, which are houses under ground. The Toion, to whose dwelling we were then conducted, was a plain decent man, sprung from a Russian mother, and a Kamtscadale father. His house, like all others in this country, consisted of only two apartments. All the furniture in the outer room, was a long narrow table, with a bench round it; and the inner apartment, which was the kitchen, was also very scantily furnished. But, the hearty welcome, and kind attention of our host, amply compensated for the poverty of his habitation. His wife, an excellent cook, served us with various sorts of fish and game, and different kinds of heathberries, which had been preserved since the last year. Whilst we were dining in this miserable hut, the guests of absolute strangers, and at the extremity of the habitable globe, a solitary half-worn pewter spoon attracted our attention. Its form was familiar to us, and the word London was stamped upon the back of it. It is impossible to express the anxious hopes, and tender remembrances, this circumstance excited in us. Those who have been long absent from their

native

native country, will readily conceive what inexpressible pleasure such trifling incidents can give.

We had now quitted the river, and the next part of our journey was to be performed on sledges; but the thaw had been so great in the day-time, as not to permit us to set out, till the snow was become hard and firm by the coldness of the evening. This furnished us with an opportunity of walking about the village, which was the only place in this country, that we had seen free from snow. It was situated on a flat, of about a mile and an half in circuit. The leaves of the trees were just budding, and the verdure was strongly contrasted with the surrounding hills, which remained covered with snow. The soil appearing to be capable of producing common vegetables, we were surprized to find that not a spot of it was cultivated. Neither were the inhabitants possessed of cattle of any sort. In short, their situation, during the winter months, must be wretched beyond conception. They were now removing from their jourts to their balagans, which gave us an opportunity of observing both these sorts of habitations. The people invited us, very civilly, into their houses; chearfulness and content were visible in every countenance, to which the approaching change of season might perhaps contribute. On returning to our host's, supper was prepared for us, consisting of the same articles which composed our former repast. When we had finished our meal, we entertained the Toion and his wife with punch made of some of our spirits; and Captain Gore, with his wonted generosity, made them some valuable presents: after which, they retired to the kitchen, leaving us in the other room; on the benches of which we spread our bear-skins, and sought a little repose; having first settled with our conductors, to proceed on our journey, when the ground was judged to be in a suitable condition. The melancholy howlings of the dogs awakened us about nine

the

the same evening. During the whole time our baggage was lashing upon the sledges, their horrid noise continued; but, when they were yoked, and prepared for travelling, a chearful yelping succeeded, which ceased the instant they marched off. We shall here give our readers an accurate description of a sledge brought over by Captain King, and now in the possession of Sir Ashton Lever. The length of the body is about four feet and an half, and the breadth one foot. It is made in the form of a crescent, of light tough wood, fastened together with wicker work; and, among the principal people, is elegantly stained with red and blue; the seat being covered with furs or bear-skins. It has four legs, about two feet in height, resting on two long flat pieces of wood, of the breadth of five or six inches, extending a foot beyond the body of the sledge, at each end. These turn up before, somewhat like a skait, and are shod with the bone of some sea-animal. The carriage is ornamented, at the fore-part, with tassels of coloured cloth, and leather thongs. It has a cross-bar, to which the harness is joined; and links of iron, or small bells, are hanging to it, which, by the jingling, is supposed to encourage the dogs. They seldom carry more than one person at a time, who sits aside, with his feet on the lower part of the sledge, having his baggage and provisions in a bundle behind him. The usual number of dogs employed in drawing this carriage, is five; four of them yoked two and two, and the other acting as leader. The reins, being fastened to the collar, instead of the head, have no great command: and are therefore usually hung upon the sledge; the driver depending principally on their obedience to his voice. Great care and attention are consequently used in training up the leader, which frequently becomes very valuable on account of his steadiness and docility; the sum of forty roubles (or ten pounds) being no unusual price for one

one of them. The rider has also a crooked stick, answering the purpose both of whip and reins; with which, by striking in the snow, he can regulate the speed of the dogs, or even stop them at his pleasure. When they are inattentive to their duty, he often chastises them by throwing it at them. The dexterity of the riders, in picking this stick up again, is very remarkable, and is the most difficult manœuvre in the exercise of their profession: nor is it, indeed, surprising that they should be skilful in a practice in which they are so materially interested; for, they assured us, that if a driver should happen to lose his stick, the dogs immediately discover it; and, unless their leader is both steady and resolute, they will instantly set off full speed, and never stop till their strength is exhausted; or till the carriage is overturned and dashed to pieces, or hurried down a precipice, when all are buried in the snow. The accounts of the speed of these animals, and of the hardships and fatigues they suffer, would have appeared incredible, had they not been supported by the greatest authority. We ourselves were witnesses of the extraordinary expedition with which the messenger returned, who had been dispatched to Bolcheretsk with the news of our arrival at St. Peter and St. Paul's, though the snow was exceedingly soft. The governor of Kamtschatka assured us, that this journey was usually performed in two days and a half; and that he had once received an express from that harbour in 23 hours. Throughout the winter, the dogs are fed on the offals of dried and stinking fish; and, even this miserable food is withheld from them, a day before they set out on a journey; and they are not permitted to eat a morsel of any thing till they arrive at the end of it. They are frequently kept fasting for two entire days, in which time they will perform a journey of great extent. The shape of these dogs resembles that of

the

the Pomeranian breed, but they are considerably larger.

As we did not chuse to rely upon our own skill, we had each of us a man to conduct the sledge, which, in the condition the roads then were, proved a very laborious business: for, as the thaw had been prevalent in the vallies, through which was our regular road, we were obliged to travel along the sides of the hills; our guides being under the necessity of supporting the sledges, on the lower sides, with their shoulders, for many miles together. Mr. King was attended by a good natured Cossack, who was so imperfect in his business, that he was continually overturned, which afforded entertainment to his companions. The party consisted of ten sledges in the whole. That which conducted Captain Gore, was formed of two lashed together, and was plentifully furnished with furs and bear-skins. It was drawn by ten dogs, yoked four abreast; and those which were laded with heavy baggage, were drawn by the same number. We had not proceeded more than four miles on our journey, when it began to rain, which, together with the darkness of the night, threw us into some confusion. It was, after some little consultation, agreed, that we should coninue where we were, till day-light: we therefore secured our sledges, wrapped ourselves up in furs, and waited patiently for the morning. At three o'clock we were summoned to proceed; our guides expressing their apprehensions, that if we waited any longer, the thaw would perhaps stop us, and prevent our advancing or returning. Though we had many difficulties to encounter, owing principally to the bad condition of the road, we got safe to an ostrog about two in the afternoon. It is called Natcheekin, and is situated on a small stream, which falls into the Bolchoireka, at some distance below the town. It is 25 miles from Karatchin; which, by their account, we could have compassed in four hours,

hours, had the frost continued; but the snow was so soft that the poor animals sunk up to their bellies at almost every step; and it was indeed surprizing that they should be able to support themselves under so fatiguing a journey. This inconsiderable ostrog consists of one log-house, the residence of the Toion, one jourt, and five balagans. We were received here with the same civility and hospitality as at Karatchin; and, in the afternoon, were conducted to a remarkable hot spring, at a small distance from this village. Before we came very near it, we saw a steam rising from it, as from a boiling caldron; and, when we approached it, we perceived a strong sulphureous effluvia. A bason of about three feet in diameter, is formed by the main spring; besides which, there are several lesser springs, of equal heat, in the adjacent ground; by which means the whole spot, consisting of about an acre, was so very hot that we could not remain two minutes in the same place. The water issuing from these springs, supplies a small bathing pond, and afterwards a little rivulet, which conducts it into the river, at the distance of about 150 yards. Great cures, they informed us, had been effected by this bath, in rheumatisms, scorbutic ulcers, swelled and contracted joints, and many other disorders. Where these springs flow, the ground is on a gentle ascent; having a green hill of a moderate size behind it. Some plants seemed to thrive here with great luxuriance, among which we observed the wild garlick.

Monday, the 10th, in the morning, we embarked on the Bolchoireeka; and, going with the stream, expected to arrive at our journey's end the following day. Though Bolcheretsk is 80 miles from Natcheekin, we were informed, that, in the summer, when the melting of snow on the mountains has rendered the river full and rapid, the canoes have often gone there in a single day: but now they told us we should be much longer, the ice having
broken

broken up only three days before our arrival, and our's being the first boat that had attempted to pass. There was but too much truth in this intelligence; for we were greatly impeded by the shallows; and, though the stream was rapid in many places, we frequently had ripplings and shoals, and were under the necessity of hauling the boats over them. On each side of the river, the country was romantic, but not diversified; the course of it being between craggy mountains, of a most dreary and barren aspect; with nothing to vary the scene, except now and then the sight of a bear, or a flock of wild-fowl. This, and the following night, we slept under our marquée, on the banks of the river, and suffered greatly from the severity of the weather.

Wednesday the 12th, at day-light, we had passed the mountains, and were proceeding through a low extensive plain, on which were a number of shrubby trees. At nine in the morning, we reached an ostrog, called Opatchin, of about the same magnitude as Karatchin, and supposed to be 50 miles from Natcheekin. A serjeant and four Russian soldiers had been here two days, waiting for our arrival; who instantly dispatched a light boat to Bolcheretsk to give intelligence of our approach. A magnificent canoe, plentifully furnished with skins and furs, was prepared for our reception, and we were very commodiously equipped; but our fellow-travellers were excluded. It gave us some concern to be separated from our old companion Mr. Port, who daily grew more shy and distant, as we drew nearer to the completion of our journey. He acknowledged, indeed, before we set out, that he was not entitled to the respect we had shewn him; but, finding him discreet, and not presuming, we had insisted on his faring as we did, throughout the journey. We performed the remainder of our passage, with the utmost ease and expedition;

expedition; for as we descended, the river grew more rapid, and had very few obstructions. On our approaching Kamtschatka, we judged, from an appearance of great stir and bustle, that our reception was to be in form. This circumstance was disagreeable to us, as decent cloathing had long been scarce among us; and our travelling habits formed a strange assemblage of the modes of India, Europe and Kamtschatka. To make a parade through the metropolis in this motley trim, we thought would appear ridiculous; and, as we observed a crowd of people collected on the banks of the river, and were informed that the commander would receive us at the water-side, we stopped at the house of a soldier, about a quarter of a mile before we came to the town. Here we dispatched Mr. Port with a message to his excellency, acquainting him, that, as soon as we had put off our travelling dresses, we would attend him at his own house to pay our respects to him; and entreated him not to think of waiting to conduct us. He persisted, however, in his resolution of paying us this compliment, and we immediately proceeded to join him at the entrance of the capital. We were all remarkably aukward and defective in making our first salutations; not having been accustomed to bowing and scraping, for at least two years and an half. The commander received us in a most engaging manner; but we had the mortification to discover, that he had almost wholly forgot the French language; so that only Mr. Webber had the satisfaction of conversing with him, as he spoke the German, which was his native tongue. Major Behm was accompanied by Captain Shmaleff, the next in command, and another officer; the whole body of merchants attended also. We were conducted to the commander's house, where we were politely and respectfully received by his lady, who had prepared tea and other refreshments for us. The

first

first compliments being over, Captain Gore desired Mr. Webber to acquaint the Major, that we were distressed for want of naval stores, fresh provisions, flour, and other necessaries; and that we were convinced we could not receive much assistance from him, in the country about Awatska Bay, from what we had already seen and heard; that the impossibility of conveying heavy stores over the peninsula, at that season, we were but too sensible of, from the difficulties we had encountered in our journey; and that we could not delay the prosecution of our voyage, to wait for any material change. Here the Major interrupted Mr. Webber, by observing, that we knew not what they were capable of doing; that he should not bestow a thought upon the difficulties of supplying our wants: he only wished to know what articles we stood in need of, and the time he could be allowed for procuring them. After expressing our acknowledgments for his obliging condescension, we presented him an account of the naval stores, cattle, and flour, we were directed to purchase; and informed him, that we intended to prosecute our voyage about the 5th of June. After this, the conversation became more general, and it might naturally be supposed, that we were anxious to obtain some information respecting our native country. Having been three years absent, we entertained the most flattering expectations, of receiving some interesting intelligence from Major Behm: but we were greatly disappointed, when he assured us, that he could not communicate any intelligence of a much later date than that of our quitting England. The commander, supposing we might be fatigued, and desirous of repose, begged leave to conduct us to our lodgings, at about seven o'clock. It was useless to protest against a compliment, to which we had no other title than that of being strangers. That alone, with this generous Livonian, was sufficient to counterbalance

terbalance every other confideration. In going along, we paffed two guard-houfes, where the men were under arms, in compliment to Captain Gore, and were conducted to a neat decent houfe, which the Major had appointed for our refidence, while we continued at Kamtfchatka. We had two fentinels pofted at our door, and a ferjeant's guard in an adjoining houfe. Having difpofed of us in our apartments, the Major took his leave, promifing to vifit us the next day. We were now at leifure to difcover the conveniencies which he had amply provided for us. Our fellow traveller, Mr. Port, and a foldier, of a rank between that of a ferjeant and a corporal, (called a pulproperfckack) were fixed upon to be our male domeftics. We had alfo a houfekeeper, and a cook, who were ordered to obey Mr. Port's directions in dreffing us a fupper, after the Englifh mode of cookery. In the courfe of the evening, we were favoured with a number of civil meffages, from the principal inhabitants of the town, politely obferving, that their attending to pay their refpects to us at that time, would add to our fatigues, but they would do themfelves that honour the next morning. Such attention and politenefs, in fo uncultivated and defolate a country, formed a contraft highly in favour of its inhabitants; and, in addition to their civility, at fun-fet, the ferjeant brought the report of his guard to Captain Gore. In the morning of the 13th, compliments were fent us by the Major, Captain Shmaleff, and the moft refpectable people of the town, from all whom we were honoured with vifits foon after. The two former having, after we had retired to reft, enquired of Mr. Port what articles we ftood in the greateft need of on board the fhips; they infifted on our fharing with their garrifon, in the fmall ftock of provifions they had then remaining; lamenting, at the fame time, that our arrival fhould happen to be in that feafon

of

of the year, when scarcity reigned universally among them; the sloops from Okotsk not being yet arrived with their annual supply. We thankfully accepted the liberal offer of these hospitable strangers; on condition, however, that we should be made acquainted with the price of the articles we received from them, that Captain Clerke might draw upon the Victualling Office, in London, for the amount. This was refused in the most positive terms; and, though repeatedly urged, the Major always stopped us short, by saying, that his mistress would be highly gratified at his rendering every assistance in his power to the English, who are her good friends and allies; and that it would give her a peculiar satisfaction to find, that, in such remote regions, her dominions had afforded any relief to vessels engaged in such important services. He added, that he could not, therefore, act so contrary to the principles of his Empress, as to think of receiving any bills; but, if we insisted on it, we might give him a bare certificate of the articles he might supply us with, which he would transmit to the court of Russia, as evidence of having performed his duty. All farther acknowledgments, continued he, must be submitted to the two courts; but you must excuse me from acceding to your proposal. This matter being adjusted, he requested to be informed respecting our private wants, saying he should consider it as offering him an affront, if we applied to any of the merchants, or had dealings with any other person except himself.

Not having it in our power to make an adequate return for such singular generosity, he had only our thanks and admiration. At this moment, Mr. King recollected, that Captain Clerke had sent by him a set of the engravings to Captain Cook's second voyage, desiring him to present it, in his name, to the commander. Nothing could have been more acceptable to him than this present, the Major being

ing an enthusiast in all matters relative to discoveries. Captain Clerke had also given Mr. King a discretionary power, of permitting the commander to see a chart of the discoveries made in the present voyage; and, judging from his situation and disposition of mind, that he would be highly gratified by such a communication; though, from motives of delicacy, he had only asked a few general questions on the subject, Mr. King reposed in him that confidence, which his whole conduct so justly merited. He felt this compliment as it was intended he should, and was struck at beholding, in one view, the whole of that coast on the side of Asia and America, which his countrymen had been so long employed in acquiring an imperfect knowledge of. Except this mark of confidence, and the set of copper-plates already mentioned, we had nothing with us deserving of his acceptance; for it was hardly worth noticing, that Mr. King prevailed on his son (who was quite a youth) to accept of a silver watch; and contributed to his little daughter's happiness, by presenting her with two pair of earrings, of French paste. He also gave Captain Shmaleff the thermometer which he had used on his journey, when he engaged to keep a register of the temperature of the air for one whole year, and to transmit it to Mr. Muller, with whom he was acquainted. This day we dined at the commander's, who, ever studious to gratify our curiosity, had prepared variety of dishes dressed after the Russian and Kamtschadale manner, besides a number of others in the English style. In the afternoon, we took a survey of the town, and the adjacent country. The situation of Bolcheretsk is in a low swampy plain, extending to the sea of Okotsk, being about 40 miles in length, and of a considerable breadth. It lies north of the Bolchoi-reka, (or great river) and on a peninsula, which has been separated from the continent by a large canal, under the

the directions of the present commander; which has added strength to it as a fortress, and rendered it much less subject to inundations. The depth of the river, below the town, is from six to eight feet, and the breadth about a quarter of a mile. At the distance of 22 miles, it empties itself into the sea of Okotsk, where it is capable of admitting pretty large vessels. No corn, of any kind, is cultivated in this part of the country; and the Major assured us, that his was the only garden that had been planted. In general, the earth was covered with snow; the parts which were free from it, were full of black turfy hillocks. We saw about 20 or 30 cows, and the commander had six good horses. These, and their dogs, are their only tame animals: being obliged to keep a great number of the latter, they can rear only such cattle as are a match for them in strength and size. For, during the whole of the summer season, the dogs are turned loose, to provide entirely for themselves; and are sometimes so ravenous, that they will even venture to attack the bullocks. In Bolcheretsk the buildings are all in the same style; they consist of logs of wood, and are thatched. The Major's house is considerably larger than the rest, and has three capacious rooms, neatly papered; but the talc, which covered the windows, gave them a disagreeable and mean appearance. The town consists of low buildings, in rows of five or six habitations each, connected together by a passage extending the whole length of them; having the kitchen and storehouse on one side, and the dwelling apartments on the other. There are also barracks for the Russian soldiers and cossacks, a tolerable church, a courtroom; and, at the end of the town, a number of balagans. The number of the inhabitants is between five and six hundred. A handsome entertainment was given by the Major, in the evening, to which were invited all the respectable inhabitants of both sexes. The next day we made a private application to Fedositsch, the merchant, in order to purchase some tobacco; the sailors having been without that favourite commodity for upwards of a year. This, however, like other similar transactions, came immediately to the knowledge of the commander; and, in a very short time after, we were surprized to find four bags of tobacco in our house, each containing upwards of 100 pounds; which the Major requested might be presented to our sailors, in his name, and that of the garrison under his command. By the same conveyance, we received 20 loaves of sugar, and as many pounds of tea, which they requested the officers to accept of; as they understood that we were almost destitute of those articles. A present was also sent by Madame Behm, for Captain Clerke, which consisted of honey, butter, figs, rice, and other articles; accompanied with her best wishes, that, in his infirm state, they might prove serviceable to him. We strenuously endeavoured to oppose this profusion of bounty, and were extremely anxious to restrain it; fully convinced that they were giving us almost the whole stock of their garrison. But the answer we received from the Major, on these occasions, generally was, That he had been in distress himself, and he was sensible that we must now be in that situation. The length of time, indeed, since we had touched at any known port, appeared to them almost incredible, and seemed to require the evidence of our maps, and other concurrent circumstances, to obtain their credit. Among the latter, we shall mention a curious fact, which Major Behm related to us this morning, and which he said he should not have known how to account for, but for our arrival. Among the people of the north of Asia, it is well known, that the Tschutski only have maintained their independence, and resisted all the efforts of the Russians to reduce them. The last attempt

was

was in 1750, and, after variety of temporary advantages on each side, the Russian forces retreated, after having lost their commanding officer. The Russians afterwards removed their frontier fortress, from the Anadyr to the Ingiga, a river which runs into the northern extremity of the sea of Okotsk, and gives its name to a gulph, west of that of Penshinsk. On the day of our arrival at Bolcheretsk, the Major had received dispatches from this fort, acquainting him, that a party of the Tschutski had arrived there, with voluntary offers of friendship and a tribute. That, on asking the cause of so unexpected an alteration in their sentiments, they had acquainted his people, that two large Russian boats had visited them, towards the end of the preceding summer; that they had been shewn the greatest kindness by the people who were in them, and had entered into a league of amity with them; and that, in consequence of this, they came to the Russian fort, in order to settle a treaty upon terms agreeable to both nations. This remarkable tale had given rise to much speculation, both at Iginsk and Bolcheretsk; and must have remained utterly unintelligible, had it not been elucidated by us. It was no small satisfaction to us, to have thus shewn the Russians, even by accident, the best method of collecting tribute, and extending their dominions; in hopes that the good understanding, which this event has produced, may rescue a brave people from such powerful invaders.

This day being Friday, the 14th, we were engaged to dine with Captain Shmaleff, who, in order to vary our amusements, entertained us with an exhibition of dancing, in the Russian and Kamtschadale style. It is impossible to convey an adequate idea of this uncouth exhibition. The figure of the Russian dance, resembled those of our hornpipes, and consisted of one, two, or four performers at a time. Their steps were exceedingly short and quick, their feet being raised but a very little way from the ground; their arms were hung down close to the sides, the body being kept, the whole time, erect and immoveable, except when the performers passed each other, when the hand was suddenly raised with an awkward motion. But, if the Russian dance was unmeaning and ridiculous, the Kamtschadale was infinitely more so. The principal aim, in their performances, is to represent the clumsy gestures of the bear, which the inhabitants of this country have frequent opportunities of observing in various situations. To describe the awkward postures, exhibited on these occasions, would appear tedious and uninteresting. In general, however, the body was bowed, and the knees bent, whilst the arms were employed in imitating the motions of that awkward animal. Much time had been spent in our journey to Bolcheretsk, and being informed that our return might, perhaps, be more difficult and tedious, we were obliged to acquaint the Major this evening, with our intention of departing the next day. We could not think of leaving our new acquaintance without regret: and were agreeably surprized, when the Major promised to accompany us, if we would stay but one day longer. He told us, that he had made up his dispatches, and resigned the command of Kamtschatka to Captain Shmaleff; having made the necessary preparations for his departure to Okotsk, which was shortly to take place; but that he should be happy in postponing his journey, and attending us to St. Peter and St. Paul's, in order to be satisfied, that nothing which could be done to serve us, should be omitted. For the articles which Mr. King had given to the Major's children, he received, the next morning, a most magnificent Kamtschadale dress, such as the principal Toions wear on the most solemn occasions. This habit, as we were informed by Fedositsch, must have cost, at least, 120 roubles.

He also, at the same time, was presented with a handsome sable muff, as a present from his daughter.

Saturday, the 15th, we dined with the commander, who, willing to give us an opportunity of seeing as much as we could of the manners and customs of the country, invited all the principal inhabitants of the town, to his house this evening. The dresses of the women were splendid, after the Kamtschadale manner. Captain Shmaleff's lady, and the wives of the other officers of the garrison, were dressed in a pretty taste, partly in the Siberian, and partly in the European mode. Madame Behm, in particular, appeared in a grand European dress. The richness and variety of the silks worn by the women, as well as the singularity of their dress, was very striking: and the whole had the air of some enchanted scene, in the midst of the most desert and dreary country in the universe. The entertainments of this night were dancing and singing. As we had fixed upon the next morning for our departure, we retired early to our apartments, where three travelling dresses presented themselves to our view, made after the Kamtschadale mode, which had been provided for us by the commander. He came to us himself soon after, to see that proper care was taken in packing up our things. We had, indeed, no inconsiderable load of baggage; for, exclusive of his liberal presents, Captain Shmaleff, and several other individuals, shewed us many instances of kindness and generosity. On the 16th, early in the morning, we were preparing for our departure, when we were invited to take our leave of Madame Behm, in our passage to the boats. Already impressed with sentiments of the warmest gratitude, for the benevolent and generous treatment we had received at Bolcheretsk, they were much heightened by the affecting scene which followed. On quitting our apartments, we saw all the

the soldiers and cossacks of the garrison drawn up on one side; and, on the other, were all the male inhabitants of the town, in their best cloathing; the whole body of the people joining in a melancholy song, which, we were informed, it was usual to sing on the departure of friends. Thus we marched till we arrived at the commander's house, preceded by the drums and music belonging to the garrison. Here we were received by Madame Behm, accompanied by several ladies, habited in long silk cloaks, lined with furs of various colours; forming a most splendid appearance. Having partook of some refreshment which had been provided for us, we proceeded to the water-side, attended by the ladies, who joined with the rest of the people in the song; and, having taken leave of Madame Behm, after assuring her that the sense of the hospitality of Bolcheretsk would be indelible in our hearts, we were too much affected not to hasten into the boats. At putting off, we received three cheers, which we immediately returned; and, on doubling a point, where we last beheld our friendly entertainers, they still added to our feelings, by a farewell cheer! On our return, the stream was so exceedingly rapid, that, notwithstanding the utmost exertions of our conductors, we did not arrive at the first village, Opatchin, till the 17th in the evening, which did not exceed the rate of 20 miles a day. On the 19th, we reached Natcheekin, and crossed the plain to Karatchin on the 20th. The road was in much better order than when we passed it before, as it froze smartly in the night of the 19th. We proceeded down the Awatska river on Friday, the 21st, and passed over the shoals, at the entrance of the bay, before it was dark. During the whole of our journey, we were highly pleased with the willingness and alacrity, with which the Toions and their Kamtschadales assisted us at the different ostrogs. On seeing the Major, joy appeared

in

in every countenance; and they were much affected
upon being informed that he would shortly leave
them. A messenger had been dispatched from Bolcheretsk to Captain Clerke, acquainting him with
the nature of our reception; and that the Major
intended to accompany us on our return; apprizing
him, at the same time, of the day he might expect
us. We observed, with pleasure, as we approached
the harbour, all our boats coming towards us. The
men were all clean, and the officers as well arrayed
as their wardrobes would then permit them to be.
The Major was struck at the healthy appearance of
our sailors, and was surprized to see that many of
them had no other covering than a shirt and trowsers, though it actually snowed at that very instant.
Major Behm had expressed an inclination to visit the
ships before he landed; but, being informed that
Captain Clerke was extremely ill, he thought it
would be improper to disturb him, at so late an
hour; it being then after nine o'clock. Mr. King
therefore attended him to the serjeant's house, and
afterwards went on board to communicate to Captain Clerke what had happened at Bolcheretsk. He
was much concerned to find that, during his absence, that officer's health was considerably impaired,
instead of growing better, as we flattered ourselves
it might, from undisturbed repose in the harbour,
and a milk and vegetable diet. The next morning,
Mr. King conducted the Major to the ships; where
he was received with every possible mark of distinction, and saluted with 13 guns. He was attended
by the commander of a Russian galliot, two merchants from Bolcheretsk, a master of a sloop, and
the priest of the village of Paratounca. Having
visited the captain, and taken a view of the two
ships, he returned to dine on board the Resolution.
In the course of the afternoon, the curiosities which
we had collected were shewn him, and an assortment of each article presented to him by Captain
Clerke.

Clerke. Here we cannot suppress an instance of great generosity and gratitude in our sailors; who, being informed of the handsome present which had been made them by the Major, voluntarily requested that their grog might be withheld, and their allowance of spirits presented to the garrison of Bolcheretsk; saying they knew brandy was extremely scarce in that country, the soldiers on shore having offered four roubles a bottle for it. We could not but admire this extraordinary sacrifice, knowing how much the sailors felt, when abridged or deprived of their grog. Indeed, they never had that article withheld from them but in warm weather, that they might enjoy a greater proportion when it was most necessary; but this generous proposal would deprive them of it, even in the inclement season we had naturally to expect in our northern expedition. The officers, however, would not permit them to suffer by their generosity, and substituted, in the room of the small quantity of brandy, which the Major consented to accept, an equal quantity of rum. A dozen or two of Cape wine for Madame Behm, and some other trifling presents which we were enabled to make, were accepted with great politeness. The tobacco was distributed the next morning, among the crews of both vessels; every man that chewed or smoked tobacco being allowed three pounds, and the others who did not, only one. We have already observed that the Major had resigned the command of Kamtschatka, and was speedily to repair to Petersburgh; and he now expressed his willingness to convey any dispatches we might chuse to commit to his care. Such an opportunity was not to be neglected; and Captain Clerke requested him to take the charge of some papers relative to our voyage, to the British ambassador at the Russian court. At first, we intended to transmit only a concise journal of our proceedings; but, after mature consideration, Captain Clerke was

of

of opinion, that the whole account of our discoveries might safely be committed to the care of a man, who had given the strongest proofs of probity and virtue. Considering also, that a very hazardous part of the voyage was still to be performed, he resolved to send, by him, the whole of Captain Cook's journal; together with his own, from the death of that commander, till our arrival at Kamtschatka; and also a chart of our discoveries. Mr. Bayly and Mr. King also determined to send an account of our proceedings to the board of longitude. From these precautions, had any accident befallen us, the admiralty would have become possessed of the principal facts of our voyage. It was farther resolved, that a smaller packet should be dispatched from Okotsk, which the Major supposed would reach Petersburgh by December; and that he expected to arrive there himself in February or March. The Major was entertained alternately in the two ships, as well as we were able, the three following days. On Thursday, the 25th, he departed, and was saluted with 13 guns; the sailors, at their own request, expressing their regard for him by three cheers. Mr. King and Mr. Webber attended him, the next morning, some few miles up the Awatska river, where the Russian priest and his family were waiting to bid a last adieu to their commander. When taking our leave of the Major, it is difficult to say, whether the worthy priest and his family or ourselves were most affected. Though our acquaintance had been of short duration, his behaviour had inspired us with the highest esteem for him; and we could not part (perhaps for ever) with one, to whom we were under such infinite obligations, without indulging the most tender feelings. Exclusive of the stores, which might probably be carried to a public account, the value of the private presents he bestowed on us, must have amounted to upwards of 200 pounds. But, however extraordinary this generosity may appear, it was exceeded by his delicacy in conferring favours, and his ingenious endeavours to prevent our feeling the weight of obligations, which he knew we were unable to requite. In supporting a public character, and maintaining the honour of his sovereign, he is still more entitled to our admiration, as he was actuated by sentiments the most noble and enlarged. The service in which we were engaged, he told us, was for the general benefit of mankind; and entitled us to the offices of humanity, and the privileges of citizens, in whatever country we might be driven. That, by affording us such relief as was in his power, he was certain that he was acting agreeably to the wishes of his empress; and that he could not so entirely forget her character, or his own honour, as to barter for the performance of a duty. Among other things, he said, he made a particular point of setting a good example to the Kamtschadales, who were just emerging from a state of barbarism; that they considered the Russians as their patterns, in every respect; and that he hoped they would, in future, think it a duty incumbent on them to render strangers every assistance in their power, and believe it to be the universal practice of all polished and civilized nations. The Major having, so far as he was capable, relieved our present distresses, he was not unmindful of our future wants; and, imagining we should not be able to discover the passage we were in search of, and that we should return to Kamtschatka; he procured from Captain Clerke, the particulars of what flour and cordage he should want, promising to send them from Okotsk, to wait our arrival. He also presented the captain with a written paper, enjoining every Russian subject to assist us to the utmost of their abilities. Having thus given a narrative of the journey of our party to, and their return from Bolcheretsk, their reception there, and the departure of Major Behm,

we

we shall now recount the transactions which passed at Petropaulowska during our absence.

On Friday, the 7th of May, not long after we had quitted the bay of Awatska, a great piece of ice drove against the Resolution, and brought home the small bower anchor; in consequence of which the other anchor was weighed, and the ship was moored again. The carpenters, who were occupied in stopping the leak, were under the necessity of taking off great part of the sheathing from the bows; and many of the trunnels were found to be so loose and rotten, that they were drawn out easily with the fingers. On Tuesday the 11th, heavy gales blew from the N. E. which obliged both vessels to strike their yards and top-masts; but the weather becoming more moderate in the afternoon, and the ice having drifted away as far as the mouth of the harbour of Petropaulowska, they warped close to the shore for the greater convenience of procuring wood and water, and again moored, as before; the mouth of the bay shut in by the most southerly point of Rakowina harbour, bearing S. and the town N. half W. at the distance of half a mile. On the 12th, a party was detached to cut wood, but made little progress in that service, on account of the snow, which still covered the ground. A convenient spot, abreast of the ships, was cleared, where there was a good run of water; and a tent being pitched for the cooper, the empty casks were landed, and the sail-makers sent ashore. On Saturday, the 15th, as the beach was then clear of ice, a party was sent to haul the seine, and caught a plentiful supply of fine flat-fish for the companies of both ships. From this time, indeed, till we quitted the harbour, we were even overpowered with the great quantities of fish which came in from every quarter. The Toions, both of this town, and of Paratounca, a neighbouring village, had received orders from Major Behm to employ, in our service, all the Kamtschadales;

dales; so that it frequently happened, that we could not take into the ships the presents which were sent us. They generally consisted of herrings, trout, flat-fish, and cod. The former, which were in their highest perfection, and of a delicious flavour, were in extreme plenty in this bay. The people of the Discovery, at one time, surrounded such an amazing quantity in their seine, that they were obliged to throw out a very considerable number, left the net should be broken to pieces; and the cargo they landed was still so abundant, that, besides having a sufficient stock for immediate use, they filled as many casks as they could conveniently spare for salting; and, after sending on board the Resolution a tolerable quantity for the same purpose, they left behind several bushels upon the beach.

The ice and snow now began rapidly to disappear, and plenty of nettle-tops, celery, and wild garlick, were gathered for the use of the crews; which being boiled with portable soup and wheat, furnished them with an excellent and salutary breakfast; and with this they were every morning supplied. The birch-trees were also tapped, and the sweet juice, of which they produced great quantities, was constantly mixed with the brandy allowed to the men. On the 16th, a small bullock was killed, which the serjeant had procured for the ships' companies. Its weight was 272 pounds. It was served out to both the crews for their Sunday's dinner, and was the first fresh beef which they had tasted since the departure of our vessels from the Cape of Good Hope, in December, 1776; a period of almost two years and a half. This evening John Macintosh, the carpenter's mate expired, after having been afflicted with a dysentery ever since we had left the Sandwich Isles. He was a peaceable and industrious man, and greatly regretted by his messmates. Though he was the fourth person that we had lost by sickness during our voyage, he was

the

the first who, from his age and constitution, could be said to have had, on our setting out, an equal chance of life with the rest of his companions. Watman was supposed by us to be about 60 years old; and Roberts, and Mr. Anderson, from the decline which had manifestly commenced before our departure from England, most probably could not, under any circumstances, have lived to a later period than they did.

Captain Clerke's health continuing daily to decline, notwithstanding the salutary change of diet which Kamtschatka afforded him, the priest of Paratounca, as soon as he was informed of the weak state he was in, supplied him every day with milk, bread, fowls, and fresh butter, though his habitation was 16 miles from the harbour where our ships were stationed. On our arrival, the Russian hospital, near the town of St. Peter and St. Paul, was in a very deplorable state. All the soldiers were, in a greater or less degree, afflicted with the scurvy, many being in the last stage of that disorder. The rest of the Russian inhabitants were likewise in a similar condition; and we observed, that our friend the serjeant, by drinking too freely of the spirits he had received from us, had brought on himself, in the course of a few days, several of the most alarming symptoms of that disease. Captain Clerke, desirous of relieving them from this lamentable state, put them all under the care of our surgeons, and gave orders, that a supply of sour krout, and malt, for wort, should be furnished for their use. A surprising alteration soon took place in the figures of most of them; and their speedy recovery was chiefly attributed to the effects of the sweet wort.

On Tuesday, the 1st of June, 250 poods, or 9,000 pounds weight of rye flour, were brought on board the Resolution; and the Discovery received a proportional quantity. We were supplied with this flour

flour from the stores of Petropaulowska. The men were now put on their full allowance of bread, which, from the time of our leaving the Cape of Good Hope, they had not been indulged in. The same day, we compleated our stock of water, 65 tons having been conveyed on board. Friday, the 4th, we had fresh breezes, and heavy rains, so that we were disappointed in our design of dressing the ships, and obliged to content ourselves with firing 21 guns, in honour of His Majesty's birth-day, and celebrating it, in other respects, in the best manner we could. Port, who, on account of his skill in languages, was left with us, partook, as well as the serjeant, (in the capacity of commandant of the place) of the entertainment of the day. The worthy priest of Paratounca, having been informed that it was the anniversary of our sovereign's birth, gave likewise a sumptuous feast, at which several of our gentlemen were present, who were highly pleased with their entertainment, of which dancing formed a part. On the 6th, 20 head of cattle arrived, having been sent us, by the directions of the commander, from the Verchnei ostrog, which stands on the river Kamptschatka, at the distance of almost a hundred miles from this place. These cattle were of a moderate size; and, though the Kamtschadales had been 17 days in driving them down to the harbour, were in good condition when they arrived. The four succeeding days were employed in making preparations for putting to sea; and on Friday, the 11th, about two o'clock in the morning, we began to unmoor. Before, however, we had got up one anchor, so violent a gale sprung up from the N. E. that we thought proper to moor again, supposing, from the position of the entrance of the bay, that the current of wind would, in all probability, set up the channel. The pinnace was dispatched to examine the passage, and returned with intelligence, that the wind blew violently from

the

the S. E. with a great swell, setting into the bay; so that any attempt to get out to sea would have been attended with considerable risque. Mr. Port now took his leave of us, carrying with him the box containing the journals of our voyage, which Major Behm was to take charge of, and the packet that was to be forwarded by express. On the 12th, the gale having abated, we began unmooring again; but, after having broken the messenger, and reeved a running purchase with a six inch hauser, which likewise broke three times, we were, at last, under the necessity of heaving a strain at low water, and waiting for the flowing of the tide to raise the anchor. This measure succeeded, though not without damaging the cable. About three o'clock in the afternoon, the best bower was weighed, and we set sail; but, at eight, the tide making against us, and the wind being inconsiderable, we anchored again in ten fathoms water, off the mouth of Rakowina harbour: the ostrog being at the distance of between two and three miles, bearing N. by E. half E. the elevated rock on the western side of the passage, bearing S. and the needle rocks, on the eastern side of the passage, S. S. E. half E.

On Sunday, the 13th, at four o'clock, A. M. we got under way with the tide of ebb; and, as there was a perfect calm, the boats were dispatched ahead for the purpose of towing the ships. About 10, a south-easterly wind springing up, and the tide having turned, we were obliged to let go our anchors again, in seven fathoms; the ostrog bearing N. half E. at the distance of a mile from the land that was nearest to us; and the three needle rocks being in the direction of S. half E. In the afternoon, Captain Gore and Lieutenant King landed on the east side of the passage, where they observed, in two different places, the remains of spacious villages; and, on the side of a hill, they saw an old ruined parapet, with four or five embrasures. It had

had guns mounted on it in Beering's time, as that navigator himself informs us; and commanded the passage up the mouth of the bay. Not far from this spot, were the ruins of subterraneous caverns, which our two gentlemen conjectured to have been magazines. About six o'clock, P. M. we weighed anchor, with the ebb tide, and turned to windward; but, two hours after, a thick fog coming on, we were under the necessity of bringing to, our soundings not affording us a sufficient direction for steering betwixt several sunken rocks, situated on each side of the passage we were to make. The next morning, the fog in some degree dispersing, we weighed as soon as the tide began to ebb; and, there being little wind, the boats were sent a-head to tow; but, about 10 o'clock, both the wind and tide set in so strong from the sea, that we were once more obliged to cast anchor, in 13 fathoms water, the high rock being at the distance of six furlongs, in the direction of W. one quarter S. We continued, during the remainder of the day, in this situation, the wind blowing fresh into the mouth of the bay. Towards the evening, the weather was extremely dark and cloudy with an unsettled wind.

On the 15th, we were surprized, before day-light, with a rumbling noise, that resembled distant thunder; and when the day appeared, we found that the sides and decks of our ships were covered, near an inch thick, with a fine dust like emery. The air was at the same time loaded and obscured with this substance; and, towards the volcano mountain, which stands to the northward of the harbour, it was exceedingly thick and black, insomuch that we were unable to distinguish the body of the hill. About 12 o'clock, and during the afternoon, the loudness of the explosions increased; and they were succeeded by showers of cinders, which, in general, were of the size of peas, though many of those that were picked up from the deck were larger than a hazel a hazel nut. Several small stones, which had undergone no alteration from the action of fire, fell with the cinders. In the evening we had dreadful claps of thunder, and vivid flashes of lightning, which, with the darkness of the sky, and the sulphureous smell of the air, produced a very awful and tremendous effect. Our distance from the foot of the mountain was, at this time, about eight leagues. On the 16th, at day-break, we got up our anchors, and stood out of the bay; but the wind falling, and the tide of ebb setting across the passage on the eastern shore, we were driven very near the three needle rocks, situated on that side of the entrance, and were under the necessity of hoisting out the boats, for the purpose of towing the ships clear of them. At 12 o'clock, we were at the distance of six miles from the land; and our depth of water was 43 fathoms, over a bottom of small stones, of the same kind with those which had fallen upon our decks, after the late eruption of the volcano. The country had now a very different appearance from what it had on our first arrival. The snow, except what remained on the summits of some very lofty mountains, had vanished; and the sides of the hills, which abounded with wood in many parts, were covered with a beautiful verdure. As our commander intended to keep in sight of the coast of Kamtschatka, as much as the weather would allow, in order to ascertain its position, we continued to steer towards the N. N. E. with variable light winds, till Friday, the 18th. The volcano was still observed to throw up immense volumes of smoke; and we did not strike ground with 150 fathoms of line, at the distance of 12 miles from the shore. This day the wind blew fresh from the S. and the weather became so thick and hazy, that it was imprudent to make any further attempts at present to keep in sight of the land. However, that we might be ready, whenever the fog should clear up, to resume our survey, we ran on in the direction of the coast, (as represented in the Russian charts) and fired signal guns for the Discovery to proceed on the same course. At 11 o'clock, just before we lost sight of land, Cheepoonskoi Nofs, so denominated by the Russians, was at the distance of seven or eight leagues, bearing N. N. E. On the 20th, at three o'clock in the morning, the weather becoming clearer, we stood in towards the land; and, in the space of an hour afterwards, saw it a-head, extending from N. W. to N. N. E. at the distance of about five leagues. The northern part we conjectured to be Kronotskoi Nofs; its position in the Russian charts, nearly agreeing with our reckoning in respect to its latitude, which was 54 deg. 42 min. N. though, in point of longitude, we differed considerably from them; for they place it 1 deg. 48 min. E. of Awatska; whereas our computation makes it 3 deg. 34 min. E. of that place, or 162 deg. 17 min. E. of Greenwich. The land about this cape is very elevated, and the inland mountains were, at this time, covered with snow. There is no appearance of inlets or bays in the coast; and the shore breaks off in steep cliffs. We had not long been gratified with this view of the land, when the wind freshened from the S. W. bringing on a thick fog, which obliged us to stand off in the direction of N. E. by E. The fog dispersing about noon, we again steered for the land, expecting to fall in with Kamtschatskoi Nofs, and gained a sight of it at day-break on the 21st. The S. W. wind being soon after succeeded by a light breeze that blew off the land, we were prevented from approaching the coast sufficiently near to determine its direction, or describe its aspect. At noon, our long. was 163 deg. 50 min. and our lat. 55 deg. 52 min. the extremes of the land bore N. W. by W. three quarters W. and N. by W. three quarters W. and the nearest part was at the distance of about 24 miles.

miles. At nine in the evening, when we had approached about 6 miles nearer the coast, it appeared to form a projecting peninsula, and to extend 11 or 12 leagues in the direction nearly of N. and S. It is level, and of a moderate elevation; the southern extreme terminates in a low sloping point; that to the northward forms a steep bluff head; and between them, 10 or 12 miles to the S. of the northern cape, there is a considerable break in the land. On both sides of this break, the land is low. A remarkable hill, resembling a saddle, rises beyond the opening; and a chain of lofty mountains, capped with snow, extends along the back of the whole peninsula. As the coast runs in an even direction, we were uncertain with respect to the position of Kamtschatskoi Nofs, which, according to Mr. Muller, forms a projecting point towards the middle of the peninsula; but we afterwards found, that, in a late Russian map, that appellation is given to the southern cape. The latitude of this, from several accurate observations, was 56 deg. 3 min. and its longitude, 163 deg. 20 min. To the S. of this peninsula, the great river Kamtschatka runs into the sea. The season being too far advanced for us to make an accurate survey of the coast of Kamtscatka, it was the design of Captain Clerke, on our course to Beering's Straights, to ascertain chiefly the respective situations of the projecting points of the coast. We therefore steered across a spacious bay, laid down between Kamtschatskoi Nofs and Olutorskoi Nofs, with a view of making the latter; which is represented by the Russian geographers, as terminating the peninsula of Kamtschatka, and as being the southern limit of the country of the Koriacs.

On Tuesday, the 22d, we passed a dead whale, which emitted a most horrible smell, perceiveable at the distance of three or four miles. It was covered with a very considerable number of gulls, petrels,

petrels, and other oceanic birds, which were regaling themselves upon it. On the 24th, the wind, which had shifted about during the three preceding days, settled at S. W. bringing on clear weather, with which we proceeded towards the N. E. by N. across the bay, having no land in sight. In the course of this day we observed a great number of gulls, and were disgusted with the indelicate manner of feeding of the arctic gull, which has procured it the appellation of the parasite. This bird, which is rather larger than the common gull, pursues the latter species whenever it meets them; the gull, after flying about for some time, with loud screams, and manifest indications of extreme terror, drops its excrement, which its pursuer instantly darts at, and catches in his beak before it falls into the sea.

On Friday, the 25th, at one o'clock, P. M. when in the latitude of 59 deg. 12 min. and in the longitude of 168 deg. 35 min. a very thick fog came on, about the time we expected to obtain a view of Olutorskoi Noss, which (if Muller's position of it, in the latitude of 59 deg. 30 min. and in the longitude of 167 deg. 36 min. is right) could then have been only 12 leagues from us; at which distance, we might easily have discerned land of a moderate height. Our depth of water, at present, was so great, that we had no ground with 160 fathoms of line. The fog still continuing, prevented us from making a nearer approach to the land, and we steered E. by N. at five o'clock, which is a little more easterly than the Russian charts represent the trending of the coast from Olutorskoi Noss. The next day, a fresh gale blew from the S. W. which lasted till noon on the 27th, when the weather clearing up, we steered to the N. with an intention of making the land. Our latitude, at this time, was 59 deg. 49 min. and our longitude 175 deg. 43 min. Though we saw some shags in the morning,

ing, which are imagined never to fly far from the land, yet there was no appearance of it during the whole day. However, the next morning, about six o'clock, we had sight of it towards the N. W. The coast appeared in hills of a moderate elevation; but inland, others were observed considerably higher. The snow lying in patches, and no wood being perceived, the land had a very barren aspect. At nine o'clock, we were ten or eleven miles from the shore, the southern extreme bearing W. by S. about six leagues distant, beyond which the coast seemed to incline to the W. This point being in the longitude of 174 deg. 48 min. and in the latitude of 61 deg. 48 min. is situated according to the Russian charts, near the mouth of the river Opuka. The northern extremity, at the same time, bore N. by W. between which, and a hill bearing N. W. by W. quarter W. the coast appeared to bend towards the W. and form a deep bay. At the distance of about eight miles from the land we observed a strong rippling; and being under apprehensions of meeting with foul ground, we made sail to the N. E. along the coast. On heaving the lead, we found the depth of water to be 24 fathoms, over a bottom of gravel. We therefore concluded, that the appearance above-mentioned, was occasioned by a tide, then running to the southward. At noon, the extremes of the land bearing W. S. W. and N. N. E. we were abreast of the low land, which, we now observed, joined the two points, where we had before expected to discover a deep bay. The coast bends a little towards the W. and has a small inlet, which is, perhaps, the mouth of some inconsiderable river. Our longitude was now 175 deg. 43 min. and our latitude 61 deg. 56 min. During the afternoon, we continued our course along the coast, which exhibited an appearance of sterility, and the hills rose to a considerable elevation inland, but the clouds on their tops prevented us from determining

their

their height. About eight o'clock in the evening, some of our people thought they saw land to the E. by N. upon which we stood to the southward of E. but it proved to be nothing more than a fog bank. At midnight, the extreme point bearing N. E. quarter E. we conjectured that it was St. Thadeus's Nofs; to the S. of which the land inclines towards the W. forming a deep bight, wherein the river Katirka, according to the charts published by the Ruffians, is situated. On Tuesday the 29th, the weather was unsettled, with the wind at the N. E. point. On the 30th, at noon, we observed in longitude 180 deg. and latitude 61 deg. 48 min. At this time, St. Thadeus's Nofs bore N. N. W. at the distance of 23 leagues; and beyond it we perceived the coast extending almost directly N. The easternmost point of the Nofs is in the latitude of 62 deg. 50 min. and in the longitude of 179 deg. The land about it, from its being discerned at so great a distance, may justly be supposed to be of a considerable height. During this and the preceding day, we saw numbers of sea-horses, whales, and seals; also albatrosses, gulls, sea-parrots, guillemots, and other birds.

CHAP. XVIII.

ON Thursday, the 1st of July 1779, at noon, Mr. Bligh, master of the Resolution, found by experiment, that the ship made a course to the N. E. at the rate of about half a mile in an hour: this he attributed to the effect of a southerly swell, rather than to that of any current. The wind towards the evening, freshening from the S. E. we steered to the N. E. by E. for the point that Beering calls Tschukotskoi Nofs, which we had observed on the 4th of September the preceding year, at the

same

same time that we perceived, towards the S. E. the Isle of St. Lawrence. This cape, and St. Thadeus's Nofs, form the north-eastern and south-western extremes of the extensive Gulph of Anadir, into the bottom of which the river of that name discharges itself, separating, as it passes, the country of the Tschutski from that of the Koriacs. On the 3d, at noon, we observed in latitude 63 deg. 33 min. longitude 186 deg. 45 min. Between twelve and one, we descried the Tschukotskoi Nofs, bearing N. half W. at the distance of 13 or 14 leagues. At five in the afternoon, we saw the island of St. Lawrence, in the direction of E. three-quarters N. and also another island, which we imagined was between St. Lawrence and Anderson's Island, about 18 miles E. S. E. of the former. As we had no certain knowledge of this island, Captain Clerke was inclined to have a nearer view of it, and immediately hauled the wind towards it: but it unfortunately happened, that we were unable to weather the Isle of St. Lawrence, and were therefore obliged to bear up again, and pass them all to the leeward. The latitude of the Island of St. Lawrence, according to the most accurate observations, is 63 deg. 47 min. and its longitude is 188 deg. 15 min. This island, if its boundaries were at present within our view, is about three leagues in circumference. The northern part of it may be discerned at the distance of ten or a dozen leagues. As it has some low land to the S. E. the extent of which we could not perceive, some of us supposed, that it might perhaps be joined to the land to the eastward of it: we were, however, prevented by the haziness of the weather, from ascertaining this circumstance. These islands, as well as the land adjoining to the Tschukotskoi Nofs, were covered with snow, and presented a most dismal aspect. About midnight, the Isle of St. Lawrence was five or six miles distant, bearing S. S. E. and our soundings were
18 fathoms.

18 fathoms. We were accompanied with sea fowl of various sorts, and observed some guillemots and small crested hawks. The weather continuing to thicken, we lost sight of land till Monday the 5th, when we had a view of it both to the N. E. and N. W. Our longitude, at this time, was 189 deg. 14 min. and our latitude 65 deg. 24 min. As the islands of St. Diomede, which are situated in Beering's Strait, between the two continents of Asia and America, were determined by us the preceding year to be in the latitude of 65 deg. 48 min. we were at a loss how to reconcile the land towards the N. E. with the position of those islands. We therefore stood for the land till three o'clock in the afternoon, when we were within the distance of four miles from it, and discovering it to be two islands, were pretty well convinced of their being the same; but the haziness of the weather still continuing, we, in order to be certain, with respect to our situation, stood over to the Asiatic coast, till about seven o'clock in the evening; at which time we had approached within two or three leagues of the eastern cape of that continent. The cape is an elevated round head of land, and extends about five miles from N. to S. It forms a peninsula, which is connected with the continent by a narrow isthmus of low land. It has a bold shore; and three lofty, detached, spiral rocks, are seen off its N. part. It was at present covered with snow, and the beach encompassed with ice. We were now convinced of our having been under the influence of a strong current setting to the northward, which had occasioned an error of twenty miles in our computation of the latitude at noon. At the time of our passing this strait the last year, we had experienced a similar effect. Having now ascertained our position, we steered N. by E. At ten o'clock in the evening, the weather clearing up, we saw, at the same instant, the remarkable peaked hill near

Cape

Cape Prince of Wales, on the North American coast, and the East Cape of Asia, with the two islands of St. Diomede between them. In the course of this day, we saw several large white gulls, and great numbers of very small birds of the hawk kind. The beak of the latter was compressed, and large in proportion to the body of the bird: the colour was dark brown, or rather black, the breast whitish, and towards the abdomen a reddish brown hue was visible. On the 6th, at twelve o'clock, our latitude was 67 deg. and our longitude 191 deg. 6 min. Having already passed many large masses of ice, and observed that it adhered, in several places, to the shore of the Asiatic continent, we were not greatly surprised when we fell in, about three o'clock, with an extensive body of it, stretching towards the W. This appearance considerably discouraged our hopes of proceeding much farther to the N. this year, than we had done the preceding. There being little wind in the afternoon, the boats were hoisted out in pursuit of the sea-horses, great numbers of which were seen on the detached pieces of ice; but they returned without success; these animals being extremely shy, and, before our people could come within gun-shot of them, always retreated into the water. At seven o'clock, P. M. having hoisted in the boats, we stood on to the north-eastward, with a fresh southerly breeze, intending to explore the American continent, between the latitudes of 68 deg. and 69 deg. which, on account of the foggy weather, we had not an opportunity of examining the last year. In this attempt we were partly disappointed again: for, on the 7th, about six o'clock in the morning, we were stopped by a large body of ice, stretching from N. W. to S. E. but, not long afterwards, the horizon becoming clear, we had a view of the American coast, at the distance of about ten leagues, extending from N. E. by E. to E. and lying between 68 deg.

deg. and 68 deg. 20 min. of northern latitude. The ice not being high, we were enabled by the clearness of the weather to see over a great extent of it. The whole exhibited a compact solid surface, not in the least thawed; and seemed also to adhere to the land. Soon after, the weather becoming hazy, we lost sight of the land; and it being impossible to approach nearer to it, we steered to the N. N. W. keeping the ice close on board; and having, by noon, got round its western extremity, we found that it trended nearly N. Our longitude, at this time, was 192 deg. 34 min. and our latitude 68 deg. 22 min. We proceeded along the edge of the ice, to the N. N. E. during the remainder of the day, passing through many loose pieces which had been separated from the main body, and against which our vessels were driven with great violence, notwithstanding our utmost caution. About eight in the evening, we passed some drift-wood: at midnight the wind veered to the N. W. and there were continued showers of snow and sleet. The thermometer had now fallen from 38 deg. to 31 deg. On Thursday, the 8th, at five o'clock, the wind shifting more to the northward, we could continue no longer on the same tack, by reason of the ice, but were under the necessity of standing towards the W. Our depth of water, at this time, was 19 fathoms; from which, upon comparing it with our remarks on the soundings in the preceding year, we inferred, that our present distance from the coast of America did not exceed six or seven leagues; but our view was circumscribed within a much narrower compass, by a heavy fall of snow. Our latitude, at noon, was 69 deg. 21 min. and our longitude 192 deg. 42 min. At two o'clock, P. M. the weather became clearer, and we found ourselves close to an expanse of ice, which, from the mast-head, was discovered to consist of very large compact bodies; united towards the exterior
edge,

edge, but, in the interior parts, some pieces were observed floating in vacant spaces of the water: it extended from W. S. W. to N. E. by N. We bore away towards the S. along the edge of it, endeavouring to get into clearer water; for the strong northerly winds had drifted down such numbers of loose pieces, that we had been encompassed with them for some time, and were unable to prevent the ships from striking against several of them. On the 9th, a fresh gale blew from the N. N. W. accompanied with violent showers of snow and sleet. We steered W. S. W. and kept as near the main body of ice as we could; but had the misfortune to damage the cut-water against the drift pieces, and rub off some of the sheathing from the bows. The shocks, indeed, which our ships received, were frequently very severe, and were attended with considerable hazard. Our latitude, at noon, was 69 deg. 12 min. and our longitude 188 deg. 5 min.

We had now sailed almost 40 leagues to the W. along the edge of the ice, without perceiving any opening, or a clear sea beyond it towards the N. no prospect therefore remained of making further progress to the northward at present. For this reason Captain Clerke determined to bear away to S. by E. the only quarter which was clear, and to wait till the season was somewhat more advanced, before he made any further attempts to penetrate through the ice. He proposed to employ the intermediate time in surveying the bay of St. Lawrence, and the coast situate to the S. of it; as it would be a great satisfaction to have a harbour so near, in case of future damage from the quantity of ice in these parts. We were also desirous of paying another visit to the Tschutski; and more particularly since the accounts we had heard of them from Major Behm. In consequence of this determination, we made sail to the southward, till the 10th at noon, when we passed considerable quantities of drift-ice, and a perfect calm enſued. The latitude, at this time, was 68 deg. 1 min. and the longitude 188 deg. 30 min. This morning we ſaw ſeveral whales; and in the afternoon, there being great numbers of ſea-horſes on the pieces of ice that ſurrounded us, we hoiſted out the boats, and diſpatched them in purſuit of thoſe animals. Our people had more ſucceſs on this occaſion, than they had on the 6th; for they returned with three large ones, and a young one, beſides having killed or wounded ſome others. They were witneſſes of ſeveral ſtriking inſtances of parental affection in theſe animals. All of them, on the approach of the boats towards the ice, took their young ones under their fins, and attempted to eſcape with them into the ſea. Some, whoſe cubs were killed or wounded, and left floating upon the ſurface of the water, roſe again, and carried them down, ſometimes juſt as our men were on the point of taking them into the boat; and could be traced bearing them to a conſiderable diſtance through the water, which was ſtained with their blood. They were afterwards obſerved bringing them, at intervals, above the ſurface, as if for air, and again plunging under it, with a horrid bellowing. The female, in particular, whoſe young one had been killed, and taken into the boat, became ſo furious, that ſhe even ſtruck her two tuſks through the bottom of the cutter. About eight o'clock in the evening, an eaſterly breeze ſprung up, with which we continued to ſteer to the ſouthward; and, at midnight, fell in with many extenſive bodies of ice. We attempted to puſh through them under an eaſy ſail, that the ſhips might ſuſtain no damage; and when we had proceeded a little further towards the S. nothing was viſible but a very large and compact maſs of ice, extending to the N. E. S. W. and S. E. as far as the eye could reach. This formidable obſtacle prevented our viſiting the Tſchutſki; for no ſpace remained open,

except

except back again to the northward. We therefore tacked, at three o'clock in the morning of the 11th, and stood to that quarter. The lat. at noon, was 67 deg. 49 min. and the long. 188 deg. 47 min. On Monday, the 12th, we had light winds and hazy weather. On examining the current, we found it set towards the N. W. at the rate of half a mile an hour. We continued our northerly course, with a breeze from the S. and fair weather, till 10 o'clock in the morning of the 13th, when we again found ourselves close in with a solid mass of ice, to which we could perceive no limits from the mast-head. This was an effectual discouragement to all our hopes of penetrating further; which had been greatly raised, by our having now advanced almost 10 leagues, through a space, which, on the 9th, had been found to be occupied by impenetrable ice. Our situation, at this time, was nearly in the middle of the channel, betwixt the two continents; our lat. was 69 deg. 37 min. and the main body of the ice extended from W. S. W. to E. N. E.

In that part of the sea where we now were, there was no probability of getting further to the north, Captain Clerke therefore determined to make a final attempt on the coast of America, for Baffin's Bay, since we had found it practicable to advance the furthest on this side, in the preceding year. We accordingly, during the remainder of the day, worked to the windward, with a fresh breeze from the east. We observed several fulmars, and arctic gulls, and passed two trees, both of which seemed to have lain a long time in the water. The larger one was, in length, ten or eleven feet, and in circumference, about three, without either the bark or branches. We continued our course to the eastward on the 14th, with thick foggy weather. The next day, the wind blowing fresh from the west, and having, in some measure, dispersed the fog, we immediately steered to the north, in order to have a nearer view of the ice; and we were soon close in with it. It extended from N. N. W. to N. E. and was solid and compact: the exterior parts were ragged, and of various heights; the inner surface was even; and, as we supposed, from 8 to 10 feet above the level of the sea. The weather becoming moderate during the rest of the day, we shaped our course according to the trending of the ice, which, in several places, formed deep bays. On Friday, the 16th, the wind freshened, in the morning, and was accompanied with frequent and thick showers of snow. At eight o'clock in the forenoon, we had a strong gale from the W. S. W. which brought us under double-reefed top-sails; when, the weather in some degree clearing up, we found ourselves, as it were, embayed; the ice having suddenly taken a turn to the south-eastward, and encompassing us in one compact body, on all sides but the south. In consequence of this, we hauled our wind to the southward, being, at that time, in 26 fathoms water, and in the lat. of 70 deg. 8 min. N. and, as we imagined, at the distance of about 25 leagues from the American coast. At four in the afternoon, the gale increasing, we got the top-gallant-yards down upon the deck, furled the mizen top-sail, and close-reefed the fore and main-top-sails. About eight o'clock, finding that our soundings had decreased to 22 fathoms, which we considered as an indication of our near approach to the coast of America, we tacked and steered to the northward. In the night we had boisterous weather, attended with snow: but the next morning it was clear and moderate; and, at eight o'clock, we got the top-gallant-yards across, and bore away, with the wind still at W. S. W. Our lat. at noon, was 69 deg. 55 min. and our long. 194 deg. 30 min. The wind slackened in the evening, and, about midnight, we had a calm. A light breeze arising from the E. N. E. at five in the morning of the

18th,

18th, we continued our progress towards the N. with a view of regaining the ice as soon as possible. We saw numbers of sea-parrots, and small ice-birds, and also many whales; and passed several logs of drift-wood. The lat. at 12 o'clock, was 70 deg. 26 min. and the long. 194 deg. 54 min. Our soundings, at the same time, were 23 fathoms; and the ice extended from N. to E. N. E. being about one league distant. At one o'clock in the afternoon, observing that we were close in with a firm united mass of ice, stretching from E. to W. N. W. we tacked, and, the wind veering to the westward, stood to the E. along the edge of it, till 11 in the evening. A very thick fog then coming on, and the depth of water decreasing to 19 fathoms, we hauled our wind to the southward. About nine o'clock in the evening, a white bear swam close by the Discovery; it afterwards went towards the ice, on which were likewise two others. The weather clearing up, at one in the morning of Monday, the 19th, we bore away to the N. E. till two o'clock, when we were again so completely embayed by the ice, that no opening remained, except to the southward; to which quarter we therefore directed our course, and returned through a very smooth water, with favourable weather, by the same way we had come in. We were unable to penetrate further towards the N. than at this time, when our lat. was 70 deg. 33 min. which was about five leagues short of the point to which we had advanced the preceding summer. We stood to the S. S. W. with light winds from the N. W. near the edge of the main body of ice, which was situated on our left-hand, extending between us and the American coast. At noon, our lat. was 70 deg. 11 min. and our long. 196 deg. 15 min. and our soundings were 16 fathoms. We supposed, from this circumstance, that the Icy Cape was at the distance of only seven or eight leagues from us: but,

though

though the weather was in general pretty clear, there was, at the same time, a haziness in the horizon; so that we could not expect to have an opportunity of seeing the cape. During the afternoon, two white bears appearing in the water, some of our people immediately pursued them in the jolly-boat, and were so fortunate as to kill them both. The larger one, which was, in all probability, the dam of the younger, being shot first, the other would not leave it, though it might have escaped with ease on the ice, while the men were re-loading their musquets; but continued swimming about, till after having been several times fired upon, it was shot dead. The length of the larger one, from the snout to the end of the tail, was seven feet two inches; its circumference, near the fore legs, was four feet ten inches; the height of the shoulder was four feet three inches; and the breadth of the fore-paw was ten inches. The weight of its fore quarters was 436 pounds. The fore quarters of the smallest weighed 256 pounds. These animals furnished us with some good meals of fresh meat. Their flesh, indeed, had a strong fishy taste, but was infinitely superior to that of the sea-horse; which, however, our people were again persuaded, with no great difficulty, to prefer to their salted provisions.

On Tuesday, the 20th, at six o'clock, A. M. a thick fog arising, we lost sight of the ice for the space of two hours; but, when the weather became clearer, we again had a view of the main body to the S. S. E. and immediately hauled our wind, which was easterly, towards it, expecting to make the American coast to the S. E. which we effected between 10 and 11 o'clock. The lat. at noon, was 69 deg. 33 min. and the long. 194 deg. 53 min. Our depth of water, at the same time, was 19 fathoms. The land was at the distance of eight or ten leagues, extending from S. by E. to S. S. W.
half

half W. being the same we had seen the preceding year; but it was, at present, much more covered with snow than at that time; and the ice seemed to adhere to the shore. We continued to sail in the afternoon, through a sea of loose ice, and to steer towards the land, as near as the wind, which blew from E. S. E. would permit. A thick fog came on at eight o'clock in the evening, and the wind abated. Observing a rippling in the water, we tried the current, and found it set to the E. N. E. at the rate of a mile an hour: we therefore resolved to steer before the wind, during the night, in order to stem it, and oppose the large pieces of loose ice, which were setting us on towards the coast. Our soundings, at midnight, were twenty fathoms. The next morning, at eight o'clock, the wind freshening, and the fog dispersing, we again had sight of the coast of America to the south-eastward, at the distance of nine or ten leagues, and hauled in for it; but the ice in a short time effectually stopped our further progress on that side, and we were obliged to bear away towards the W. along the edge of it. Our lat. at 12, was 69 deg. 34 min. our long. was 193 deg. and our soundings were 24 fathoms. A connected solid field of ice, thus baffling all our efforts to make a nearer approach to the land, and (as we had some reason to imagine) adhering to it, we relinquished all hopes of a N. E. passage to Great-Britain. Our commander now finding it impossible to advance further to the northward on the American coast, and deeming it equally improbable, that such a prodigious quantity of ice should be dissolved by the few remaining weeks that would terminate the summer, considered it as the best step that could be taken, to trace the sea over to the coast of Asia, and endeavour to find some opening that would admit him further N. or see what more could be done upon that coast, where he hoped to meet with better success. In consequence of this determination, we steered W. N. W. during the afternoon of the 21st of July, through a great quantity of loose ice. About ten o'clock in the evening, discovering the main body of ice through the fog, right a-head, and very near us, and being unwilling to stand to the southward, so long as we could possibly avoid it; we hauled our wind, which was easterly, and made sail to the N. but in the space of an hour afterwards, finding that the weather became clearer, and that we were surrounded by a compact field of ice on all sides, except to the S. S. W. we tacked, and steered in that direction, for the purpose of getting clear of it. On the 22d, at noon, our lat. was 69 deg. 30 min. and our long. 187 deg. 30 min. In the afternoon, we again came up with the ice, which extending to the N. W. and S. W. obliged us to proceed to the southward, in order to weather it. It may not here be improper to remark, that, since the 8th of July, we had twice traversed this sea, in lines almost parallel with the run we had just now made; that we were unable in the first of those traverses, to penetrate so far N. by eight or ten leagues, as in the second; and that in the last we had again met with a connected mass of ice, generally about five leagues to the southward of its position in the preceding run. This makes it evident, that the large compact fields of ice, observed by us, were moveable, or diminishing; but, at the same time, it does not authorise any expectation of advancing much farther, even in the most favourable seasons. About seven o'clock in the evening, the weather being hazy, and no ice visible, we made sail to the westward; but, between eight and nine, the haze dispersing, we found ourselves in the midst of loose ice, and very near the main body; we therefore stood upon a wind, which was still easterly, and continued to beat to windward during the night, hoping to weather the loose pieces, which the wind drove down

View of an ICE BERG, in the Island of SPITSBERGEN.

down upon us in such quantities, that we were in great danger of being blocked up by them. On Friday, the 23d, the clear water, in which we steered to and fro, did not exceed a mile and a half, and was lessening every moment. At length, after exerting our most strenuous endeavours to clear the loose ice, we were under the necessity of forcing a passage to the S. which we accomplished between seven and eight, though not without subjecting the ship to some very severe shocks. The Discovery was not so successful; for, about 11 o'clock, when she had almost got clear out, she became so entangled by several large pieces, that her progress was stopped, and she immediately dropped to leeward, and fell, broadside foremost, on the edge of a considerable body of ice; and there being an open sea to windward, the surf occasioned her to strike with violence upon it. This mass, at length, either so far broke, or moved, as to give the crew an opportunity of making another effort to escape; but, it unfortunately happened, that, before the ship gathered way enough to be under command, she fell to leeward a second time, on another fragment, and the swell rendering it unsafe to lie to windward, and finding no prospect of getting clear, they pushed into a small opening, furled their sails, and made the vessel fast with ice-hooks. We beheld them in this dangerous situation at noon, at the distance of about three miles from us, in a N. W. direction; a fresh gale from the S. E. driving more ice towards the N. W. and augmenting the body that lay between us. Our lat. at this time, was 69 deg. 8 min. our long. 187 deg. and our soundings were 28 fathoms. To add to the apprehensions which began to force themselves on our minds, between four and five in the afternoon, the weather becoming thick and hazy, we lost sight of the Discovery. However, that we might be in a situation to afford her every possible assistance, we stood on

close

close by the edge of the ice. About six o'clock the wind shifting to the north, gave us some hopes, that the ice might drift away, and release her from her danger; and in that case, as it was uncertain in what condition she might come out, we continued, every half hour to fire a gun, with a view of preventing a separation. Our fears for her safety did not cease till nine, when we heard her guns fired in answer to ours; and not long afterwards being hailed by her, we were informed, that upon the change of wind, the ice began to separate, and that her people, setting all the sails, forced a passage through it.

On Saturday, the 24th, we steered to the S. E. till 11 o'clock, A. M. when our course was again obstructed by a large body of loose ice, to which we could discover no bounds. At noon we found ourselves in lat. 68 deg. 53 min. long. 188 deg. About four in the afternoon, we had a calm, and the boats were hoisted out in pursuit of the seahorses, which appeared in prodigious numbers. Ten of them were killed by our people, as many as could be made use of by us for eating, or for converting into lamp-oil. We held on our course with a south-westerly wind, along the edge of the ice, till four in the morning of the 25th, when perceiving a clear sea beyond it, to the south-eastward, we steered to that point. During the remaining part of the day, we continued to run towards the S. E. with no ice in sight. At noon we observed in lat. 68 deg. 38 min. long. 189 deg. 9 min. and our soundings were 30 fathoms. For the remainder of the day, and till noon of the 27th, we stood backwards and forwards, to clear ourselves of different pieces of ice. At two in the afternoon, we had sight of the continent to the S. by E. and, at four, having run, since noon, to the S. W. we were encompassed by loose masses of ice, with the main body in view, stretching in the direction of

N. by

N. by W. and S. by E. as far as the eye could reach, beyond which we descried the Asiatic coast, bearing S. and S. by E. It being now necessary to come to some determination respecting the course we were next to steer, Captain Clerke dispatched a boat, with the carpenters, on board the Discovery, to make enquiries into the particulars of the damages she had lately received. In the evening they returned, with the report of Captain Gore, and of the carpenters of both vessels, that the damages sustained were such as would require three weeks to repair; and that it would be requisite, for that purpose, to make the best of their way to some port. Thus finding our farther progress to the N. as well as our nearer approach to either continent, obstructed by immense bodies of ice, we considered it as not only injurious to the service, by endangering the safety of the ships, but likewise fruitless, with respect to the design of our voyage, to make any farther attempts for the discovery of a passage. This, therefore, added to Captain Gore's representations, determined Captain Clerke to lose no more time after what he concluded to be an unattainable object, but to proceed to the bay of Awatska, to repair our damages there, and before the winter should set in, to take a survey of the coast of Japan. It is impossible to describe the joy that sparkled in the countenance of every individual, when the captain's resolution was made known. All were completely weary of a navigation full of danger, and in which the greatest perseverence had not been rewarded with the smallest prospect of success. We therefore turned our thoughts towards home, after an absence of three years, with a delight and satisfaction, as fully enjoyed, as if we had been already in sight of the Land's-end. On Wednesday, the 28th, we worked to windward, with a fresh breeze from the S. E. being still in sight of the coast of Asia. At four in the morning, Cape

Serdze

Serdze Kamen bore S. S. W. distant seven leagues. On the 29th, the wind continuing unfavourable, we made but slow progress to the southward. We had no land in view till seven in the evening of the 30th, when the fog dispersing, we saw Cape Prince of Wales bearing S. by E. distant six leagues; and the island of St. Diomede S. W. by W. We now stood to the W. and at eight made the East Cape, which at midnight, was four leagues distant, bearing W. by N. On Saturday, the 31st, at four o'clock, A. M. the East Cape bore N. N. E. and the N. E. part of the Bay of St. Lawrence, W. by S. distant 12 miles. At noon, we observed in latitude 65 deg. 6 min. longitude 189 deg.

We had now passed Beering's Straits, and taken a final leave of the N. E. coast of Asia; and here we shall state our reasons for adopting two general conclusions relative to its extent, in opposition to the sentiments of Mr. Muller. The first is, that the promontory, called East Cape, is actually the most easterly point of that quarter of the globe; or in other words, that no part of that continent extends in longitude beyond 190 deg. 22 min. E. The second is, that the latitude of the north-easternmost extreme is somewhat to the southward of 70 deg. N. With regard to the former, if such land really exists, it must certainly be to the N. of the 69th deg. of latitude, where the discoveries made in our present voyage terminate.

We propose therefore in the first place to investigate the probable direction of the coast beyond this point. Now, Russia, being the only nation, that has hitherto navigated this part of the ocean, all our information respecting the position of the coast to the northward of Cape North, is derived from the journals and charts of the persons who have been engaged, at different times, in determining the bounds of that extensive empire, and these are, in general, so confined, contradictory, and imperfect,
that

that we cannot easily form a distinct idea of their pretended, much less collect the particulars of their real discoveries. On this account, the extent and figure of the peninsula, inhabited by the Tschutski still remains a point, on which the Russian geographers are divided greatly in their opinions. Mr. Muller, in the map which he published in 1754, supposes that this country extends towards the N. E. as far as the latitude of 75 deg. and to the longitude of 190 deg. E. of Greenwich; and that it ends in a round cape, which he denominates Tschukotskoi Noss. To the S. of this cape, the coast, as he imagines, forms a bay to the W. bounded in the latitude of 67 deg. 18 min. by Serdze Kamen, the most northerly point observed by Beering in his expedition in 1728. The map published in 1776 by the academy of St. Petersburg, gives a new form to the whole peninsula, placing its north-easternmost extreme in the latitude of 73 deg. longitude 178 deg. 30 min. and the most easterly point in latitude 65 deg. 30 min. longitude 189 deg. 30 min. All the other maps we have seen, both manuscript and printed, vary between these two, apparently more according to the fancy and conjectures of the compiler, than on any grounds of more accurate intelligence. The only particular in which there is a general coincidence, with very little variation, is the position of the East Cape, in the latitude of 66 deg. The form of the coast both to the N. and S. of the East Cape, in the map of the academy, is extremely erroneous, and may be entirely disregarded. In Mr. Muller's map, the coast towards the N. has some degree of resemblance to our survey, as far as the latter extends, except that he does not make it trend sufficiently to the W. but makes it recede only about 5 deg. of longitude, between the latitude of 66 and 69 deg. whereas it actually recedes near ten. Between the latitude of 69 and 74 deg. the coast, according to him, bends round to the N. and N. E. and

and forms a large promontory. On what authority he grounds this reprefentation of the coaſt, comes next under our confideration.

Mr. Coxe, whofe accurate refearches into this fubject, give great weight to his fentiments, is of opinion, that the extremity of the Nofs in queſtion, was never paſſed except by Deſhneff and his party, who failed in the year 1648, from the river Kovyma, and are imagined to have got round it into the Anadyr. As the narrative of this expedition, the fubſtance of which has been given by Mr. Coxe, in his account of Ruſſian diſcoveries, comprehends no geographical delineation of the coaſt along which they failed, our conjectures reſpecting its pofition muſt be derived from incidental circumſtances; and from theſe it evidently appears, that the Tſchukotſkoi Nofs of Deſhneff, is, in reality, the promontory named by Captain Cook, the Eaſt Cape. Speaking of the Nofs, he fays, that a perfon may fail from the iſthmus to the Anadyr, with a favourable wind, in three days and three nights. This perfectly agrees with the fituation of the Eaſt Cape, which is about 120 leagues from the mouth of the river Anadyr; and there being no other iſthmus to the N. between that and the latitude of 69 deg. it feems evident, that, by this defcription, he certainly means either the cape in queſtion, or fome other fituated to the S. of it. He fays, in another place, that, oppofite to the iſthmus, there are two iſlands in the fea, upon which he obſerved fome of the Tfchutfki nation, in whofe lips pieces of the teeth of the fea-horfe were fixed. This defcription coincides exactly with the two iſlands that lie to the S. E. of the Eaſt Cape. We obferved, indeed, no inhabitants upon them; but it is by no means improbable, that a party of Americans from the oppofite continent, whom this defcription fuits, might have been accidentally there at that time, and he might eafily miſtake them for a tribe of the Tfchutfki.

Theſe

These two circumstances seem to us to be conclusive on the point of the Tschukotskoi Noss, though there are others of a more dubious nature from the same authority, and which now remain to be investigated. Deshneff, in another account, says, that in going from the Kovyma to the Anadyr, a great promontory which projects very far into the sea, must be doubled; and that this cape extends between N. and N. E. It was, perhaps, from these expressions, that Muller was induced to represent the country of the Tschutski, in the form we find in his map; but, if he had been acquainted with the position of the East Cape, as determined by Captain Cook, and the striking agreement between that and the promontory or isthmus, (for it must be remarked, that Deshneff still appears to be speaking of the same thing) in the circumstances above-mentioned, we are confident that he would not have thought those expressions of sufficient weight to authorise his extending the north-eastern extreme of Asia, either so far to the N. or E. For these words of Deshneff may be reconciled with the opinion we have adopted, if we suppose that navigator to have taken these bearings from the small bight lying to the W. of the cape. The next authority, on which Muller has proceeded, seems to have been the deposition of the Cossac Popoff, taken at the Anadyrskoi ostrog, in 1711. This Cossac was sent by land, in company with several others, to demand tribute from the independent Tschutski tribes, who inhabited the parts about the Noss. The first circumstance, in the narrative of this journey, that can tend to lead to the situation of Tschukotskoi Noss, is its distance from Anadirsk; and this is represented as a journey of ten weeks, with loaded rein-deer; for which reason, it is added, their day's journey was very inconsiderable. We cannot, indeed, conclude much from so vague an account, but as the distance between the East Cape and the ostrog, exceeds

200 leagues in a direct line, and consequently may be supposed to allow 12 or 14 miles a day, its situation is not incompatible with Popoff's calculation. Another circumstance stated in this deposition is, that their rout lay at the foot of a rock, named Matkol, situate at the bottom of a spacious gulph. This gulph Muller conjectures to be the bay he had laid down between the latitudes of 66 deg. and 72 deg. and he accordingly places the rock Matkol in the center of it; but it appears to be more probable, that it might be a part of the Gulph of Anadyr, which they would doubtless touch upon in their journey from the ostrog to the East Cape. What seems, however, to put this point beyond all dispute, and to prove that the cape which Popoff visited cannot be to the northward of the latitude of 69 deg. is that part of his deposition which relates to an island lying off the Noss, from whence the opposite continent might be discerned. For, as the two continents, in latitude 69 deg. diverge so far as to be upwards of 100 leagues distant, it is certainly very improbable, that the coast of Asia should again trend in such a manner to the E. as to come almost within sight of the American coast. If these arguments are allowed to be conclusive against the form and extent of the peninsula of the Tschutski, it must be evident that the East Cape is the Tschukotskoi of the earlier Russian navigators: we say earlier, because Beering, and, after him, the late Russian geographers, have affixed this appellation to the S. E. cape of the peninsula of the Tschutski, which was formerly distinguished by the name of the Anadyrskoi Noss: and, consequently, hence it will follow, that the undescribed coast, extending from the latitude of 69 deg. to the mouth of the Kovyma, must trend more or less towards the W. As an additional proof of this, we may observe, that the Tschukotskoi Noss is constantly laid down as dividing the sea of Kovyma from that of Anadyr,

which

which we think could not possibly be, if any large cape had projected to the N. E. in the more advanced latitudes.

Another question arising on this point is, to what degree of northern latitude this coast extends, before it inclines more immediately to the W. If the position of the mouth of the Kovyma, both with regard to its latitude and longitude, were ascertained accurately, it might perhaps be easy to form a plausible conjecture on this head. Captain Cook was always strongly induced to believe, that the northern coast of Asia, from the Indigirka eastward, has hitherto been usually laid down above two degrees to the northward of its true situation: and he has therefore, on the authority of a map that was in his possession, and on the intelligence which he received at Oonalaskka, placed the mouth of the Kovyma, in his chart of the N. E. coast of Asia, and the N. W. coast of America, in the latitude of 68 deg. Should the captain be right in this conjecture, it is probable, for the reasons we have already stated, that the coast of Asia does not, in any part, exceed 70 deg. before it trends towards the W. and consequently, that we were within one degree of its north-eastern extremity. For if the continent be imagined to extend any where to the north of Shelatskoi Noss, it can scarcely be supposed that such an interesting circumstance would have been omitted by the Russian navigators, who mention no remarkable promontory between the Anadyr and the Kovyma, except the East Cape. Another particular, which Deshneff relates, may, perhaps, be deemed a farther confirmation of this opinion, namely, that he met with no obstruction from ice in sailing round the north-eastern extremity of Asia; though he adds, that this sea is not, at all times, so free from it; as indeed appears evidently from his not succeeding in his first expedition, and, since that, from the failure of Shalauroff, as well as from the interruptions

ruptions and impediments we met with, in two successive years, in our present voyage. That part of the continent between Cape North, and the mouth of the Kovyma, is 125 leagues in longitudinal extent. About a third of this distance from the Kovyma, eastward, was explored in 1723, by Fedot Amossoff, a Sinbojarskoi of Jakuts, who informed Mr. Muller, that its direction was easterly. Since that time, it has been surveyed, with some degree of accuracy, by Shalauroff, whose chart makes it trend to the N. E. by E. as far as Shelatskoi Noss, which he places at the distance of about 43 leagues to the E. of the Kovyma. The space, therefore, between this Noss and Cape North, upwards of 80 leagues, is the only part of the Russian dominions now remaining unexplored. If the Kovyma, however, be erroneously laid down, in point of longitude as well as latitude (a supposition by no means improbable) the extent of the unexplored coast will diminish in proportion. The reasons which incline us to imagine, that in the Russian charts, the mouth of the river is placed considerably too far to the W. are the following. First, because the accounts that have been given of the navigation of the Frozen Ocean, from that river, round the northeastern extreme of Asia, to the Gulph of Anadyr, do not agree with the supposed distance between those places. Secondly, because the distance from the Anadyr to the Kovyma, over land, is represented by former Russian travellers as a journey of no very great length, and easily performed. Thirdly, because the coast from the Shelatskoi Noss of Shalauroff appears to trend directly S. E. towards the cape. If this be really the case, it may be inferred, that, as we were, in all probability, not more than one degree to the southward of Shelatskoi Noss, only 60 miles of the coast of Asia are unascertained.

We are of opinion, thinking it highly probable,
that

that a N. W. passage from the Atlantic into the Pacific Ocean, does not exist to the southward of the 56th deg. of latitude. If therefore a passage really exists, it must certainly be either through Baflin's Bay, or by the N. of Greenland, in the western hemisphere; or in the eastern, through the Frozen Sea, to the N. of Siberia; and on which ever side it is situated, the navigator must pass through the straits distinguished by the name of Beering's Straits. The impracticability of penetrating into the Atlantic Ocean, on either side, through these strai is therefore all that now remains to be offered to the reader's consideration. Here we must previously observe, that the sea to the northward of Beering's Straits, was found by us to be more free from ice in August than in July, and perhaps in some part of September it may be still more clear of it. But, after the autumnal equinox, the length of the days diminishes so fast, that no farther thaw can be expected; and we cannot reasonably attribute so great an effect to the warm weather in the first fortnight of the month of September, as to imagine it capable of dispersing the ice from the most northern parts of the coast of America. Admitting this, however, to be possible, it must at least be allowed, that it would be highly absurd to attempt to avoid the Icy Cape, by running to the known parts of Baflin's Bay, (a distance of 420 leagues, or 1260 miles) in so short a space of time as that passage can be supposed to remain open. On the side of Asia there appears still less probability of success, not only from what came to our knowledge, relative to the state of the sea to the southward of Cape North, but likewise from what we have gathered from the experience of the lieutenants under the direction of Beering, and the journal of Shalauroff, respecting that on the N. of Siberia. But, the possibility of sailing round the north-eastern extremity of Asia, is undoubtedly proved

proved by the voyage of Deshneff, if its truth be admitted; yet when we reflect, that since the time of that navigator, near a century and a half has elapsed, during which, in an age of curiosity and enterprize, no person has yet been able to follow him, we can entertain no very great expectations of the public benefits to be derived from it. But even on the supposition, that, in some remarkably favourable season, a vessel might find a clear passage round the coast of Siberia, and arrive safely at the mouth of the Lena, still there remains the Cape of Taimura, extending to the 78th deg. of latitude, which no navigator has hitherto had the good fortune to double. Some, however, contend, that there are strong reasons for believing, that the nearer approach we make to the pole, the sea is more clear of ice, and that what masses we observed in the lower latitudes, had originally been formed in the great rivers of Siberia and America, by the breaking up of which the intermediate sea had been filled. But even if that supposition be true, it is no less certain, that there can be no access to those open seas, unless this prodigious mass of ice should be so far dissolved in the summer, as to admit of a ship's making her way through it. If this be a real fact, we made choice of an improper time of the year for attempting to discover this passage, which should have been explored in the months of April and May, before the rivers were broken up. But several reasons may be alledged against such a supposition. Our experience at Petropaulowska, gave us an opportunity of judging what might be expected farther northward; and upon that ground, we had some reason to entertain a doubt, whether the two continents might not, during the winter, be even joined by the ice; and this coincided with the accounts we received in Kamtschatka, that, on the coast of Siberia, the inhabitants, in winter, go out from the shore upon the ice, to distances that exceed

ceed the breadth of the sea, in some parts, from one continent to the other. The following remarkable particular is mentioned in the deposition above referred to. Speaking of the land seen from the Tschutski Nofs, it is said, that, during the summer, they sail in one day to the land in baidares, a kind of vessel, formed of whale-bone, and covered with the skins of seals; and, in the winter, as they go swift with rein-deer, the journey may be performed in one day. Müller's account of one of the expeditions, undertaken for the purpose of discovering a supposed island in the Frozen Sea, is still more remarkable. His narrative is to the following purport. In 1714 a new expedition was prepared from Jakutsk, under the conduct of Alexei Markoff, who was to set sail from the mouth of the Jana; and if the Schitiki were not well adapted for sea voyages, he was to build, at a convenient place, proper vessels for prosecuting the discoveries without any great risque. Upon his arrival at Ust-janskoe Simovie, the port where he was to embark, he dispatched an account, dated the 2nd of February 1715, to the Chancery of Jakutsk, intimating, that it was impracticable to navigate the sea, as it was constantly frozen both in winter and summer; and that, consequently, the expedition could only be prosecuted in sledges drawn by dogs. He accordingly set out in this manner, accompanied with nine persons the 10th of March, in the same year, and returned to Ust-janskoe Simovie on the 3d of the succeeding month. The account of his journey is as follows: that for the space of seven days, he travelled with as much expedition as his dogs could draw, (which in good tracks, and favourable weather, is from 80 to 100 werfts a day) to the northward, upon the ice, without observing any island: that he was prevented from proceeding farther by the ice, which rose like mountains in that part of the sea: that he had ascended some of these, whence

whence he could see to a great distance around him, but could discern no land: and that, at length, provisions for his dogs being deficient, many of them died, which reduced him to the necessity of returning.

Besides the above-mentioned arguments, which proceed upon an admission of the hypothesis, that the ice in this ocean comes from the rivers, others may be adduced, which afford good reason for suspecting the truth of the hypothesis itself. Captain Cook, whose opinion, with regard to the formation of ice, had originally coincided with that of the theorists we are now endeavouring to confute, found sufficient grounds, in the present voyage, for changing his sentiments. We observed, that the coasts of both continents were low; that the depth of water gradually decreased towards them, and that a striking resemblance prevailed between the two; from which circumstances, as well as from the description given by Mr. Hearne of the Copper-mine River, we have room for conjecturing, that, whatever rivers may discharge themselves into the Frozen Ocean, from the continent of America, are of a similar nature with those on the Asiatic side; which are said to be so shallow at their entrance, as to admit only vessels of inconsiderable magnitude; whereas the ice seen by us, rises above the level of the sea, to a height that equals the depth of those rivers; so that its entire altitude must be, at least, ten times greater. Another circumstance will naturally offer itself in this place to our consideration, which seems to be very incompatible with the opinion of those who suppose that land is necessary for the formation of ice, we mean the different state of the sea about Spitsbergen, and of that which is to the northward of Beering's Straits. It is incumbent on those objectors to explain how it happens, that in the former quarter, and in the neighbourhood of much known land,

navigators

navigators annually penetrate to near 80 deg. of northern latitude; whereas, on the other fide, no voyager has been able to proceed with his utmoſt efforts beyond the 71ſt deg. where, moreover, the continents diverge nearly in the direction of E. and W. and where there is not any land known to exiſt in the vicinity of the pole. For the farther ſatisfaction of our readers on this ſubject, we refer them to Dr. Forſter's " Obſervations round the world," where they will find the queſtion of the formation of the ice, diſcuſſed in a full and ſatisfactory manner, and the probability of open polar ſeas diſproved by many forcible arguments.

In order to give theſe obſervations their full force, we beg leave to ſubjoin a comparative view of the progreſs made by us to the northward, at the two different ſeaſons in which we were occupied in that purſuit; together with ſome general remarks reſpecting the ſea, and the coaſts of the two continents, which lie to the N. of Beering's Straits. In 1778, we did not diſcover the ice, till we advanced to the latitude of 70 deg. on the 17th of Auguſt; and when we found it in compact bodies, which extended as far as the eye could diſcern, and of which the whole, or a part, was in motion, ſince, by its drifting down upon our ſhips, we were almoſt hemmed in between that and the land. After we had experienced, both how fruitleſs and dangerous it would be to attempt to penetrate farther to the northward between the land and the ice, we ſtood over towards the ſide of Aſia, between the latitudes of 69 deg. and 70 deg. After having encountered in this track very large fields of ice, and though the fogs and thickneſs of the weather prevented us from entirely tracing a connected line of it acroſs, yet we were certain of meeting with it before it reached the latitude of 70 deg. whenever we made any attempts to ſtand to the N. On the 26th of Auguſt, we were in latitude 69 deg. 45 min. longitude 184 deg. obstructed by it in such a manner, and in such quantities, that we could not pass either to the N. or W. and were under the necessity of running along the edge of it to the S. S. W. till we perceived land, which proved to be the Asiatic coast. With the season thus far advanced, the weather setting in with snow and sleet, and other indications of the approach of winter, we relinquished our enterprize for that time.

When we made a second attempt, the following season, in 1779, we did little more than confirm the remarks made by us in the first; for we never had an opportunity of approaching the continent of Asia in a higher latitude than 67 deg. nor that of America in any parts, except a few leagues between the latitude of 68 deg. and 68 deg. 20 min. that we had not seen the preceding year. We now met with obstructions from the ice 3 deg. lower; and our efforts to make farther progress to the northward, were chiefly confined to the middle space between the two coasts. We penetrated near 3 deg. farther on the side of America, than that of Asia, coming up with the ice both years sooner, and in more considerable quantities, on the latter coast. As we advanced in our northerly course, we found the ice more solid and compact: however, as in our different traverses from one side to the other, we passed over spaces which had before been covered with it, we imagined, that the greatest part of what we saw was moveable. Its height, on a medium, we estimated at eight or ten feet, and that of the highest at 16 or 18 feet. We again examined the currents twice, and found that they were unequal, though they never exceeded one mile an hour. We likewise found the currents to set different ways, but more from the S. W. than from any other quarter; yet whatever their direction might be, their effect was so inconsiderable, that no conclusions, with respect to the existence of any

passage

passage towards the N. could possibly be drawn from them. We found July much colder than August. The thermometer, in the 1st of these months, was once at 28 deg. and frequently at 30 deg. whereas, during the last season, in 1778, it was very uncommon in August, to have it so low as the freezing point. In both seasons, we experienced some high winds, all of which blew from the S. W. Whenever the wind was moderate from any quarter, we were subject to fogs; but they were observed to attend southerly winds more constantly than others. The straits, between the American and Asiatic continents, at their nearest approach, in lat. 66 deg. were ascertained by us to be 13 leagues, or 39 miles, beyond which they diverge to N. E. by E. and W. N. W. and in the lat. of 69 deg. their distance from each other is about 300 miles, or 100 leagues. In the aspect of the two countries to the N. of the straits, a great resemblance is discernible. Both of them are destitute of wood. The shores are low, with mountains farther inland, rising to a great height. The soundings, in the midway of the straits, were 29 and 30 fathoms, gradually decreasing as we approached either continent; with this difference, however, that the water was somewhat shallower on the coast of America, than on that of Asia, at an equal distance from land. The bottom, towards the middle, was a soft slimy mud; and near either shore, it was a brownish sand, intermixed with a few shells, and small fragments of stones. We found but little tide or current, and that came from the W. But on the 30th of July, in the present year 1779, when in Beering's Straits, and steering to the southward, we found a current so strong as to make our passage both difficult and dangerous. It set at this time to the N. W. We might to these observations, which, we doubt not, will be highly acceptable to our very numerous friends and subscribers, add some others;

but

but we apprehend, they will think, with us, that it is now time to refume the narrative of our voyage, which was broken off on the 31ft of July, on which day, at noon, we had proceeded 18 leagues to the fouthward of the Eaft Cape.

CHAP. XIX.

ON Sunday, the 1ft of Auguft, 1779, we obferved in lat. 64 deg. 23 min. long. 189 deg. 15 min. at which time the Afiatic coaft extended from N. W. by W. to W. half S. diftant 12 leagues, and the land to the E. of St. Lawrence bore S. half W. On the 2d, the weather being clear, we faw the fame land again, at noon, extending from W. S. W. half W. to S. E. and forming feveral elevated hummucks, which had the appearance of feparate iflands. Our lat. this day, at noon, we found to be 64 deg. 3 min. long. 189 deg. 28 min. and our foundings were 17 fathoms. We were not near enough to this land to afcertain, whether it was a group of iflands, or only a fingle one. We had paffed its moft wefterly point in the evening of the 3d of July, which we then fuppofed to be the Ifle of St. Lawrence; the eafternmoft we failed clofe by in September, the preceding year, and this we denominated Clerke's Ifland, and found it compofed of a number of lofty cliffs, connected by very low land. Though thofe cliffs were miftaken by us, laft year, for feparate iflands, till we made a very near approach to the fhore, we are ftill inclined to conjecture, that the Ifle of St. Lawrence is diftinct from Clerke's Ifland, as there appeared between them a confiderable fpace, where we did not obferve the leaft appearance of rifing ground. In the afternoon, we likewife faw what had the appearance of a fmall ifland, to the N. E. of the land that we had feen at noon,

noon, and which, from the thickness of the weather, we had only sight of once. We supposed its distance to be 19 leagues from the Island of St. Lawrence, in the direction of N. E. by E. half E. On the 3d, we had light variable winds, and steered round the N. W. point of the Isle of St. Lawrence. In the afternoon, a fresh breeze rising from the E. we steered to the S. S. W. and quickly lost sight of St. Lawrence. On Saturday, the 7th, at noon, we observed in lat. 59 deg. 38 min. long. 183 deg. At four o'clock, having a dead calm, part of the companies of both ships were employed in fishing, and caught a great number of fine large cod, in 17 fathoms water, which were distributed equally among the crews. To this place we gave the name of the Bank of Good Providence, and as soon as the breeze sprung up we made sail, and stood to S. W. but we were forced more to the eastward than we wished, it being our intention to make Beering's Island. On Tuesday, the 10th, we were, by observation, in lat. 56 deg. 37 min. Friday, the 13th, we dispatched a boat to the Discovery, for the purpose of comparing time, and she carried the disagreeable intelligence, that Captain Clerke had been given over by the surgeon. The weather falling calm, we hove to, in order to get some fish for the sick: a few were caught, and distributed accordingly.

On Tuesday, the 17th, at five o'clock, A. M. the man at the mast-head called out, Land to the N. W. This we imagined to be the Island of Mednoi, which, in the Russian charts, is placed to the S. E. of Beering's Island. It is elevated land, and was at this time apparently free from snow. By our reckoning, it lies in lat. 54 deg. 28 min. long. 167 deg. 52 min. Captain Clerke, now perceiving his end drawing near, signified his desire, that the officers would receive their orders from Mr. King; and directed, for the last time, that we should repair, with all convenient speed, to the Bay of Awatska.

The

The wind continuing westerly, we held on a southerly course, till Thursday, the 19th, when, after a few hours continuance of rain, early in the morning, it blew from the E. and became a strong gale. We made the most of it, by standing towards the W. with all the sail we could carry. On the 20th, the wind varying to the S. W. we steered a W. N: W. course. At noon, we observed in lat. 53 deg. 7 min. long. 162 deg. 49 min. On Saturday, the 21st, between five and six o'clock, A. M. we descried a very lofty peaked mountain, on the coast of Kamtschatka, known by the name of Chepoonskoi Mountain, bearing N. W. by N. and distant near 30 leagues. At noon, the coast was observed to extend from N. by E. to W. with a very great haziness upon it. and distant about 12 leagues.

On Sunday the 22nd, at nine o'clock, A. M. a boat was sent off to the Discovery, to announce to Captain Gore, the death of our commodore, Captain Charles Clerke, who paid the debt of nature when in the 38th year of his age. His death was occasioned by a consumption, which had manifestly commenced before his departure from England, and of which he had lingered during the whole continuance of the voyage. His very gradual decay had for a long time rendered him a melancholy object to his friends; but the firmness and equanimity with which he bore the slow approaches of death, the constant flow of good spirits which he retained even to the last hour, and a chearful resignation to the decree of heaven, furnished them with some consolation. It was impossible not to feel an uncommon degree of compassion for a gentleman, who had experienced a series of those difficulties and hardships, which must be the inevitable lot of every seaman, and under which he at last sunk. He was bred to the navy from his youth, and had been in many engagements during the war which commenced in 1756. In the action between the Bellona and Courageux,

rageux, he was stationed in the mizen-top, and was carried over-board with the maſt; but was taken up, without having received the leaſt injury. He was midſhipman on board the Dolphin, commanded by Commodore Byron, when he firſt ſailed round the world; and was afterwards on the American ſtation. In the year 1768, he engaged in a ſecond voyage round the world, in the ſituation of maſter's mate of the Endeavour; and, during that expedition, ſucceeded to a lieutenancy. In the Reſolution he made a third voyage round the world, in the capacity of ſecond lieutenant: and, in a ſhort time after his return, he was appointed maſter and commander. In the preſent expedition, he was appointed captain of the Diſcovery, and to accompany Captain Cook. By the calamitous death of the latter, he ſucceeded of courſe, as we have already related, to the chief command. It would favour of injuſtice and ingratitude, not to mention, that, during the ſhort time he was commodore, we always obſerved him to be remarkable zealous for the ſucceſs of the expedition. When the principal command devolved upon him, his health began rapidly to decline; and he was unequal, in every reſpect, to encounter the ſeverity of a high northern climate. The vigour of his mind, however, was not, in the leaſt, impaired by the decay of his body: and though he was perfectly ſenſible, that his delaying to return to a warmer region, was depriving himſelf of the only chance of recovery; yet, ſo attentive was he to his duty, that he was determined not to ſuffer his own ſituation to bias his judgment to the prejudice of the ſervice: he therefore perſevered in the ſearch of a paſſage, till every officer in both ſhips, declared they were of opinion it was impracticable, and that any farther attempts would be equally hazardous and ineffectual.

The meſſenger who was ſent to the Diſcovery with the melancholy news of our Commodore's death,

death, brought a letter from Captain Gore, containing an order for Captain King to exert his utmost endeavours to keep in company with the Discovery, and, if a separation should happen, to repair as soon as possible to St. Peter and St. Paul. At noon, we were by observation in lat. 53 deg. 8 min. long. 160 deg. 40 min. E. Cheepoonskoi Noss bearing W. On the 23d, we steered for the entrance of Awatska Bay, which we saw in the evening, at the distance of 5 leagues. At eight o'clock, the light-house, which now furnished a good light, bore W. N. by W. 3 miles distant. It was now a perfect calm, but, the tide being favourable, our boats were sent a-head, which towed us beyond the narrow parts of the mouth of the harbour. On the 24th, at one o'clock, A. M. we dropped anchor, the ebb tide setting against us. At nine, we weighed, and before three, P. M. we anchored in the harbour of St. Peter and Paul; having up our ensign half staff, as the body of our late Captain was in the vessel; and the Discovery followed us in a very short time. Both ships were moored in four fathoms water, muddy bottom. From the time we had set sail out of this bay, till the present time of our return, we had been in no harbour to refit, and had been driven from island to island, and from one continent to the other, till our ships had in a manner lost their sheathing, and were otherwise in a miserable condition; we therefore thought ourselves exceeding happy in arriving at port. Soon after we had anchored, we were visited by our old friend the Serjeant, still the commanding officer, who brought with him a present of berries, intended for our late commodore. He was much affected at hearing of his death, and seeing the coffin that contained his remains. As the deceased had particularly requested to be buried on shore, and gave the preference to the church at Paratounca, we consulted the Serjeant about the

necessary

necessary steps to be taken on this occasion, who referred us to the priest, as being the person best qualified to give us information on this subject. At the same time he signified his intention of sending an express to the commander of Bolcheretsk, with an account of our arrival; when Commodore Gore begged to avail himself of that opportunity of conveying a letter to him, wherein he requested that 16 head of black cattle might be sent with all possible dispatch. At this time, we received intelligence of Sopofnicoff's arrival from Oonalashka, who took charge of the pacquet sent by Captain Cook to the Admiralty, and which we had the pleasure to find, had been forwarded.

Wednesday, the 25th, in the morning, Captain Gore, in consequence of the death of our late commodore, made out the new commissions. He himself succeeded to the chief command in the Resolution; and our lieutenant, Mr. King, was appointed captain of the Discovery. Mr. Lanyan, master's mate of the Resolution, and who had been in that capacity, in a former voyage, on board the Adventure, was appointed to the vacant lieutenancy. In consequence of these arrangements, the following promotions took place. Lieutenants Burney and Rickman (from the Discovery) were appointed first and second lieutenants of the Resolution; and lieutenant Williamson first lieutenant of the Discovery. Captain King, by the permission of the commodore, took in four midshipmen, who had rendered themselves useful to him in astronomical calculations; and whose assistance was become the more necessary, as we had not an ephemeris for the present year. And that astronomical observations might not be neglected to be made in either ship, Mr. Bayly took Captain King's place in the Resolution, for these purposes. This day we were attended by the Pope Romanoff Vereshagen, the worthy Priest of Paratounca. His expressions of sorrow

sorrow for the death of Captain Clerke did honour to his feelings; but the good old gentleman, though much concerned, started several difficulties, and appeared rather unwilling to comply with the request of the deceased. He urged, among other objections, that the church was soon to be pulled down; that every winter it was three feet deep in water; and that in a few years no vestige of it would remain, as the new church was to be erected near the ostrog of Awatska, upon a drier and more convenient spot. He therefore advised, that the remains of our late commodore should be deposited at the foot of a tree, the scite of which was to be included in the body of the new church, where the bones of the captain might probably rest for ages undisturbed: however, he submitted the choice of either place entirely to Captain Gore. These reasons, whether real or fictitious, the officers who had charge of the funeral could not disprove, and therefore some of our people had orders to dig the grave where the priest should direct.

The Discovery having suffered great injury from the ice, especially on the 23d of July, and continued exceeding leaky ever since, it was apprehended that some of her timbers might have started: our carpenters were therefore sent to assist those of the Discovery in repairing her. To accommodate those who were to be employed on shore, a tent was erected, and a party was sent into the country, north of the harbour, to fell timber. The observatories were placed at the west end of the village, near which was erected a tent, as an abode for the commodore and Captain King. When the carpenters began to rip the damaged sheathing from the larboard bow, it was discovered, that three feet of the third strake were staved, and the timbers started: and as they proceeded, the decayed state of the ship's hull became more and more apparent. The season being now far advanced, Captain King
was

was unwilling that any hindrance or delay should happen through him, to Captain Gore's farther views of discovery, and therefore ordered the carpenters to rip off no more of the sheathing, than should be absolutely necessary for repairing the damages occasioned by the ice. He was apprehensive of their meeting with more decayed planks, which he thought had better remain in that state, than have their places supplied with green birch, even supposing it could be procured. All hands were now fully employed in their separate departments, that we might be perfectly ready for sea, by the time the carpenters had completed their business. Four men were set apart to haul the seine for salmon, which were caught in immense quantities, and we found them of most excellent quality. After the wants of both ships were sufficiently supplied, we daily salted down almost a hogshead. We had four invalids, who were employed in gathering greens, and cooking for those who were ashore. We also landed our powder, in order to have it dried; and the blubber of the sea-horses, with which both ships had completely furnished themselves, in our passage to the north, was now boiled down for oil, and was become a very necessary article, having long since expended all our candles. The cooper was also employed in his department. Both ships companies were thus engaged till Saturday, the 28th, in the afternoon, which was allowed to every man (except the carpenters) to wash their linen, and get their clothes in tolerable order, that on Sunday they might make a decent appearance.

On Sunday, the 29th, we performed the last affecting offices at the interment of Captain Clerke, our late much respected commodore; and to make the funeral the more solemn, every officer was desired to appear in his uniform; the marines were ordered to be drawn up under arms; and the common men to be dressed as nearly alike as possible, in order to attend the corpse from the water-side to the grave. All the Russians in the garrison assembled on the occasion, assisting respectfully in the solemnity, and the worthy pastor of Paratounca joined in the procession, walking with the gentleman who read the service. The ships, at the same time, fired minute guns, and the drums, muffled as usual, beat the dead march. When the corpse arrived at the grave, it was deposited under a triple discharge of three vollies, fired by the marines, which concluded the burial service. When the grave was covered, it was thought proper to fence it in by piles driven deep in the ground, and afterwards to fill up the space inclosed with stones and earth, to preserve the body from being devoured in the winter by bears, or other wild beasts, who are remarkable for their sagacity in scenting out the bodies of dead passengers, when any happen to perish, and are buried near the roads. This mournful ceremony being over, an escutcheon was prepared, and neatly painted by the ingenious Mr. Webber, with the captain's coat of arms properly emblazoned, and placed in the church of Paratounca. Underneath the escutcheon was the following inscription.

There lies interred at the foot of a tree,
near the Ostrog of St. Peter and St. Paul,
The Body of
CHARLES CLERKE, Esquire,
Commander of his Britannic Majesty's
Ships, the Resolution and Discovery;
To which he succeeded on the Death of
JAMES COOK, Esquire,
Who was killed by the natives of an Island we discovered in the South Sea, after having explored the Coast of America, from 42 deg. 27 min. to 70 deg. 40 min. 57 sec. N.
in search of a N. W. passage
from EUROPE to the
EAST-INDIES.

The Second Attempt being made by
Captain Clerke, who sailed within some few
Leagues of Captain Cook; but was brought
up by a solid body of Ice, which he found
from the America to the Asia shore,
and almost trended due East and
West—He died at Sea,
on his return to the
Southward, on the
22nd Day of
August, 1779,
Aged 38 Years.

Another inscription was affixed to the tree under which he was interred. This tree stands on a little eminence, in the valley, north of the harbour, (and at some distance from the town), where the storehouses and hospital are situated, and round which several Russian gentlemen had been buried; but none so high upon the eminence as the spot pointed out for the grave of Captain Clerke, and which Captain Gore supposed to be such a situation, as was most consonant to the wishes of the deceased. The inscription, at this place, was nearly the same as that in the church, and is as follows:

Beneath this tree lies the Body of
Captain CHARLES CLERKE, Esquire,
Commander of His Britannic Majesty's
Ships, the Resolution and Discovery:
Which Command he succeeded to, on the 14th
of February, 1779, on the Death of
Captain JAMES COOK,
Who was killed by the Natives of some
Islands he discovered in the South
Sea, on the Date above.
CAPTAIN CLERKE died at Sea,
of a lingering Illness, on the 22d Day of
August, 1779,
In the 38th Year of his Age:
And was Interred on Sunday, the 29th following.

On this occasion the crews of both ships were suffered to continue on shore, and to divert themselves, each as he liked best. It was Captain Clerke's desire that they should have double allowance for three days successively, and all that while to be excused from every other duty, than what the ordinary attendance in the ships required; but the season being far advanced, and a long track of unknown sea to traverse before they could reach China, the officers representing the hardships and inconveniences that so much lost time might bring upon themselves, they very readily gave up that part of the captain's request, and returned to their respective duties early the next day. Accordingly, on Monday the 30th, the several parties reassumed their allotted employments; and on the 2nd of September, the carpenters proceeded to rip off such of the sheathing as had been injured by the ice, from the starboard-side; having first shifted the damaged planks, and repaired and caulked the sheathing of the larboard-bow. Four feet of the plank were discovered in the third strake under the wale, so much shaken as to require to be replaced; which was accordingly done; and on the 3d the sheathing was repaired. In the afternoon we got some ballast on board; after which we unhung the rudder, and caused it to be conveyed on shore, the lead of the pintles being much worn, and a considerable part of the sheathing rubbed off. This day an ensign arrived from Bolcheretsk, with a letter from the commander of that place to Captain Gore; from which, by the assistance of the serjeant, we understood, that proper orders had been given respecting the cattle; and that in a few days we might expect to see them: to which was added, that Captain Shmaleff, who succeeded Major Behm in his command, would pay us a visit on the arrival of a sloop which he expected from Okotsk. The bearer of the letter was a son of Captain Lieutenant Synd, who about eleven years ago, was appointed to the command of an expedition on difcovery, between Afia and America, and now refided at Okotík. He told us he was appointed to receive our directions, and to fupply us with every thing that our fervice might require: that he fhould remain with us, till it was convenient for the commander to leave Bolcheretík; and then he was to return, or the garrifon would be without an officer. The Ruſſians, in Kamtſchatka, could not furniſh us with a better account of Synd than Mr. Coxe has given us; though they feemed difpofed to communicate, without referve, what they really knew. From Major Behm we had received only this general information; that the expedition had mifcarried, and that the commander had been cenfured. It was evident, that he had been on the coaſt of America, fouth of Cape Prince of Wales; and as he was too far north to meet with fea otters, which the Ruſſians feem to have in view in all their attempts at difcoveries, it is probable, that his return without having made any, from whence commercial advantages might be reaped, was the caufe of his difgrace, and on that account his voyage is fpoken of with contempt by all the Ruſſians. On Sunday, the 5th, all the parties that were on fhore returned to the fhip, and were employed in fcrubbing her bottom, and getting in fome fhingle ballaft. On Wedneſday, the 8th, we hauled the Refolution on fhore, in order to repair fome damages fhe had received from the ice, in her cut-water. We began, about this time, to make a ftrong decoction from a fpecies of dwarf pine, which is very plentiful in this country, judging it would hereafter be ufeful in making beer, and that we might perhaps be able to procure fugar, or a fubftitute, to ferment with it, at Canton. We knew, however, it would be an admirable medicine for the fcurvy, and therefore were particularly defirous of procuring a confiderable fupply; as moſt

of

of the preventatives with which we had furnished ourselves, were either consumed, or had lost their efficacy through long keeping. When we had prepared about a hogshead of it, the ship's copper was found to be remarkably thin, and that, in many places, it was even cracked. This obliged us to desist, and orders were given, that, for the future, it should be used as sparingly as possible. Those navigators, who may hereafter be engaged in long voyages, would act judiciously if they provided themselves with a spare copper, or, at least, they should be fully convinced, that the copper, usually furnished, should be remarkably strong and durable. These necessary utensils are employed in so many extra services, particularly in that important one of brewing antiscorbutic decoctions, that some such provision seems absolutely necessary; and the former appears the more eligible, because a much greater quantity of fuel would be consumed in heating coppers that are very thick.

Friday, the 10th, in the morning, the boats from both the ships were ordered to tow a Russian galliot into the harbour, which had just arrived from Okotsk. She had been no less than 35 days on her passage, and, from the Light-house, had been observed a fortnight before, beating up towards the mouth of the bay. The crew had, at that time, dispatched their boat on shore, in order to procure water, which they much wanted; but, the wind increasing, the boat was lost: the galliot was again driven to sea, and those who were passengers suffered, with the crew, inconceivable hardships. On board this galliot were fifty soldiers, with their wives and children; they had also other passengers, and the crew consisted of 25 seamen, making, in the whole, upwards of 100 persons; which, for a vessel of 80 tons, was a great number, especially as she was heavily laden with stores and provisions. This galliot, and the sloop which we saw here in May, are

built

built in the manner of the Dutch doggers. Soon after the vessel had come to anchor, we were visited by a Put-parouchich, or sub-lieutenant, who arrived in her, and sent to take the command of this place. Some of the soldiers were intended to reinforce the garrison; and two pieces of cannon were brought on shore, to serve as an additional defence to the town; for, the honest serjeant observed shrewdly, that, as we had found the way here, others might do the same, who would not be so welcome as ourselves. On the 11th, the damages of the Resolution being repaired, we hauled her off from the shore, and, in the course of the day, we got some pitch, tar, cordage, and twine from the galliot. She also furnished us with 140 skins of flour, amounting to 13,782 English pounds troy-weight. On the 12th, Ensign Synd left us to return to Bolcheretsk, with the remainder of the soldiers who had arrived in the galliot. During his abode here, he had been our constant guest; and, on his father's account, we thought him in some degree belonging to us; and, as one of the family of discoverers, entitled to a share of our esteem. The serjeant, as being commander of the place, had hitherto been admitted to our tables; and his company was additionally welcome to us, because he was sensible and quick in his conceptions; and comprehended, better than any other person, the few Russian words that we had acquired. Whilst Ensign Synd remained among us, he very politely permitted him to enjoy the same privileges; but when the new commander arrived from Okotsk, the serjeant, for what cause we did not understand, fell into disgrace, and was no longer permitted to sit in the company of his own officers. Our endeavours to obtain indulgence for him, we perceived would have been ineffectual; for, though highly agreeable to us, it was, perhaps, incompatible with their discipline.

On Wednesday, the 15th, we had completed the stowage

stowage of the holds, got our wood and water on board, and were ready for sea; but we could not think of taking our departure, because the cattle were not yet arrived from Verchnei; and fresh provisions were now become the most important article of our wants, and essentially necessary for preserving the health of our people. Having before us a prospect of fine weather, we considered this as a favourable opportunity of engaging in some amusement on shore, and of acquiring some knowledge of the country. A party for bear-hunting was therefore proposed by Captain Gore; and on Friday, the 17th, we set out on this expedition; which was deferred to that day, in order to give a lettle rest to the Hospodin Ivaskin, a new acquaintance, who had arrived here on Wednesday, and intended to be one of our party. Major Behm had desired this gentleman, who resided usually at Verchnei, to attend us on our return to the harbour, and assist us as an interpreter; and, from what we had heard of him before his arrival, our curiosity to see him was much excited. He is allied to a considerable family in Russia, and his father was a general in the service of the Empress. He received his education partly in France; he had been a page to the Empress Elizabeth, and bore an ensign's commission in her guards. At 16 years of age he was knowted, had his nose flit, and was banished to Siberia. He was afterwards transported to Kamtschatka, and had resided there 31 years. His person was tall and thin, and his visage furrowed with deep wrinkles. Old age was strongly depicted in his whole figure, though only 53 years of his existence had scarcely elapsed. Great was our disappointment when we discovered, that he had so totally forgotten the French and German languages, as not to be able to speak a single sentence, nor to comprehend readily any thing that was said to him in either of those languages. Thus were we deprived

prived, unfortunately, of what we expected would have furnished a favourable opportunity of acquiring further information respecting this country. The cause of his banishment remained a secret to every one in this country, but it was generally supposed, he had been guilty of some atrocious offence; especially as several of the commanders of Kamtschatka have exerted their interest to get him recalled, in the reign of the present Empress; but, so far from succeeding in their applications, they were not able to change the place of his banishment. He assured us that, for 20 years, he had not tasted a morsel of bread, nor had been allowed any kind of subsistence; but had lived, all that time, with the Kamtschadales, on what he had procured from the chace by his own activity and toil. Afterwards a small pension was allowed him, and his situation has been rendered much less intolerable, since Major Behm was appointed to the command. Being noticed by so respectable a character, who often invited him to become his guest, others were induced to follow his example. The major had also occasioned his pension to be augmented to 100 rubles a year, which is an ensign's pay in every other part of the Empress's dominions, but in this province, all the officers have double pay. Major Bhem informed us, that he had obtained permission for him to go to Okotsk, where he was to reside in future; but that, at present, he should leave him behind, as he might probably be useful to us as an interpreter, on our return to the bay.

We now set out on our hunting party, directing our course to the northward, towards a pool of water, that lies near the mouth of the river Paratounca, and which was a known haunt of the bears. We had scarce landed, when unfortunately the wind changed to the eastward, and destroyed all hopes of coming up with our game; for the Kamtschadales assured us, that it was in vain to expect to meet with bears, when to the windward of them; owing to their being poffeffed of an uncommon acutenefs in fcenting their purfuers, which enabled them, under fuch circumftances, to avoid the danger, though at a very great diftance from them. We returned therefore to the boat, and paffed the night on the beach, having brought a tent with us for that purpofe. The next morning, being the 18th, we croffed the bay, and purfued our courfe on foot along a plain, abounding with berries, on which the bears feed; but though feveral of thefe animals were feen at a diftance, we could never contrive, the weather being fhowery and unfavourable, to get within fhot of them. Thus difappointed again, we changed our diverfion to that of fpearing falmon, which we faw pufhing in great numbers through the furf into a fmall river. Fortunately the water afforded us a little provifion; for ill fuccefs had not only attended us in the chace by land, but we had failed in our expectations of fhooting wild-fowl, after having almoft depended folely upon a fupply of them for our fubfiftence; and on its failure, we began to think it time to return to head quarters. Thefe fentiments entirely correfponded with thofe of the Hofpodin, whom former feverities had rendered unable to endure fatigue. On Sunday, the 19th, at night, we reached the fhips, after having been full 12 hours upon our legs. Poor Ivafkin feemed perfectly overcome with fatigue, and was probably the more fenfibly affected by it, for want of a fupply of fnuff; for, almoft at every ftep, his hand funk mechanically into his pocket, and rofe inftantly again with his huge empty box. When arrived at the tent, the Hofpodin's box was immediately replenifhed, and, regaling upon a good fupper, we forgot the fatigues and difappointments of our fruitlefs excurfion.

On Monday, the 20th, we received the difagreeable intelligence, that our much efteemed friend, the

the serjeant, had suffered corporal punishment, which had been inflicted on him by command of the old Put-parouchick. None of us could learn the cause of his displeasure; but it was supposed to have arisen from some little jealousy, which had been excited by our civility to the former. We were unwilling to remonstrate on this subject, till Captain Shmaleff should arrive; however, when we were next visited by the Put-parouchick, the coolness with which we received him, must have testified fully our chagrin. The 22d, being the anniversary of the King's coronation, we fired 21 guns; and, in honour of our royal master, prepared as elegant a feast as our situation would allow of. The arrival of Captain Shmaleff was announced the very moment we were sitting down to dinner. We were equally pleased and surprized at this unexpected visit: first, because the captain came so opportunely to take a share in the festivity of the day; and also, because we were lately informed, that the effects of a late illness had rendered him unequal to the journey. We had the satisfaction to hear this had been merely an excuse; and that, knowing we were distressed for tea and sugar, &c. he was hurt at the idea of coming empty handed, and therefore had deferred his setting out, waiting impatiently for the arrival of a sloop from Okotsk; but hearing no intelligence of her, and fearing we should sail before he had visited us, he was resolved to prosecute the journey, though he had nothing to present to us but apologies for the poverty of Bolcheretsk. At the same time he informed us, that the reason of our not having received the black cattle, was, that the heavy rains at Verchnei, had prevented their setting out. So much generosity and politeness demanded the best answer we were capable of making; and on coming on board the next day, we saluted him with 11 guns. Friday, the 24th, he was entertained on board the Discovery; and the day

day following, being the 25th, he returned to Bolcheretſk. No intreaties could prevail on him to extend his viſit, having, as he aſſured us, ſome expectations that the ſub-governor-general would arrive in the ſloop expected from Okotſk, he being on a tour through all the provinces of the governor-general of Jakutſk. Without any application from us, he reinſtated the ſerjeant in his command, before his departure, having reſolved to take the Putparouchick with him. We alſo underſtood, that he was much offended with him for puniſhing the ſerjeant, as there did not appear to be the ſlighteſt grounds for inflicting ſuch chaſtiſement. Encouraged by the captain's great readineſs to oblige us, we ventured to requeſt a ſmall favour for another inhabitant of Kamtſchatka. It was to requite an honeſt old ſoldier, who kept a kind of ordinary for the inferior officers, and who had done a thouſand good offices both for them and the whole crew. The captain obligingly complied with our wiſhes, and dubbed him inſtantly a corporal, telling him, at the ſame time, to thank the Engliſh officers for his very great promotion. It may not here be unneceſſary to remark, that the lower claſs of officers in the Ruſſian army, have a greater pre-eminence above the private men, than thoſe in the Britiſh ſervice can poſſibly conceive. It was, indeed, a matter of aſtoniſhment to us, to ſee a ſerjeant aſſume all the ſtate, and exact as much homage from thoſe beneath him, as though he had been a field-officer. Beſides there are ſeveral gradations of rank among them, of which other countries are wholly ignorant; there being no leſs than four intermediate ſteps between a ſerjeant and a private ſoldier. But the diſcipline of the Ruſſian army, though ſo extremely remote from the ſeat of government, is remarkable for its ſtrictneſs and ſeverity; not exempting even the commiſſioned officers. Impriſonment, and bread and water diet, is the puniſhment

of

of the latter for inconsiderable offences. A good friend of ours, an ensign in this place, informed us, that the punishment he received for having been concerned in a drunken frolic, was three months imprisonment in the black hole, with a daily allowance only of bread and water for his subsistence; which so affected his nervous system, that he has never since enjoyed a sufficient flow of spirits to qualify him for a convivial meeting. Captain King attended Captain Shmaleff as far as the entrance of Awatska river, and, having taken leave of him, embraced that opportunity of visiting the priest of Paratounca.

On Sunday, the 26th, Captain King attended him to his church, where his whole congregation consisted of his own family, three men, and the same number of boys, who assisted in the singing; and the whole of the service was performed with great solemnity and devotion. Though the church is of wood, it is much superior to any other edifice, either in this town, or that of St. Peter and St. Paul. Among several paintings with which it is ornamented, are two pictures of St. Peter and St. Paul, the Apostles, presented by the navigator, Beering, and which may vie with the first European performances, in the intrinsic richness of their draperies, the principal parts thereof being composed of thick plates of real solid silver, so fashioned as to imitate the foldings of the robes which decorate the figures, and fixed upon the canvass. Monday, the 27th, was spent by another party in the diversion of bear-hunting; when Captain King submitted himself to the directions of the parish-clerk, who had acquired great reputation as a bear hunter. About sun-set they arrived at one of the larger lakes, where it was deemed necessary to conceal themselves; and this was effected easily among some long grass, and brush-wood, of which we saw great plenty near the water's edge. We had not been

been long under our covert, before our ears were agreeably faluted with the growling of bears, in almoſt every quarter round about us; and we foon had the pleaſure of beholding one of them in the water, ſwimming in a direct courſe to where we lay concealed. At this time the moon ſhone, ſo as to afford a confiderable light; and as the bear advanced towards us, three of us fired at it, almoſt at the ſame inſtant. Immediately the animal turned ſhort on one ſide, and ſet up a moſt horrible noiſe, which was neither yelling, growling, nor roaring, but a very extraordinary mixture of the whole three. We could eaſily perceive, that the beaſt was wounded ſeverely, and that it reached the bank with difficulty; whence it retreated to ſome thick buſhes not far diſtant, ſtill continuing to make a hideous noiſe. The Kamtſchadales ſuppoſed it to be mortally wounded; but judged it an act of imprudence to attempt to rouſe it again immediately. It was then nine o'clock; and as the night became overcaſt, and a change of weather was to be apprehended, we thought it adviſeable to return home, and wait till morning for the gratification of our curioſity, when we accordingly repaired to the ſpot, and found the bear dead from the wounds it had received. It was a female, and larger than the ordinary ſize.

This account of our hunting party may convey a wrong idea of the method purſued uſually in this ſport; to prevent which, it may not be amiſs to ſubjoin a few words to this ſubject. The natives generally contrive to reach the ground about ſunſet, where the bears uſually frequent. They firſt look out for their tracks, and attend particularly to the freſheſt of them; always paying a regard to the ſituation with reſpect to concealment; and taking aim at the animal as it paſſes by, or advances, or goes from them. Theſe tracks are numerous between the woods and the lakes, and are often found

among

WHITE BEAR, found in CAPT^N: COOK'S LAST VOYAGE.

among the long sedgy grass and brakes on the margin of the water. Having determined upon a convenient spot for concealment, the hunters fix their crutches in the ground, on which they rest their firelocks, pointing them in a proper direction. They afterwards kneel or lie down, as the circumstances of their situation may require; and, having their bear-spears in readiness by their side, wait the arrival of their game. These precautions are extremely necessary, that the hunters may make sure of their mark: for the price of ammunition is so high at Kamtschatka, that the price of a bear will not purchase more of it than will load a musquet four or five times. It is much more material on another consideration; for, if the first shot should not render the bear incapable of pursuit, fatal consequences too frequently ensue. The enraged beast makes immediately towards the place from whence the sound and smoke issue, and furiously attacks his adversaries. They have not sufficient time to reload their pieces, as the bear is seldom fired at till he comes within the distance of 15 yards; therefore, if he should not happen to fall, they immediately prepare to receive him upon their spears; their safety depending, in a great measure, on their giving him a mortal stab as he advances towards them. Should he parry the thrust (which these animals are sometimes enabled to do, by the strength and agility of their paws) and break in upon his opponents, the conflict becomes bloody; for it is seldom that the loss of a single life will satisfy the beast's revenge. This business, or diversion, is particularly dangerous at two seasons of the year: in the spring, when they first issue from their caves, after having subsisted the whole winter (as it is here positively asserted) solely on sucking their paws; and especially if the frost should continue to be severe, and the ice in the lakes is not broken up; as they cannot then have recourse to their customary and expected food. Thus becoming exceedingly famished, they grow fierce and savage in proportion; pursuing the inhabitants by the scent; and prowling about at a distance from their usual tracks, dart upon them unawares. Under such circumstances, as the natives have no idea of shooting flying, or running, or in any manner without resting their piece, they often fall a sacrifice to their savage rapacity. The time of their copulation, is the other dangerous season to meet with them, and that is usually about September. Many instances of natural affection in these animals are frequently related by the Kamtschadales, who hence derive considerable advantages in hunting. They never presume to fire at a young bear if the dam is upon the spot; for, if the cub should happen to be killed, she becomes enraged to an immoderate degree; and, if she can only obtain a sight of the offender, she is sure to be revenged of him, or die in the attempt. On the other hand, if the mother should be shot, the cubs continue by the side of her after she has been a long time dead; exhibiting, by affecting gestures and motions, the most poignant affliction. The hunters, instead of commiserating their distresses, embrace these opportunities of destroying them. If the varacity of the Kamtschadales may be depended on, the sagacity of the bears is as extraordinary as their natural affection. Innumerable are the stories which they relate to this effect. They likewise acknowledge infinite obligations to the bears, for all the little progress they have hitherto made in several arts. They confess themselves indebted wholly to those animals for all their knowledge in physic and surgery; that, by observing what herbs they have applied to the wounds they have received, and what methods they have pursued when they were languid, and out of order, they have acquired a knowledge of most of those simples which they have now recourse to, either as external or internal applications. But the most singular circumstance of all is, that they admit

mit the bears to be their dancing-masters, though the evidence of our own senses places this matter beyond dispute; for in the bear-dance of the Kamtschadales, every gesture and attitude peculiar to that animal, is faithfully exhibited. All their other dances are similar to this in many particulars; and those attitudes are thought to come nearest to perfection, which most resemble the motions of the bear.

On Tuesday, the 28th, Captain King returned from his excursion to the ships, not a little pleased, as it had afforded him an opportunity of seeing a part of the country, and of observing the manners and behaviour of the people, when under no restraint, evidently not the case when they were in company with the Russians. On the 30th, our commodore went to Paratounca; but, before his departure, ordered Captain King to get the ships out of the harbour, that they might be in readiness to sail.

On Friday, the 1st of October, we had a violent gale of wind, which continued the whole day; but, on the 2nd, both ships warped out of the harbour, and anchored in 7 fathoms water, about a quarter of a mile from the ostrog. Fortunately for us, the day before we quitted the harbour, the cattle from Verchnei arrived; and that the men might have the full enjoyment of this seasonable supply, by eating it whilst it was fresh, the commodore determined to stay in our present station five or six days longer. This time, however, was far from being misapplied; for the pumps, sails, and rigging of each ship, received an additional repair. Captain King having obtained permission to use the copper belonging to the Resolution, and being supplied with molasses from Captain Gore, he was enabled to brew a sufficient quantity of beer to last the crew a fortnight, and to make ten additional puncheons of strong spruce essence. This supply was the more acceptable, as our last cask of spirits was now serving out, except a small quantity reserved for cases of emergency. The 3d being the name-day of the Empress of Russia, we were cordially disposed to shew it every possible respect. The pastor of Paratounca, Ivaskin, and the serjeant, were invited to dine with us; and an entertainment was prepared for the two Toions of Paratounca, and St. Peter and St. Paul; as well as for the inferior officers of the garrison, and the most respectable of the inhabitants. All the other natives were invited to partake in common with the ships companies; a pound of excellent beef being served out to every man, and the remainder of our spirits was made into grog, and distributed among them. Twenty-one guns were fired upon the occasion; and considering we were in a very remote part of the Empress's dominions, the whole festival was conducted in a manner not unworthy so illustrious a character. On Tuesday, the 5th, we received a fresh supply of tea, sugar, and tobacco, from Bolcheretsk. Captain Shmaleff having met this present on his return, he transmitted a letter with it, informing us, that the sloop from Okotsk had arrived in his absence, and that Madame Shmaleff had instantly dispatched a courier with these few articles, requesting our acceptance of them. On the two following days we were prevented from unmooring by reason of foul weather; but on Friday the 8th, all the boats were hoisted in, and we sailed towards the mouth of the bay; when the wind, veering to the S. obliged us to drop anchor, the ostrog bearing N. distant half a league. On the 9th, at four o'clock, P. M. we again unmoored; but as we were raising our last anchor, we were informed that the drummer of the marines had fled from the boat of the Discovery, which had just left the village, and that he had lately been seen with a Kamtschadale woman, to whom he was known to be much attached, and who had importuned him frequently to stay behind. This man was entirely useless in the

the service, being lamed by a swelling in his knee; and on that very account Captain King was the more unwilling to leave him behind, lest he should become a miserable burthen to himself and the Russians. He therefore applied to the serjeant to send parties of his men after him; and, in the mean time, some sailors visited a well known haunt of his in the neighbourhood, where the drummer and his woman were found together. On his return the Discovery weighed anchor, and followed the Resolution.

Having now taken our final departure from St. Peter and St. Paul, an account of Awatska Bay, and the adjoining coast, may not be unacceptable to our friendly readers; especially as it is, perhaps, the safest and most extensive bay that has ever been discovered; and the only one, in this part of the world, that can admit vessels of a considerable burthen. The entrance thereto is in lat. 52 deg. 51 min. N. long. 158 deg. 48 min. E. It lies in the bight of another exterior bay, formed by Cape Gavareea to the S. and Cheepoonskoi Nofs to the N. The latter of these head-lands bears from the former N. E. by N. and is 32 leagues distant. From the Cape Gavareea to the entrance of Awatska Bay, the coast takes a northerly direction, and extends about 11 leagues. It consists of ragged cliffs and rocks, and, in many parts, presents an appearance of bays and inlets; but, on a nearer approach, low grounds was seen to connect the head-lands. From the entrance of Awatska Bay, Cheepoonskoi Nofs bears E. N. E. distant 17 leagues. The shore on this side is flat and low, with hills behind, rising gradually to a considerable height. The latitude of Cape Gavareea is 52 deg. 21 min. This remarkable difference of the land on the sides of Awatska Bay, together with their different bearings, are very proper guides to steer for it, in coming from the southward; and when it is approached from the northward, Cheepoonskoi Nofs becomes very conspicuous;

ous; it being a high projecting head-land, and is united to the continent, by a large extent of level ground, lower than the Nofs. We are rather particular in defcribing this coaft; for if we had poffeffed a good account of its form on both fides of Awatfka Bay, we fhould, when we firft vifited it, have arrived two days fooner than we did, and confequently have avoided part of the tempeftuous weather, which we experienced in plying off the mouth of the harbour. Befides, as the fogs are fo prevalent in thefe feas, it often happens, that an obfervation for afcertaining the latitude cannot be taken. It fhould alfo be confidered, that land makes a very deceptive appearance when covered with fnow, or when viewed through a hazy atmofphere; both which circumftances render it neceffary for every navigator to be acquainted with as many difcriminating objects as poffible. Should the weather be fufficiently clear to admit a view of the mountains, both on the coaft and its neighbourhood, the fituation of Awatfka Bay may be precifely known, by the two high mountains to the S. of it. That nearest the bay is in form of a fugar loaf: the other, more inland, is flat at top, and not quite fo high. There are three very confpicuous mountains to the N. of the bay: that fartheft to the W. appears to be the higheft; the next, a volcano-mountain, may readily be known by the fmoke iffuing from the top. The third is the moft northerly, and might, with fome propriety, be called a clufter of mountains, as it prefents feveral flat tops to our view. When we got within the capes, and into the outward bay, a light-houfe on a perpendicular head-land, pointed out the entrance into the harbour to the N. Many funken rocks lie to the eaftward of this head-land, ftretching two or three miles into the fea, and when this or a fwell are moderate, they will always fhew themfelves. To the S. of the entrance, about 4 miles diftant from it, lies a fmall round ifland, compofed chiefly of high pointed rocks, one of which

is

is larger, and more perpendicular than the rest. The entrance into the bay is, at first, about three miles wide; one mile and a half in the narrowest part; and it is four miles long, in a N. N. W. direction. Within the mouth is a noble bason, 20 miles in circumference, in which are the harbours of Rakoweena to the E. Tarcinska to the W. and St. Peter and St. Paul to the N. The breadth of Tarcinska harbour is three miles, and the length twelve. A narrow neck of land separates it from the sea at the bottom, and it stretches to the E. S. E. The entrance of the harbour of Rakoweena is impeded by a shoal in the middle of the channel, which, in general, makes it necessary to warp in, unless there should happen to be a leading wind. Were it not for this circumstance, this harbour would be preferable to the other two. It is one mile and a half broad, and three miles long, running in a S. E. and easterly direction.

But one of the most convenient little harbours we have seen, is that of St. Peter and St. Paul. Six ships may be commodiously moored in it, head and stern, and it is, in every respect, convenient for giving them any kind of repairs. The S. side of this harbour is formed by a low, narrow, sandy neck, whereon the ostrog is built. The mid channel is only 270 feet across, in which there was six fathoms and a half water. The deepest within is seven fathoms, over a muddy bottom. We found, however, some inconvenience from the toughness of the ground, which often broke the messenger, and occasioned some trouble in getting the anchors up. At the head of this harbour is the watering-place. Off the eastern harbour is a shoal, and within the entrance a spit, stretching from the S. W. shore, having only three fathoms water over it. To steer clear of the latter, a small island, or rather a large detached rock, on the W. shore of the entrance, must be shut in with the land to the S. of it. In order to steer clear of the former, the three

needle

needle rocks, near the light-house-head, on the E. shore of the entrance, must be kept open with the head-lands to the northward of the first small bending on the E. side of the entrance. As you come into the harbour of St. Peter and St. Paul, and approach the village, it is very necessary to keep near the eastern shore, to avoid a spit which stretches from the head-land, to the S. W. of the ostrog.

Let it be noticed, that the observatories were placed on the W. side of the village of St. Peter and St. Paul; and from the sun's meridian altitudes, and of five stars to the N. of the zenith, we found the latitude to be 53 deg. 38 sec. N. and its longitude, from 146 sets of lunar observations, to be 158 deg. 43 min. 16 sec. E. At full and change of the moon, it was high-water at 36 min. after four; and five feet eight inches, was the greatest rise. The tides were regular every twelve hours. It may be proper to observe further, in this place, that the time-keeper on board our ship, which was copied exactly from Mr. Harrison's by Mr. Kendal, stopped on the 27th of April, a few days before our first arrival in Awatska Bay. During the voyage, it had always been carefully attended to, not having been trusted, even for a moment, in any other hands than those of Captain Cook and Captain King. No accident, therefore, could possibly have happened, to which its stopping could be attributed; nor could it proceed from intense cold, the thermometer being but very little below the freezing point. When the failure of the piece was first discovered, the Commodore and Captain King consulted about the measures to be pursued; whether they should suffer it to remain in a useless state, or submit it to the inspection of a seaman on board, who had been regularly bred a watch-maker in London, and who had given many satisfactory proofs of his skill in that profession, in repairing several watches upon the voyage. Having experienced the

accuracy

accuracy of this time-piece, we were extremely unwilling to be deprived of its advantages. Besides, it should be considered, that the watch had already been sufficiently tried to ascertain its utility, as well in the former voyage, as during the three years of our having it on board: therefore, on the first clear day after we arrived in Awatska Bay, the time-piece was opened, in the presence of the two captains, Clerke and King. No part of the watch appeared to be broken; but as the watch-maker was not able to make it go, he took off the cock and balance, and cleaned the pivot-holes: these were extremely foul; and other parts of the work were in the same condition. Upon taking off the dial-plate, a piece of dirt was found between two teeth of the wheel, that carries the second hand, to which cause its stopping was principally attributed. After putting the work together, and oiling it very sparingly, the watch seemed to go with freedom and regularity. Captain King having received orders to go the next day to Bolcheretsk, the time-keeper was left with Mr. Baily, in order to get its rate, by comparing it with his watch and clock; who informed him on his return, that it had gone very regularly for some days, not losing more than 17 seconds a day; and afterwards stopped again. This we supposed to be occasioned by its having been badly put together. It was therefore now a second time opened; and when again adjusted, it gained about a minute a day; when, the watch-maker in attempting to alter the regulator, broke the balance-spring. He made a new spring, but the watch went so irregularly afterwards, that we were obliged to lay it aside as quite useless. The honest mechanic was as much vexed as we were at our ill-success; not so much owing, as we were convinced, to his want of skill, as to the improper tools he had to work with, and the callousness his hands had contracted from his employment as a mariner. We shall now proceed, to give a correct and perfect geographical and natural history of the Peninsula of Kamtschatka.

Kamtschatka is situated on the eastern coast of Asia. It extends from 52 deg. to 61 deg. N. lat. the long. of its extremity to the S. being 156 deg. 45 min. The isthmus, that joins it to the continent on the N. lies between the gulphs of Olutorsk and Penshinsk. Its extremity to the S. is Cape Lapatka. The whole peninsula is somewhat in form of a shoe; and its greatest breadth is 236 computed miles, being from the mouth of the Tigil, to that of the river Kamtschatka; and towards each extremity, it gradually becomes narrower. On the N. it is bounded by the country of the Koriacks; by the N. Pacific Ocean to the S. and E. and by the sea of Okotsk to the W. A chain of high mountains extends the whole length of the peninsula, from N. to S. and almost equally divide it; whence several rivers take their rise, and make their course into the Pacific Ocean, and the sea of Okotsk. The three principal of these are, the Bolchoireka, or great river, the Kamtschatka, and the river Awatska. To the N. W. of the mouth of the Kamtschatka, lies the gret lake Nerpitsch; from Nerpi, a seal; that lake abounding with those animals. A fort, called Nishnei-Kamtschatka Ostrog, is situated about 20 miles up the river, where an hospital and barracks have been built by the Russians; and this place, we understood, is now become the principal mart in the country.

Were we to judge of this country from what we saw of its soil and vegetable productions, it appears to be barren in the extreme. Neither about the bay, nor in our journey to Bolcheretsk, nor in any of our hunting excursions, did we ever perceive the smallest spot of ground, that had the appearance of a good green turf, or that seemed capable of improvement

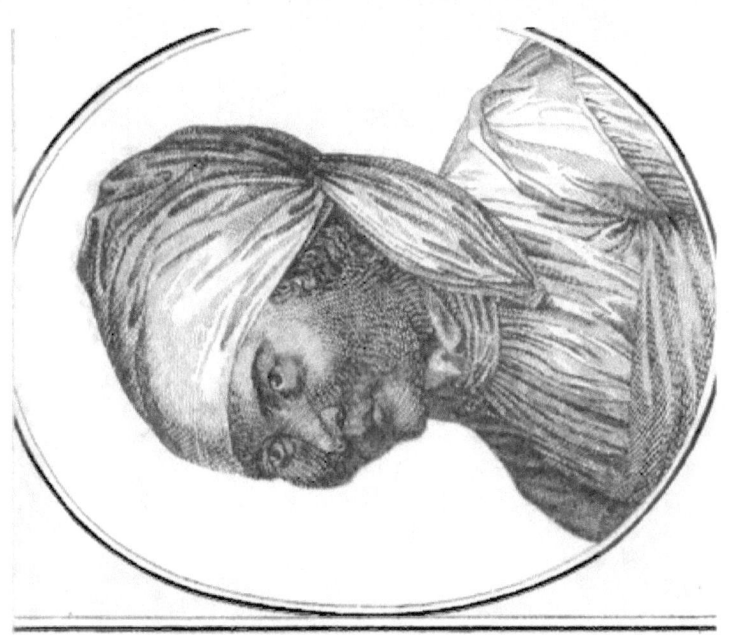

improvement by cultivation. Indeed, the whole surface of the country, in a most striking degree, resembles that of Newfoundland. At Paratounca, however, we saw some stacks of most excellent hay; and Major Behm assured us, that the banks of the Kamtschatka, and the Bistraia, as well as many other parts of the peninsula, produce a quantity of grass, of great strength and height, which is mowed twice in every summer, and that the hay is particularly adapted to the fattening of cattle, being of a very succulent quality. This agrees with Krascheninicoff's account, who relates, that the country which borders on the river Kamtschatka, is much superior, in point of fertility, to that of either the N. or S. The severity of the climate, it may naturally be supposed, must be in proportion to the sterility of the soil, of which it is perhaps the cause. We first saw this country in the beginning of May, 1779, when it was covered with snow, from six to eight feet in depth. On the 24th of August, when we returned, the foliage of the trees, and vegetation in general, appeared to be in the height of perfection. The weather, during the remainder of that month, and the whole of September, was not severe; but when October began, the new fallen snow again covered the tops of the hills. In computing the seasons here, Spring should certainly be omitted. Summer may be said to extend from the middle of June, till the middle of September. October may be considered as Autumn; from which period to the middle of June, it is all dreary winter. The climate in the country adjacent to the river Kamtschatka, is said to be as serene and temperate, as in many parts of Siberia under the same latitude. The inhabitants, however, are sometimes prevented, by the uncertainty of the summer season, from providing a sufficient stock of dried fish, for their food in winter; and the moisture of the air occasions worms to breed in them,

them, which frequently destroy or spoil the greatest part. The severity of the winter, and the dreadful hurricanes of wind and snow which attend it, oblige the natives to retire to their subterraneous habitations, both for their security and warmth. We had neither thunder nor lightning during our stay at Kamtschatka, excepting on the night of the eruption of the volcano. In this peninsula volcanoes are numerous; but only three have lately been subject to eruptions. That in the neighbourhood of Awatska we have already mentioned. The volcano of Tolbatchick is situated between the river Kamtschatka and Tolbatchick, on a neck of land. The eruptions proceed from the summit of a high mountain, which terminates in pointed rocks. On the top of the mountain of Kamtschatka, supposed to be by far the highest in the peninsula, is the third volcano. Springs of hot water are said to abound in this country.

The principal trees which fell under our notice, were the birch, the poplar, and the alder; several small species of the willow, and two sorts of dwarfish cedars. One of these sorts grows upon the coast, seldom exceeding two feet in height, and creeping on the ground. Of this our essence for beer was made, and proved to be very proper for the purpose: the other, which grows much higher, is found on the mountains, and bears a kind of nut or apple. Of the birch which appears to be the most common, we remarked three sorts. Two of them were large and fit for timber; differing from each other only in the colour and texture of the bark. The third is of a dwarfish kind. The natives apply this tree to a variety of uses. When tapped, it yields a liquor in great abundance, which they drink without mixture, or any kind of preparation, as we observed frequently in our journey to Bolcheretsk. We drank some of it ourselves, and found it pleasant and refreshing, though somewhat purgative. The bark they convert into vessels for
domestic

domestic purposes; and from the wood of this tree are made their sledges and canoes. Not only the birch, but every other kind of tree, in the neighbourhood of the bay, were stunted, and very small: the natives therefore are obliged to go a considerable distance up the country, to get wood of a proper size for their canoes, their balagans (or summerhouses) and many other purposes. This peninsula likewise produces great abundance of the shrub kind, as mountain ash, junipers, raspberry bushes, and wild roses. Also a variety of berries, as partridge-berries, blue-berries, black-berries, cran-berries, and crow-berries. These are preserved by mashing them into a thick jam; and they constitute a considerable part of their winter provisions, serving as a general sauce to their dried fish. They also eat them in puddings, and make decoctions of them for their common beverage. We found here large quantities of wholesome vegetables in a wild state, such as chervil, garlic, onions, angelica, and wild celery. We also met with some excellent turnips, and turnip-radishes, upon a few spots of ground in the vallies. This was the utmost of their garden cultivation: yet, this account of vegetables only relates to such parts of the country as fell within our observation: near the river Kamtschatka, where, as we have already observed, both the soil and climate are the best in the peninsula, garden culture is attended to, and perhaps with success; for, with the second drove of cattle which we received from Verchnei, we also received a present of cucumbers, celery, some large turnips, and other garden vegetables. Two plants are produced in this peninsula, which must not pass unnoticed. The first is called by the natives sarana, which grows wild and in great quantities. About the beginning of August, many women are employed in collecting the roots, which, after being dried in the sun, are preserved for use. It is a maxim with the Kamtschadales, that

Providence

Providence never deserts them, for the season that is prejudicial to the sarana, is alway favourable for fishing; and, on the contrary, an unsuccessful fishing month, is always amply compensated by an exuberant sarana harvest. This article is variously employed in cookery. When roasted in embers, it is a better substitute for bread than any thing the country produces. When baked in an oven, and pounded, it supplies the place of flour and meal, and is mixed in all their soups, and many other dishes. It is extremely nourishing, has a pleasant bitter flavour, and may be eaten daily without cloying. We partook of these roots, boiled as we do potatoes, and found them very agreeable. The name of the other plant is Sweet Grass. When at its full growth, it is about six feet high. This plant was formerly a principal ingredient in cookery among the natives; but since the Russians have been in possession of the country, it has been chiefly appropriated to the purpose of distillation. The liquor extracted is called raka, and has the strength of brandy. Seventy-two pounds of the plant, produce 25 pints of raka. A vulgar well-known plant remains to be noticed, as being more essential to their subsistence than all which have hitherto been mentioned: this is the nettle; which, as neither hemp nor flax are produced in this country, supplies materials for their fishing-nets; and on which their existence principally depends.

Many parts of this peninsula would probably admit of such cultivation, as might contribute to the comfort and convenience of the inhabitants; yet the number of wild animals it produces, must always be considered as its real riches; and no labour can be considered so productive of advantage, as what is employed upon its furrieries. And next to these, the animals that supply them are deserving of attention. These are the fox, the zebiline, or sable, the stoat, or ermine, the isatis, or arctic fox,

fox, the earless marmot, the varying hare, the weasel, the glutton, or wolverene, the wild sheep, the rein-deer, wolves, bears, and dogs. The most general objects of the chace are foxes, with which this country abounds, and among which are a variety of colours. The most common species is the same as the European, but their colours are more vivid and shining. Some are of a dark chesnut; others have dark-coloured stripes; the bellies of some are black, but the other part of the body is of a light chesnut. Some are wholly black, others of a dark brown, others of a stone colour, and some few are entirely white; the last, however, are very scarce. The quality of their fur is much superior to that of the same animals in Siberia or America. The sables are much larger than those of Siberia, and their fur is thicker and brighter; but those in the neighbourhood of the rivers Olekma and Vitime, are of a finer black. The sables of the Tigil and Ouka, are said to be the best in Kamtschatka; a pair of these being sold frequently for five pounds sterling. The inferior sorts are found in the southern parts.

A rifle barrel gun, of a very small bore, a net, and a few bricks, are the whole apparatus of the sable hunters. With the first they sometimes shoot them, when seen on trees: the net is used in surrounding hollow trees, in which they usually take refuge when pursued; and the bricks are put hot into the cavities, in order to drive them out with the smoke. The skin of the arctic fox is of little value; and, on the same account, the varying hare is neglected. They are very numerous, and always become perfectly white during the winter. In the beginning of May, we observed several of this colour, but they were so extremely shy, as not to suffer us to come within gun-shot. The earless marmot, or mountain rat, is a beautiful creature, much smaller than a squirrel; and, like that animal, feeds upon roots and berries. Its skin is of
high

high estimation, being warm, light, and of a bright shining colour. The ermine, or stoat, is little regarded; its fur being of a very ordinary kind. The weasel is also neglected on the same account. The skin of the wolverene, or glutton, on the contrary, is in the highest repute; a Kamtschadale looking upon himself as most splendidly attired, when a small quantity of this fur appears upon his garments. The women embellish their hair with its white pats, which is considered as the most superlative piece of finery. All the bears which we had an opportunity of seeing, were of a dun brown colour. They appear generally in a company of four or five together; and frequently in the season when the fish quit the sea, and push, in great quantities, up the rivers. In the winter months they are seldom visible. Of their skins, warm mattresses, and coverings for beds, are made; also comfortable bonnets, gloves, and harness for the sledges. The flesh, especially the fat, is held in great estimation. The wolves appear only in winter, when they are said to prowl about in large companies. Rein-deer, both wild and tame, are found in many parts of the peninsula, but none in the neighbourhood of Awatska. It is remarkable that these animals are not used here, for the purposes of carriage, as they are by their neighbours to the N. and E. Their place is indeed sufficiently supplied by dogs; yet it appears somewhat extraordinary, that they should not have preferred an animal so much more powerful and docile. The dogs resemble the Pomeranian breed, in mien and figure; but they are larger, and the hair is considerably coarser. The colour most prevalent among them, is that of a light dun, or a pale dirty yellow. These animals are all turned loose, about the latter end of May, and are obliged to shift for themselves till the ensuing winter; but they never fail to return to their respective homes, when the snow begins to make its appearance. In the winter,

winter, their food consists wholly of the head, backbones, and entrails of salmon, which are preserved and dried for that purpose; and even with this food they are very scantily supplied. The dogs must certainly be very numerous, no less than five being yoked together for a single sledge, in which only one person is carried. In our journey to Bolcheretsk, we had occasion for 139 at two stages. It is observable, that bitches are never employed in this business, nor dogs that have been castrated. The whelps are trained to the draft, by being fastened to stakes with leathern thongs, which are elastic; and having their food placed beyond their reach, by continually pulling to obtain it, they acquire strength and a habit of drawing; both of which are essentially necessary for their destined labour. We must not omit, in our catalogue of animals, the wild mountain sheep, or argali, unknown in all parts of Europe, except those of Corsica and Sardinia. Its skin resembles that of a deer's, but, in its gait and general appearance, it nearer approaches the goat. Its head is adorned with two large twisted horns, which, when the animal is full grown, weigh sometimes from 25 to 30 pounds, and are rested on the creature's back when it is running. These animals are remarkably swift and active, frequent only the most craggy and mountainous parts, and traverse the steepest rocks with an astonishing agility. Spoons, cups, and platters, are fabricated by the natives of their horns; and they often have one of the latter hanging to a belt; which serves them to drink out of, when on their hunting expeditions. This is a gregarious creature, extremely beautiful, and its flesh is sweet, and delicately flavoured.

Of northern sea-fowl, almost every kind frequent the coast and bays of Kamtschatka, and among others the sea-eagles. The inland rivers are plentifully stored with various species of wild ducks; one of which, called by the natives a-an-gitche, has a most

most beautiful plumage. Its cry is equally singular and agreeable. Another species is called the mountain duck. The plumage of the drake is remarkably beautiful. A variety of other water-fowl were seen, which, from their magnitude, appeared to be of the goose kind. We observed, in passing through the woods, some eagles of a prodigious size, but of what species we could not possibly determine. It is said, there are three different kinds. The first is the black eagle with a white head, tail and legs: the eaglets of which are perfectly white. The second is improperly called the white eagle, though, in reality, it is of a light grey. The third is the stone coloured eagle, which is a very common sort. There are great numbers of the hawk, falcon, and bustard kind in this peninsula. Woodcocks, snipes, and grouse, are also found here. Swans are very numerous, and generally make a part of the repast at all public entertainments. The vast abundance of wild fowl, in this country, was sufficiently manifest, from the many presents we received, consisting frequently of twenty brace at a time. We saw no amphibious animals on the coast, except seals, and these were extremely numerous about the bay of Awatska. The sea-otters found here, and those we met with at Nootka Sound, are exactly the same; and have already been particularly described. They were formerly in great abundance here; but since the Russians have opened a trade with the Chinese for their skins, where they bear a price superior to any other kind of fur, the hunters have been induced to be so indefatigable in the pursuit of them, that very few remain in the country. They are still found in the Kurile Islands, though the number is inconsiderable.

Fish is the main article of subsistence among the inhabitants of this peninsula, who cannot possibly derive it either from agriculture or cattle. The soil, indeed, affords some wholesome roots, and

every

every part of the country produces great quantities of berries; but fish alone may be called their staff of life, with more propriety than bread in any other country; for neither the inhabitants, nor their domestic animals of the canine species, could possibly exist without it. Whales are common in this country, and when taken serve for a variety of uses. After cleaning thier intestines, drying them, and blowing them like bladders, they deposit their oil and grease therein. Excellent snares are made of their nerves and veins; in short, no part of the whale is useless in this peninsula. We caught abundance of fine flat fish, trout, and herrings. At one haul, on the 15th of May, we dragged out above 300 flat fish, besides a considerable quantity of sea-trout. The first herring season commences about the latter end of May. They visit the coast in large shoals, but continue no considerable time. These fish are excellent, as are also large quantities of exceeding fine cod; and many of our empty casks were filled with the former. But notwithstanding this abundance, it is on the salmon fishery alone that the inhabitants depend for their winter sustenance. The fishing season begins about the middle of May, and continues to the end of June. The first shoals that enter the mouth of the Awatska, is the largest and most esteemed. Three feet and a half is their usual length; and they are more than proportionably deep; their average weight being from 30 to 40 pounds. We had one of the first that were taken, but not without being told, that it was the highest compliment the Kamtschadales could possibly confer upon us. It was formerly a custom among them to eat the first fish they caught, in the midst of great rejoicings, accompanied with many superstitious ceremonies. There is a smaller sort of salmon, weighing from about 8 to 15 pounds, known by the name of the red fish, which assemble in the bays, and at the mouths of the rivers, early in the month of June. From this time till towards the end of September, vaſt quantities of them are taken upon the eaſtern and weſtern coaſts, where the ſea receives any freſh water, and alſo up the rivers, almoſt to their very ſource. All the lakes which communicate with the ſea abound with fiſh, which have much the appearance of ſalmon, and weigh uſually about five or ſix pounds. The natives, we underſtand, do not think it worth their labour to catch them. Theſe lakes being generally ſhallow, the fiſh become an eaſy prey to bears and dogs, in the ſummer ſeaſon; and from the quantities of bones appearing upon the banks, vaſt numbers of them ſeem to have been devoured. The natives dry the principal part of their ſalmon, and ſalt but very little of it. They cut a fiſh into three pieces. The belly-piece is firſt taken off, and then a ſlice along each ſide of the back bone. The former, which is eſteemed the beſt, is dried and ſmoked: the other ſlices are dried in the air, and are either eaten whole as a ſubſtitute for bread, or pulverized for paſte and cakes. The head, tail and bones, are dried, and preſerved for their dogs.

The inhabitants of Kamtſchatka may be divided into three claſſes; the Kamtſchadales, the Ruſſians and Coſſacks, and a mixture produced by their intermarriages. The Kamtſchadales are a people of remote antiquity, and have inhabited this peninſula for many ages; and they doubtleſs deſcended from the Mangalians; though ſome have imagined they ſprang from the Tonguſian Tartars, and others from the Japaneſe. The Ruſſians, having made themſelves maſters of that vaſt extent of coaſt of the Frozen Sea, eſtabliſhed poſts and colonies, and appointed commiſſaries to explore and ſubject the countries ſtill farther to the E. They ſoon diſcovered that the wandering Koriacs inhabited part of the coaſt of the ſea of Okotſk, and they found no difficulty in making them tributary. Theſe not being

ing at a great distance from the Kamtschadales, with whom they had frequent intercourse, a knowledge of Kamtschatka must naturally follow; and the honour of the first discovery of this peninsula is attributed to Feodot Alexeieff, a merchant, in the year 1648; but a Cossack, named Volodimer Atlassoff is the unquestionable first acknowledged discoverer of Kamtschatka. He was sent in 1697, in the capacity of commissary from Jakutsk to the Anadirsk, with directions to call in the Koriacs to his assistance, in order to discover, and make tributary, the countries beyond theirs. With sixty Russian soldiers, and as many Cossacks, he penetrated, in the year 1699, into the heart of the peninsula, and gained the Tigil. In his progress he levied a tribute upon furs, and proceeded to the river Kamtschatka, on which he built an ostrog, now called Verchnei; and leaving a garrison of 16 Cossacks, returned to Jakutsk, with vast quantities of valuable tributary furs, in the year 1700. Since which time to the grand revolt of the Kamtschadales in 1731, the history of this country presents an unvaried detail of revolts, massacres, and murders, in every part of the peninsula. Though a great many of the inhabitants were lost, in quelling the rebellion of 1731, yet the country had afterwards recovered itself, and was become as populous as ever in 1767; at which period the small-pox was, for the first time, introduced among them, by a soldier from Okotsk. It broke out with fury, and, in its progress, was as dreadful as the plague; seeming almost to threaten their entire extirpation. Twenty thousand were supposed to have died by this loathsome disorder in Kamtschatka, the Kurile islands, and the Koreki country. The inhabitants of whole villages were sometimes swept away; of which sufficient proof remains to this day. There are eight ostrogs about the bay of Awatska, which, we were informed, had been completely inhabited, but now they are all become desolate,

solate, except St. Peter and St. Paul; and only seven Kamtschadales, who are tributaries, reside in that. At the ostrog of Paratounca only 36 native inhabitants remain, including men, women, and children; though it contained 360 before it was visited by the small-pox. We passed no less than four extensive ostrogs, in our journey to Bolcheretsk, which had not a single inhabitant in either of them. We were informed by Major Behm, that those who at this time pay tribute, including the Kuriles, do not exceed 3,000. The amount of the military forces, in five forts, is about 400, including Russians and Cossacks. Nearly the same number are said to be at Ingiga; which, though in the N. of the peninsula, is under the command of Kamtschatka. The Russian traders and emigrants are not very considerable.

The government, established in this country by the Russians, considered as a military one, is remarkably mild and equitable. The natives are permitted to elect their own magistrates in their antient mode. One of these, called a Toion, presides over each ostrog, to whom all differences are referred. In some districts, the only tribute exacted is a sable's skin; and in the Kurile islands, a sea otter's; but as the latter is considerably more valuable, the tribute of several persons is paid with a single skin; a tribute so inconsiderable can hardly be considered in any other light, than that of an acknowledgment of the Russian dominion over them. But the Russians are not only to be commended for the mildness of their government; they are also entitled to approbation for their successful endeavours in converting the natives to Christianity, there being now but very few idolaters remaining among them. If we form a judgment of the other missionaries from the benevolent pastor of Paratounca, more suitable persons could not possibly be engaged in this business.

The

The exports of this country consist entirely of furs; and this business is chiefly conducted by a company of merchants, appointed by the empress. Twelve was the number originally, but three have since been added. Besides a charter or grant of privileges, they are distinguished by wearing a gold medal, expressive of the empress's protection of the fur trade. There are other inferior dealers, chiefly Cossacks, in different parts of the country. At what time the principal merchants remain here, they reside either at Bolcheretsk, or the Nishnei ostrog; the trade centering wholly in those two places. This business was formerly carried on in the way of barter, but every article is at present purchased with ready money, no inconsiderable quantity of specie being circulated in that wretched country. The furs produce a high price; and the natives require few articles in return. Our sailors brought a quantity of furs from the coast of America, and were both pleased and astonished on receiving such a quantity of silver for them from the merchants; but as they could not purchase gin or tobacco, or any thing else that would afford them any degree of entertainment, the roubles were soon considered as troublesome companions, and they frequently diverted themselves by kicking them about the deck. Our men received thirty roubles of a merchant, for a sea-otter's skin, and in the same proportion for others; but the merchant understanding they had great quantities to dispose of, and perceiving they were unacquainted with traffic, he afterwards procured them at a much cheaper rate.

European articles are the principal that are imported, but they are not solely confined to Russian manufactures. They come from England, Holland, Siberia, Bucharia, the Calmucs, and China. They chiefly consist of coarse woollen and linen cloths, stockings, bonnets, and gloves; thin Persian silks, pieces of nankeen, cottons, handkerchiefs, both of silk and cotton; iron stoves, brass and copper pans, files, guns, powder and shot; hatchets, knives, looking-glasses, sugar, flour, boots, &c. These commodities, we observed, sold for three times the sum they might have been purchased for in England. And, notwithstanding the merchants have so extravagant a profit upon these imported goods, they receive still a greater advantage from the sale of the furs at Kiachta, a considerable market for them on the frontiers of China. In Kamtschatka, the best sea-otter skins usually produce about thirty roubles a-piece; at Kiachta, the Chinese merchant gives more than double that price, and disposes of them again at Pekin for a much greater sum; after which, an additional profit is made of many of them at Japan. If, then, the original value of a skin at Kamtschatka is thirty roubles, and it is afterwards transported to Okotsk, thence by land 1364 miles to Kiachta, thence 760 miles to Pekin, and after that to be transported to Japan, what a lucrative trade might be established between Kamtschatka and Japan, which is not above three weeks sail from it, at the utmost? It may be necessary to observe, that the principal and most valuable part of the fur trade, lies among the islands between Kamtschatka and America. Beering first discovered these in 1741, and as they were found to abound with sea-otters, the Russian merchants sought anxiously for the other islands seen by that navigator, S. E. of Kamtschatka, named in Muller's Map the islands of St. Abraham, Seduction, &c. They fell in with no less than three groups of islands, in these expeditions. The first, about 15 deg. E. of Kamtschatka; another, 12 deg. E. of the former; and the third, Oonalashka, and the neighbouring islands. These mercantile adventurers also proceeded as far as Shumagin's Islands, of which Kodiak is the largest. But here they met with so warm a reception, for attempting to compel the payment of a tribute, that

they

they never ventured so far again. The three groups before-mentioned, however, were made tributary. The whole sea between Kamtschatka and America is, according to the Russian charts, covered with islands; for, as those who were engaged in these expeditions, frequently fell in with land, which they supposed did not tally with the situation laid down by preceding adventurers, they immediately supposed it to be a new discovery, and reported it accordingly on their return; and, as these vessels were usually out three or four years, and sometimes longer, such mistakes could not immediately be rectified. It is pretty certain, however, that only those islands which have been enumerated, have been discovered in that sea by the Russians, S. of 60 deg. latitude. The sea-otter skins, which are certainly the most valuable article in the fur trade, are principally drawn from these islands; which being now under the Russian dominion, the merchants have factors residing in settlements there, for the sole purpose of bartering with the natives. To extend this trade, an expedition was fitted out by the admiralty of Okotsk, to make discoveries to the N. and N. E. of the above-mentioned islands, and the command of it given to Lieutenant Synd. But, as this gentleman directed his course too far N. he did not succeed in the object of his voyage; for, as we never found a sea-otter N. of Bristol Bay, they, perhaps, avoid those latitudes where large amphibious sea-animals are numerous. The Russians have not since undertaken any expedition for making discoveries to the eastward; but they will, probably, make an advantageous use of our discovery of Cook's River. Notwithstanding the general intercourse between the natives, the Russians, and Cossacks, the former are as much distinguished from the latter by their habits and disposition, as by their features and general figure.

As the persons of the natives have already been described,

described, we shall only add, that, in their stature, they are below the common height, which Major Behm attributes to their marrying so very early; both sexes usually engaging in the conjugal state at 13 or 14 years of age. They are exceedingly industrious, and may be properly contrasted with the Russians and Cossacks, who frequently intermarry with them, apparently, for no other reason, but that they may be supported in laziness and sloth. To this inactivity may be attributed those scorbutic complaints, which most of them are dreadfully afflicted with; whilst the natives, who exercise in the open air, entirely escape them.

Their habitations consist of three distinct sorts; jourts, balagans, and log-houses, which are here called isbas; they inhabit the first in the winter, and the second in the summer; the third are introduced by the Russians, wherein only the wealthier people reside. The jourts are thus constructed. A kind of oblong square is dug about six feet deep in the earth; the dimensions must be proportioned to the numbers who are to inhabit it, for it is usual for several to live together in the same jourt. Strong wooden posts, or pillars, are fastened in the ground, at equal distances from each other, on which the beams intended to support the roof are extended; which is formed by joists, one end of which rest upon the ground, and the other on the beams. Between the joists, the interstices are filled up with wicker-work, and turf is spread over the whole. The external appearance of a jourt, resembles a round squat hillock. A hole, serving for a chimney, window, and door, is left in the center, and the inhabitants go in and out by the assistance of a long pole, having notches deep enough to afford a little security for the toe. On the side, and even with the ground, there is another entrance, appropriated to the use of the women; but if a man passes in or out of this door, he becomes as much

an

an object of ridicule, as a sailor who descends through lubber's hole. A jourt consists of one apartment, forming an oblong square. Broad platforms, made of boards, are extended along the sides, at the height of about six inches from the ground; which serve them for sitting on, and on which they repose; first taking care to cover them with mats and skins. The fire-place is on one side, and, on the other, their provisions and culinary utensils are stowed. When they make entertainments, the compliment is considered in proportion to the heat of the jourts; the hotter they are made, the more gracious is the reception of the guests considered. We always found them so extremely hot as to be intolerable. They generally retire to their jourts about the middle of October, and continue in them till the month of May is more than half expired. To erect a balagan, nine posts are fixed into the earth, in three regular rows, at equal distances from each other, to the height of about 12 or 13 feet from the surface. About 10 feet from the ground, rafters are laid from post to post, and securely fastened by strong ropes. The joists are laid upon these rafters, and a turf covering completes the platform or floor of the balagan. A roof of a conical figure is raised upon this, by means of long poles, which are fastened to the rafters at one end, and meet together in a point at the top. The whole is covered, or rather thatched, with a coarse kind of grass. These summer habitations have two doors, placed directly opposite to each other, to which they ascend by the same kind of ladders that are used in the jourts. In the lower part, which is left entirely open, they dry their fish, vegetables, and other articles intended for the consumption of the winter. Though six families usually live together in one jourt, a balagan is seldom occupied by more than one at a time. The isbas, or log-houses, are thus erected: long timbers are piled horizontally, with the ends let into each other, and the seams are filled up or caulked with moss. Like those of our common cottages, the roof is sloping, and thatched either with grass or rushes. Each log-house has three apartments in the inside. One end may be said to be a kind of entry, which extends the whole width and height of the house, and seems to be a kind of receptacle for their bulky articles, as sledges, harness, &c. This has a communication with their best apartment, which is in the middle, and is furnished with broad benches, calculated both for eating and sleeping upon. A door leads from this into the kitchen, almost half of which is taken up with an oven, or fire-place; which is let into the wall that separates the middle apartment and the kitchen, and is so constructed as to communicate the heat to both rooms at the same time. There are two lofts over the kitchen and middle apartment, to which the inhabitants ascend by a ladder placed in the entry for that purpose. Each apartment has two small windows made of talc, and, among the inferior people, of fish-skin. The boards and beams of their habitations, are smoothed only with a hatchet, for they are strangers to the plane; and the smoke has rendered them of a deep shining black.

In Kamtschatka, an ostrog is called a town, and consists of several houses or habitations of the various kinds above-mentioned. Balagans are considerably the most numerous; and it is remarkable that we never saw a house of any kind that was detached from an ostrog. There are, in St. Peter and St. Paul, seven log-houses, nineteen balagans, and three jourts. Paratounca is nearly of the same size. Karatchin and Natcheekin have not so many log-houses as the former, but rather more balagans and jourts; whence it may be concluded that such is the most general size of an ostrog.

The dress of the Kamtschadale women having
already

already been described, we shall proceed to that of the men. The upper garment resembles that of a waggoner's frock. If for summer wear, it is made of nankeen; if intended for winter, it is made of a skin, (generally that of a deer or dog) having one side tanned, and the hair preserved on the other, which is worn innermost. A close jacket of nankeen, or some other cotton stuff, is the next under this; and beneath that, a shirt made of thin Persian silk, of a red, blue, or yellow colour. They wear also a pair of long breeches, or tight trowsers, of leather, reaching below the calf of the leg. They have likewise a pair of boots, made of dog or deer skin, with the hair innermost. They have a fur cap, having two flaps that are usually tied up close to the head, but are permitted to fall round the shoulders in bad weather. The fur dress, which was presented by Major Behm's son to Captain King, is one of those worn on ceremonious occasions by the Toions. It is shaped like the exterior garment we have just described, and consists of small triangular pieces of fur, chequered brown and white, and so ingeniously joined as to appear to be of the same skin. A border, of the breadth of six inches, curiously wrought with different coloured threads of leather, surrounds the bottom, and produces a rich effect. A broad edging of the sea-otter's skin is suspended to this. The sleeves are ornamented with the same materials. An edging of it also encircles the neck, and surrounds the opening at the breast. It is lined with a beautiful white skin. And the present was accompanied with a pair of gloves, a cap, and a pair of boots, executed with the utmost neatness, and composed of the same materials. The Russians who reside in Kamtschatka, wear the European dress; and the uniform worn by the troops here, is of a dark green turned up with red.

CHAP.

CHAP. XX.

THE people situated to the N. and S. of Kamtschatka, being but imperfectly known, we shall, before we proceed to the continuation of our voyage, give such information as we have been able to acquire respecting the Kurile Islands, the Koreki, and Tschutski. The Kuriles are a chain of islands, extending from the southern promontory of Kamtschatka to Japan, in a S. W. direction. The inhabitants of the neighbourhood of Lopatka, who were called Kuriles, gave these islands the same name, as soon as they became acquainted with them. Spanberg makes their number amount to 22, exclusive of the very small ones. The northernmost island is called Shoomska, and lies about three leagues distant from the promontory of Lopatka, its inhabitants consisting of a mixture of natives and Kamtschadales. The next, named Paramousir, is considerably larger than Shoomska, and is inhabited by the real natives, whose ancestors, they say, came from an island called Onecutan, a little farther to the S. The Russians paid their first visit to these two islands in 1713, and added them to the dominions of the empress. The others, as far as Ooshesheer inclusive, are now made tributary, if we may rely upon the information of the worthy pastor of Paratounca, their missionary; who pays them a visit once in three years, and mentions the islanders in the most respectable terms, extolling them for their hospitality and humanity; and that they excel their Kamtschadale neighbours as much in the gracefulness of their persons, as in their docility and understanding. Though the island of Ooshesheer is the farthest to the S. of any under the dominion of Russia, yet they are said to trade to Ooroop, which is the 18th in order; and is the only one that has a good harbour for vessels of burthen.

burthen. Nadeegſda lies to the S. of this, and is said to be inhabited by a race of men who are remarkably hairy, and who live in a ſtate of perfect independence, like thoſe of Oorogp. Nearly in the ſame direction lie a group of iſlands called Jeeſo, by the Japaneſe; a name alſo given by them to the chain of iſlands between Kamtſchatka and Japan. That called Matmai, the fartheſt to the S. belongs to the Japaneſe, and has a garriſon and fortifications on the ſide towards the continent. The iſlanders of Kunachir, and Zellany, to the N. E. of Matmai, and three others, called the Three Siſters, ſtill farther to the N. E. are entirely independent. The inhabitants of Matmai barter with thoſe of the iſlands laſt-mentioned, as well as with thoſe of the Kuriles to the northward. Many of the inhabitants of thoſe iſlands that are under the dominion of Ruſſia, are now converted to Chriſtianity. And perhaps the time is not far diſtant, when an advantageous commerce will be carried on between Kamtſchatka and this extenſive chain of iſlands, which may afterwards produce a communication with Japan itſelf. The advantages that muſt infallibly accrue to the Ruſſians by eſtabliſhing a commerce with the Japaneſe are ſufficiently obvious.

In the country of Koreki are two diſtinct nations, called the wandering and fixed Koriacs. Part of the iſthmus of Kamtſchatka is inhabited by the former, as well as all the coaſt of the eaſtern ocean, from thence to the Anadir. The nation of the wandering Koriacs, extends weſtward towards the river Kovyma, and along the N. E. of the ſea of Okotſk, as far as the river Penſkina. The reſemblance between the fixed Koriacs, and the Kamtſchadales, is very ſtriking: both countries depend alike on fiſhing for ſubſiſtence. Their cloathing and habitations are equally ſimilar. The fixed Koriacs are under the diſtrict of Ingiga, and are tributary to Ruſſia. The wandering Koriacs are employed

ployed wholly in breeding and pasturing deer, and are said to have immense numbers in their possession; it being common for a single chief to have a herd of 5,000. Upon the flesh of these animals they subsist, having an aversion to every kind of fish. They erect no balagans; their only habitations being somewhat like the Kamtschadale jourts, except that, in winter, they are covered with raw deerskins, and, in summer, with such as have been tanned. Their sledges are drawn only by deer, and those that are used in drawing them feed in the same pasture with the others. When they are wanted, the herdsman makes use of a certain cry, which, being very familiar to them, they obey, and quit the herd immediately. The two nations of the Koriacs, and the Tschutski, make use of different dialects of the same language; but it has not the smallest affinity to that of the Kamtschadale. The Tschutski are a courageous, well made, warlike race of people; and are formidable neighbours to the Koriacs of both nations, who often experience their depredations. The country inhabited by the Tschutski, is bounded by the Anadir on the S. and extends to the Tschutskoi Noss. Their attention, like that of the wandering Koriacs, is confined chiefly to their deer, with which their country abounds. The Russians have long endeavoured to bring them under their dominion: but, though they have lost a great number of men in different expeditions, they have not yet been able to accomplish this purpose. It is now time to return to the history of our voyage, and to make known the plan of our future operations.

In the instructions for the regulation of the present voyage, the Lords of the Admiralty had intrusted the commanding officer of the expedition with a discretionary power, in case of not succeeding in the discovery of a passage from the Pacific Ocean into the Atlantic, to make choice, in his return

return to England, of whatever rout he should judge proper; the commodore therefore desired, that the principal officers would deliver their sentiments, in writing, relative to the mode in which these instructions might most effectually be carried into execution. The result of their opinions, which, to his great satisfaction, he found unanimous, and perfectly agreeing with his own, was, that the condition of the ships, their sails, cordage, &c. rendered it hazardous and unsafe to make any attempt, as the winter was now approaching, to navigate the sea between Asia and Japan, which would otherwise have opened to us the most copious field for discovery; that it was therefore most prudent to steer to the eastward of that island, and in our way thither, to sail along the Kuriles, and examine particularly those islands that are situated nearest to the northern coast of Japan, which are said to be of considerable extent, and not subject to the Russians or Japanese. Should we have the good fortune to meet with some secure and commodious harbours in any of these islands, we supposed they might prove of considerable importance, as convenient places of shelter for subsequent navigators, who might be employed in exploring the seas, or as the means of producing a commercial intercourse among the adjacent dominions of the two above-mentioned empires. Our next object was to take a survey of the Japanese Isles; after which we designed to make the coast of China, as far to the N. as might be in our power, and then to proceed to Macao. This plan being adopted, Captain King received orders, in case the two ships should separate, to repair, without delay, to Macao.

On Saturday, the 9th of October, at six o'clock, P. M. having cleared the entrance of the Bay of Awatska, we made sail to the S. E. At midnight we had a dead calm, which continued till noon of the following day. A breeze springing up from the

W. about three o'clock, P. M. we steered to the S. along the coast. A head-land now opened with Cape Gavareea, in the direction of S. by W. situated nearly 20 miles beyond it. On Monday, the 11th, at noon, we observed in lat. 52 deg. 4 min. long. 158 deg. 31 min. Cape Gavareea bearing N. by W. one quarter W. and the southern extremity S. W. half W. We were now at the distance of 9 or 10 miles from the nearest part of the coast, and perceived the whole inland country covered with snow. A point of land towards the S. formed the northern side of a deep bay, distinguished by the name of Achachinskoi, to the southward of which, the land did not exhibit such a rugged and barren aspect, as was observable in that part of the country which we had before passed. On Tuesday, the 12th, at six o'clock, P. M. we discerned, from the mast-head, Cape Lopatka, which is the most southern extreme of Kamtschatka. This, by accurate observations, we found to be in lat. 51 deg. and in the long. of 156 deg. 45 min. We perceived, to the N. W. of it, a very lofty mountain, whose summit was lost in the clouds. At the same instant, the first of the Kurile Islands, named Shoomska, made its appearance, in the direction of W. half S. On Wednesday, the 13th, at day-break, we descried the second of the Kurile Islands, named Paramousir by the Russians, extending from W. half S. to N. W. by W. This land was exceedingly high, and almost covered with snow. The island is the largest of the Kuriles; and its southern extremity stands, according to our computation, in lat. 49 deg. 58 min. the northern extremity we place in lat. 50 deg. 46 min. long. 10 deg. W. of Cape Lopatka. During the two following days, the wind, blowing fresh from the W. obliged us to steer to the southward, and consequently prevented us from seeing any more of the Kuriles. On Saturday, the 16th, our lat. was 45 deg. 27 min. our long. deduced from many lunar

lunar observations taken the three preceding days, was 155 deg. 30 min. and the variation 4 deg. 30 min. E. In this situation, we were almost encompassed by the real or pretended discoveries of prior navigators; not one of which we were fortunate enough to meet with in our course. The wind having veered in the afternoon to the northward, we hauled round to the W. In the course of this day, we observed several albatrosses, fulmars, and numerous flocks of gulls: we also saw a number of fish, called grampusses by our sailors; but we were rather inclined to judge, from the appearance of those which passed close by our vessels, that they were the kasatka, or sword-fish. Sunday, the 17th, we observed in lat. 45 deg. 7 min. long. 154 deg. On the 19th, at two o'clock, A. M. we hauled our wind, and stood to the southward till five, at which time a violent storm reduced us to our courses. Though from the unfavourable state of the weather, there was but little probability of our making the land, our attention was still anxiously directed to this object; and on the appearance of day-light, we ventured to steer W. by S. We proceeded on the same course till 10 o'clock, when the wind suddenly veered round to the S. W. attended with fair weather. Scarce had we availed ourselves of this, by letting out our reefs, and setting the top-sail, when it began to blow with such vehemence, that we were under the necessity of close reefing again; and, about noon, the wind shifting more to the W. we were prevented from continuing any longer on this tack: we therefore put about, and stood towards the S. We were now in lat. 44 deg. 12 min. long. 150 deg. 40 min. so that, after all our exertions, we had the mortification of finding ourselves, according to the Russian charts, upon the same meridian with Nadeegsda, which they represent as the most southerly of all the Kurile Islands. Though the violent and adverse winds that we had met with for six days past, had deprived us of an

opportunity

opportunity of getting in with these islands, yet the course on which we had been obliged to proceed, did not prove altogether destitute of geographical advantages: for the group of Islands, comprehending Zellany, Kunashir, and the Three Sisters, which, in the maps of M. D'Anville, are laid down in the track we had just crossed, are, by this means, demonstrably removed from that position; and thus an additional proof is obtained of their being situated to the W. where Captain Spanberg has placed them, between the longitudes of 142 and 147 deg. But this space being occupied, in the French charts, by Staten Island, and part of the supposed land of Jeso, the opinion of Muller becomes highly probable, that they are all the same lands; and, as we have no reason to call in question the accuracy of Spanberg, we have, in our general chart, reinstated Kunashir, Zellany, and the Three Sisters, in their proper situation, and have totally omitted the rest. When we consider the manner in which the Russians have multiplied the islands of the northern Archipelago, not only from the want of accuracy in ascertaining their real position, but likewise from the desire, natural to mankind, of propagating new discoveries, we shall not be surprized, that the same causes should produce similar effects. It is thus that the lands of Jeso, which appear, as well from the earliest traditions among the Russians, as from the accounts of the Japanese, to be no other than the Kurile Islands, have been imagined to be distinct from the latter. De Gama's land is next on record; and this was originally represented as being nearly the same in situation with those we have just mentioned; but it was afterwards removed, in order to make room for Staten's Island, and the Company's land; and as Jeso, and the most southerly of the Kuriles, had likewise possession of this space, that nothing might be lost, the former had a place provided for it westward, and the latter towards the E. As, according to the Russian charts, the isles of of Kunashir and Zellany, were still to the S. we entertained some hopes of being able to make them, and, with this view, kept the head of the Resolution towards the W. as much as the wind would permit. On Wednesday, the 20th, at noon, we observed in lat. 43 deg. 47 min. long. 150 deg. 30 min. We were then standing to the W. by S. with a gentle breeze from the S. E. but about three o'clock, P. M. the wind, shifting to the N. W. point, began to blow with such violence, that we were brought under our mizen stay-sail, and fore-sail. For the following 24 hours we had heavy rain, and vehement squalls; and as the wind continued to blow from the N. W. our attempts to make the land were rendered abortive; and we were at length obliged to relinquish all further thoughts of discovery to the northward of Japan. To this disappointment we submitted with the greater reluctance, as our curiosity had been considerably excited by the accounts that are given of the natives of these islands. On the 21st, in the afternoon, an accident befel our ship, the Resolution; for the leach-rope of her fore-top-sail gave way, and split the sail. This having frequently happened during the life of Captain Cook, he had, on such occasions, ordered the foot and leach-ropes of the top-sails to be taken out, and larger ones to be fixed in their room; and these likewise proving incapable of supporting the strain that was on them, gave him good reason to observe to us, that the just proportion of strength between the sail and those ropes, is extremely miscalculated in our service. On the 22d, in the morning, we let out the reefs of our top-sails, and carried more sail. At noon, we found ourselves to be in lat. 40 deg. 58 min. long. 148 deg. 17 min. variation of the needle 3 deg. E. This day some birds afforded us clear indications that we were not at any considerable distance from land: with this hope we steered to the W. N. W. in which direction were situated, at the distance of about 50 leagues, the southernmost

southernmost islands, seen by Captain Spanberg, and said to be inhabited by hairy men. At eight o'clock, the following morning, a fresh breeze springing up, with which we continued our course till the evening, when we had violent squally gales, accompanied with rain; and as we had, in the course of this day, passed some patches of green grass, and observed a number of small land birds, a shag, and many flocks of gulls, we did not think it consistent with prudence, having all these signs of the vicinity of land, to stand on for the whole night: about midnight therefore we tacked, and for the space of a few hours steered S. E.

Sunday, the 24th, we again bore away to the W. N. W. and carried a press of sail till seven o'clock, P.M. when the wind veered round to the N. and blew a fresh gale. At this time our lat. was 40 deg. 57 min. long. 145 deg. 20. min. This second disappointment in our attempts to get to the N. W. the tempestuous weather with which we had been harrassed, and the small probability, at this season of the year, of its becoming more favourable to our designs, were the motives that now induced Captain Gore to abandon finally all further search for the islands situate to the northward of Japan, and to direct our course to the W. S. W. for the northern part of that island. On the 25th, at noon, we were in lat. 40 deg. 18 min. and in long. 144 deg. Flights of wild ducks were this day observed by us; a pigeon lighted upon our rigging; and many small birds, resembling linnets, flew about the ships, with a degree of vigour, that gave us reason to imagine they had not been long on the wing. We also passed a piece either of bamboo, or sugar-cane, and several patches of long grass. These indications of our being at no great distance from land, determined us to try for soundings; but we could not reach the bottom with 90 fathoms of line. On the approach of evening, the wind gradually veered round to the S. with which we continued our course to
the

the W. S. W. On Tuesday, the 26th, at day-break, we had the satisfaction of perceiving high-land towards the W. which proved to be Japan. At eight o'clock, it was at the distance of ten or twelve miles, and extended from S. by W. to N. W. A low flat cape, which apparently constituted the southern part of the entrance of a bay, bore N. W. three quarters W. Near the S. extremity, a hill of a conic figure appeared, bearing S. by W. three quarters W. To the N. of this hill, there seemed to be an inlet of very considerable depth, the northern side of whose entrance is formed by a low point of land; and, as well as we were enabled to judge by the assistance of our glasses, has a small island near it towards the S. Having stood on till nine o'clock, we had, by that time, approached within five or six miles of the land, which bore W. three quarters S. We now tacked, and stood off; but as the wind failed us, we had proceeded, at noon, to no greater distance than 3 leagues from the shore. This part of the coast extended from N. W. by N. to S. half E. and was principally bold and cliffy. The low cape above-mentioned, was about six leagues distant, bearing N. W. by W. and the northern point of the inlet was in the direction of S. three quarters W. Our lat. by observation, was 40 deg. 5 min. and our long. 142 deg. 28 min. The most northerly land in view, was supposed by us to be the northern extreme of Japan. It is somewhat lower than the other parts; and from the range of the elevated lands that were discerned over it from the masthead, the coast manifestly appeared to trend to the westward. The northern point of the inlet was imagined by us to be Cape Nambu; and we conjectured, that the town, which Jansen calls Nabo, stood in a break of the high land, towards which the inlet apparently directed itself. The neighbouring country is of a moderate elevation, and has a double range of mountains. It is well furnished with wood, and exhibits a variety of pleasing hills and
dales.

dales. We perceived the smoke arising from several villages or towns, and saw many houses in delightful and cultivated situations, at a small distance from the shore. While the calm continued, that we might lose no time, we put our fishing lines overboard, in ten fathoms water, but had no success. This being the only diversion which our present circumstances would permit us to enjoy, we very sensibly felt our disappointment; and looked back with regret to the cod banks of the dismal regions we had lately quitted, which had furnished us with so many salutary meals, and by the amusement they had afforded, given a variety to the tedious recurrence of astronomical observations, and the wearisome succession of calms and gales. At two o'clock, P. M. the wind blew fresh from the S. and, by four, had reduced us to close-reefed top-sails, and obliged us to stand off to the south-eastward; in consequence of which course, and the gloominess of the weather, we soon lost sight of land. We kept on during the whole night, and till eight o'clock the following morning, when the wind shifting to the N. and becoming moderate, we made sail, and steered a W. S. W. course, towards the land, which, however, we did not make before three in the afternoon; at which time it was seen to extend from N. W. half W. to W. The most northerly extremity was a continuation of the elevated land, the southernmost we had observed the preceding day. The land to the westward, we conjectured to be the High Table Hill of Jansen. The coast, between the two extremes, was low, and could scarcely be perceived, except from the mast-head. We proceeded towards the coast till eight in the evening, when our distance from it was about five leagues, and having shortened sail for the night, we steered in a southerly direction, sounding every four hours; but our depth of water was so great, that we did not find ground with 160 fathoms of line.

On Thursday, the 28th, at six o'clock, A. M. we again

again saw land, 12 leagues to the southward of that we had seen the day before, and extended from W. by N. to W. S. W. At ten o'clock we saw more land in the same direction. At noon, the northern extremity of the land in view bore N. W. by N. and a peaked hill, over a steep head-land, was 15 or 16 miles distant, bearing W. by N. By observation, our lat. was 38 deg. 16 min. and our long. 142 deg. 9 min. During the remainder of the day, we continued our course to the S. W. and, at midnight, found our depth of water to be 70 fathoms, over a bottom of fine brown sand. We therefore hauled up towards the E. till the next morning, when we again had sight of land, eleven leagues to the S. of that we had seen the preceding day. The ground was low towards the sea, but gradually swelled into hills of a moderate elevation. At nine o'clock, the sky being over-cast, and the wind veering to the S. we tacked and stood off to the E. Not long after, we observed a vessel, close in with the land, standing to the N. along the shore; and we also saw another in the offing, coming down on us before the wind. Objects belonging to a country so celebrated, and yet so imperfectly known, excited a general eagerness of curiosity; in consequence of which, every person on board came instantaneously upon deck to gaze at them. As the vessel to windward approached us, she hauled off to a greater distance from the shore; upon which being apprehensive of alarming those who were on board of her by the appearance of a pursuit, we brought to, and she sailed a-head of us. We might have spoken to them; but Captain Gore perceiving, by their manœuvres, that they were highly terrified, was unwilling to increase their apprehensions; and, imagining that we should have many better opportunities of a communication with the Japanese, suffered them to retire without interruption. According to the most probable conjectures we were enabled to form, the vessel was of the burthen of 40 tons;

tons; and there seemed to be six men on board her. She had only one maft, whereon was hoifted a quadrangular fail, extended aloft by a yard, the braces of which worked forwards. Three pieces of black cloth came half way down the fail, at an equal diftance from each other. The veffel was lower in the middle than at each end; and from her figure we fuppofed, that fhe could not fail otherwife than large. At noon, the wind blew frefh, accompanied with much rain. By three o'clock it had increafed in fo great a degree, that we were reduced to our courfes. The fea, at the fame time, ran as high as any of our people ever remember to have feen it. About eight o'clock, in the evening, the gale, without the fmalleft diminution of violence, fhifted to the W. and by producing a fudden fwell, in a direction contrary to that which had before prevailed, caufed our fhips to labour and ftrain exceedingly. During the ftorm, we had feveral of our fails fplit. They had, indeed, been bent for fo long a time, and were worn fo thin, that this accident had happened lately in both veffels almoft daily; particularly when the fails were ftiff, and heavy with rain, in which cafe, they became lefs capable of bearing the fhocks of the boifterous and variable winds we experienced occafionally. On Saturday, the 30th at noon, we obferved in lat. 36 deg. 41 min. long. 142 deg. 6 min. In the afternoon, the wind fhifting to the N. E. we ftood to the S. at the diftance of 18 leagues from the fhore. On the 31ft, at two o'clock, A. M. the wind veered round to the W. and blew in violent fqualls, accompanied with lightning and rain.

Monday, November the 1ft, the wind fhifted to the S. E. and was attended with fair weather; in confequence of which, we obtained, with four different quadrants, 42 fets of diftances of the moon, from the fun and ftars, each fet comprehending fix obfervations. Thefe nearly coinciding with each other, we determined, at noon, by obfervation, our
lat,

lat. to be 35 deg. 17 min. and our long. with great accuracy, to be 141 deg. 32 min. At two o'clock, we again made land towards the W. distant 13 leagues. A hummock to the northward, which had an insular appearance, bore N. N. W. half W. We steered for the land till between five and six, when we hauled our wind to the S. At this time we descried to the westward a mountain of extraordinary height, with a round summit rising far inland. In its neighbourhood the coast is of a moderate elevation; but, to the S. of the hummock island, there appeared, at a considerable distance up the country, a ridge of hills, extending towards the mountain, and which might perhaps join it. As the weather, in the morning of the 2nd, had a very threatening appearance, and the wind was at S. S. E. we thought it adviseable to quit the neighbourhood of the shore, and stand off towards the E. that the ships might not be entangled with the land. We were not deceived in our prognostications; for not long afterwards, a heavy gale began to blow, which continued till the next day, and was attended with rainy and hazy weather. On Wednesday the 3d, in the morning, we found ourselves by our reckoning, upwards of 50 leagues from the coast; which circumstance, united to the consideration of the very uncommon effect of currents we had already experienced, the advanced period of the year, the variable and uncertain state of the weather, and the small prospect we had of any alteration for the better, induced Captain Gore to form the resolution of leaving Japan, and prosecuting our voyage to China: to which facts may be added, that the coast of Japan, according to Kæmpfer's description of it, is the most dangerous in all the known world; that it would have been exceedingly hazardous, in case of distress, to have run into any of the harbours of that country; where, if we may credit the most authentic writers, the aversion of the natives to a communication with strangers, has prompted them to the commiffion of the moft flagrant acts of barbarity; that our veffels were in a leaky condition; that the rigging was fo rotten as to require continual repairs; and that the fails were almoft entirely worn out, and incapable of withftanding the vehemence of a gale of wind. As the violent currents, which fet along the eaftern coaft of Japan, may perhaps be attended with dangerous confequences to thofe navigators, who are not acquainted with their extreme rapidity, we will here fubjoin a fummary account of their direction and force, as remarked by us from the 1ft to the 8th of November. On the 1ft, at the time when we were about 18 leagues to the E. of White Point, the current fet at the rate of 3 miles in an hour, to the N. E. and by N. On the 2nd, as we made a nearer approach to the fhore, we obferved, that it continued in a fimilar direction, but was augmented in its rapidity to five miles an hour. As we receded from the coaft, it again became more moderate, and inclined towards the E. On the 3d, at the diftance of 60 leagues from the fhore, it fet, at the rate of three miles an hour, to the E. N. E. On the two following days, it turned to the fouthward, and, at 120 leagues from the coaft, its direction was S. E. and its rate did not exceed one mile and a half an hour. It again, on the 6th, and 7th, fhifted to the N. E. and its force diminifhed gradually till the 8th, at which time we could not perceive any current.

During the 4th and 5th of November, we proceeded to the fouth-eaftward, with very unfettled weather, having much lightening and rain. On Saturday, the 6th, we changed our courfe to the S. S. W. but about eight o'clock, in the evening, we were obliged to ftand towards the S. E. On the 9th, at noon, we obferved in lat. 31 deg. 46 min. long. 146 deg. 20 min. Friday, the 12th, a moft violent gale arofe, which reduced us to the mizen-ftay-fail and fore-fail. At noon, we were in lat. 27 deg. 36 min. and in long. 144 deg. 25 min.

On

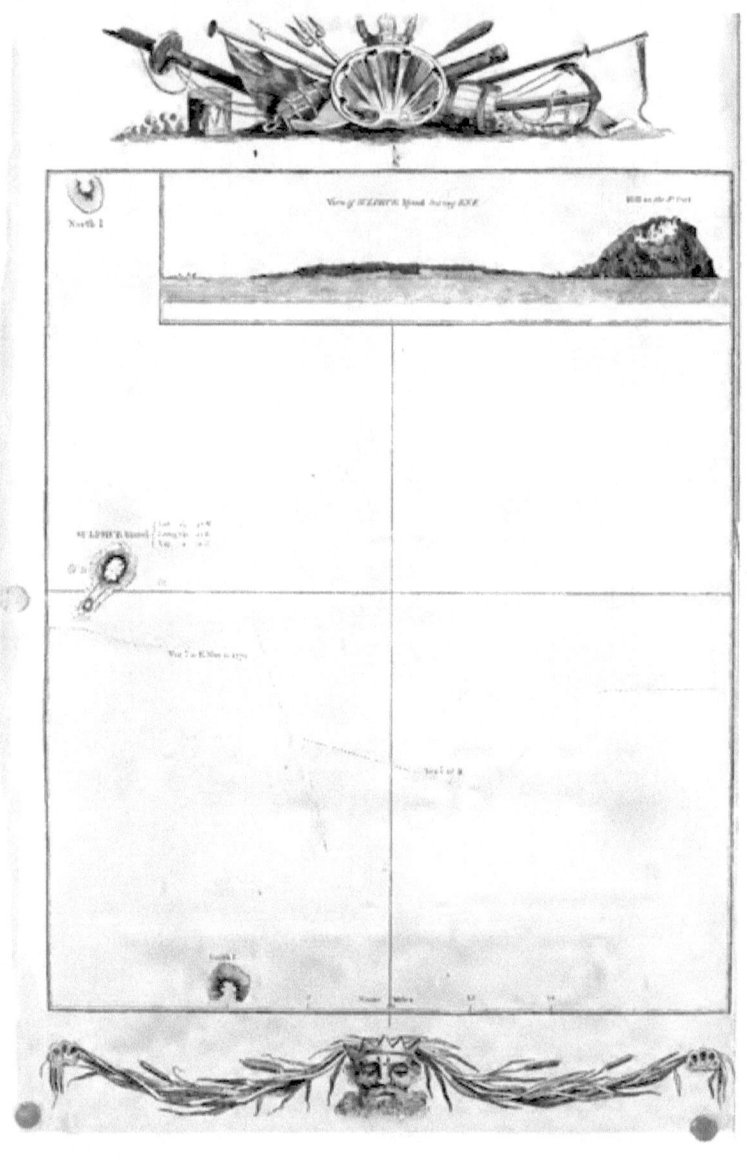

On the 13th, we were nearly in the same situation attributed to the island of St. Juan, yet we saw not the least appearance of land. At six o'clock, P. M. we steered to W. S. W. Captain Gore thinking it useless to stand any longer to the S. S. W. as we were nearly in the same meridian with the Ladrones, or Marianne Islands, and at no very considerable distance from the track of the Manilla galleons. On Monday, the 15th, we saw three islands, and bore away for the S. point of the largest, upon which we observed a high barren hill, flattish at the top and when seen from the W. S. W. presents an evident volcanic crater. The earth, rock, or sand, for it was not easy to distinguish of which its surface is composed, exhibited various colours, and a considerable part we conjectured to be sulphur, both from its appearance to the eye, and the strong sulphureous smell perceived by us in our approach to the point. The Resolution having passed nearer the land, several of our officers thought they discerned steams proceeding from the top of the hill. These circumstances induced the commodore to bestow on this discovery, the name of Sulphur Island. On Friday, the 26th, at six o'clock, A. M. the wind having considerably abated, we set our top-sails, let out the reefs, and bore away to the westward. At noon, we observed in lat. 21 deg. 12 min. long. 120 deg. 25 min. In the course of this day, we saw many tropic birds, and a flock of ducks; also porpoises and dolphins; and continued to pass many pumice-stones. We spent the night on our tacks; and on the 27th, at six o'clock, A. M. we again made sail to the W. in search of the Bashee Isles. On the 28th, at four o'clock, A. M. we had sight of the island of Prata. At noon, our lat. was 20 deg. 39 min. long. 116 deg. 45 min. The extent of the Prata shoal is considerable; for it is about six leagues from N. to S. and extends four leagues to the E. of the island: its limits to the westward, we had not an opportunity of ascertaining. We carried

carried a press of sail during the remainder of the day, and kept the wind, which now blew from the N. E. by N. in order to secure our passage to Macao.

On Monday, the 29th, in the morning, we passed some Chinese fishing-boats, the crews of which eyed us with marks of great indifference. At noon, our lat. by observation, was 22 deg. 1 min. and, since the preceding noon, we had run 110 miles upon a N. W. course. On the 30th, in the morning, we ran along the Lema Isles, which, like the other islands situated on this coast, are destitute of wood, and, as far as we had an opportunity of observing, devoid of cultivation. We now fired a gun, and displayed our colours, as a signal for a pilot. On the repetition of the signal, there was an excellent race between four Chinese boats; and Captain Gore engaged with the person who arrived first, to conduct the ship to the Typa, for the sum of 30 dollars, sending word, at the same time, to Captain King, that as he could easily follow with the Discovery, that expence might be saved to him. In a short time afterwards a second pilot got on board, and immediately laying hold of the wheel, began to order the sails to be trimmed. This gave rise to a violent altercation, which was at length compromised, by agreeing to divide the money between them. In obedience to the instructions from the Lords of the Admiralty, it now became necessary to demand of the officers and men, belonging to both ships, their journals, and what other papers they might have in their possession, relative to the history of the voyage. At the same time Captain King gave the Discovery's people to understand, that whatever papers they wished should not be sent to the Lords of the Admiralty, he would seal up their presence, and preserve in his custody till the intentions of their Lordships, respecting the publication of the history of the voyage, were accomplished, after which, he said they should be faithfully restored to them. The captain observes upon

this

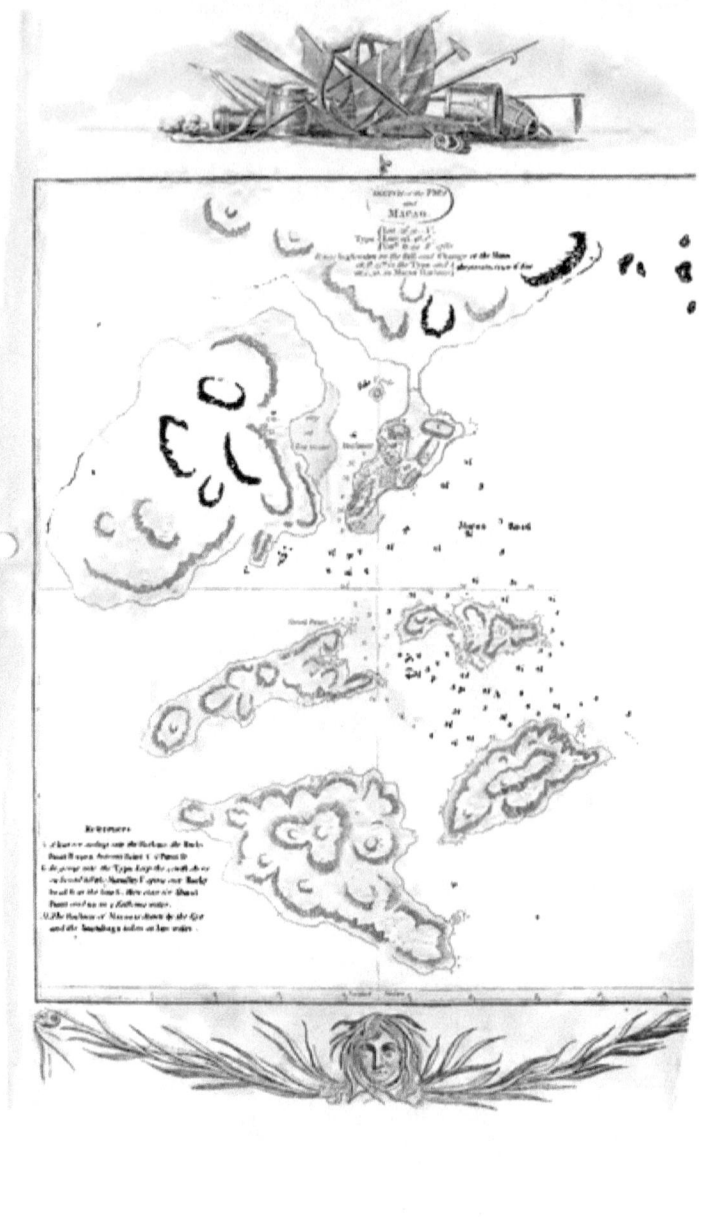

this occasion, that it is but doing justice to his company to declare, that as to the crew, they were the best disposed, and the most obedient men he ever knew, though the greatest part of them were very young, and had never served before in a ship of war. The same proposals were made to the people of the Resolution, and instantly complied with.

We continued working to windward, by the direction of our pilot, till about six o'clock, P. M. when we let go our anchors, he being of opinion, that the tide was now setting against us. During the afternoon, we stood on our tacks, between the Grand Ladrone and the island of Potoe, having passed to the east of the latter. At nine o'clock we again cast anchor in six fathoms water; the town of Macao being at the distance of nine or ten miles, in a N. W. direction; and the island of Potoe bearing S. half W. seven miles distant.

On the 2d of December, in the morning, one of the Chinese contractors, called compradors, came on board, and sold us as much beef as weighed 200 weight, together with a considerable quantity of greens, oranges, and eggs. In the evening Captain Gore sent Mr. King on shore to visit the Portuguese Governor, and to request his assistance in procuring refreshments, which he thought might be done on more reasonable terms than the comprador would undertake to furnish them; with whom we had agreed for a daily supply; for which, however, he insisted on our paying him before-hand. Upon Mr. King's arrival at the citadel, the Fort-Major informed him that the governor was sick, and not able to see company. Having acquainted the Major with his desire of proceeding immediately to Canton, the former told him, that they could not presume to provide a boat, till permission had been obtained from the Hoppo, or officer of the customs; and that it was necessary to apply, for this purpose, to the Chinese government at Canton. When the captain was returning, the Portuguese officer asked him,

him, if he did not mean to visit the English gentlemen at Macao? This question gave him inexpressible pleasure. He proceeded immediately to the house of one of his countrymen; from whom he received information of the French war, and of the continuance of the American war; and that five sail of English ships were now at Wampu, near Canton, in China. The intelligence we had gained concerning the state of affairs in Europe, rendered us the more anxious to accelerate our departure as much as we possibly could. The first thing that claimed the attention of the commodore, was to provide as well as he could for the general safety of the people under his command, on their return home. The news of a French war, without letting us know the order issued by the King of France in our favour, gave us much concern. Our ships were ill fitted for war: the decks, fore and aft, being finished flush, had no covering for men or officers; it was therefore thought necessary to raise a kind of parapet, musquet proof, on both decks; and likewise to strengthen the cabins as much as possible in case of action. On Thursday, the 9th, we received an answer from the English supercargoes at Canton, in which they promised to exert their most strenuous endeavours in procuring the supplies of which we were in want, with all possible dispatch; and that a passport should be sent for one of our officers. Friday, the 10th, an English merchant, from one of our East-Indian settlements, made application to Captain Gore for the assistance of a few of his people, to navigate as far as Canton a vessel which he had purchased at Macao. The commodore considering this as a good opportunity for Captain King to repair to that city, gave orders, that he should take with him his second lieutenant, the lieutenant of the marines, and 10 sailors. Accordingly, they quitted the harbour of Macao, on Saturday, the 11th; and as they approached the Bocca Tygris, which is near 40 miles distant from Macao, the

coast

coast of China appeared to the eastward in white steep cliffs. Their progress being retarded by contrary winds, and the lightness of the vessel, they did not arrive at Wampu, which is only nine leagues from the Bocca Tygris, till Saturday, the 18th. Wampu is a small town, off which the ships of various nations, who trade with the Chinese, are stationed, in order to receive their respective ladings. At Wampu, Captain King embarked in a Sampane, or Chinese boat, the most convenient for passengers that we ever saw; and in the evening we reached Canton, and disembarked at the English factory, where the captain was received with every mark of civility and respect. Messrs. Fitzhugh, Bevan, and Rapier, composed, at this time, the Select Committee; and the former of these gentlemen acted as president. They immediately gave the captain an inventory of those stores with which the East-India ships were able to supply us, and he had the pleasure to find, that they were ready to be shipped, and that the provisions we might have occasion for might be had at a day's notice. Being desirous of making our stay here as short as possible, the captain requested, that the gentlemen would endeavour to procure junks for us the next day; but we were soon convinced by them, that patience is an indispensible virtue in China. After the captain had waited several days for the issue of his negociation with the Chinese, and was considering what steps he should take, the commander of a country ship presented him with a letter from Captain Gore, whereby he was informed of that commander being engaged to bring our party from Canton, and to deliver our supplies, at his own hazard, in the Typa. All difficulties being thus removed, Captain King had leisure to bestow some attention on the purchase of our stores and provisions, which he completed on Sunday, the 26th, and, on the following day, the whole stock was conveyed on board. As Canton was likely to be the most advantageous market for furs, the commodore had desired Captain King to take with him about 20 skins of sea-otters; most of which had been the property of our deceased commanders; and to dispose of them at the best price he could obtain. The English supercargoes being informed of these circumstances, they directed him to a member of the Hong (a society of the principal merchants of the city) who being fully apprised of the nature of the business, seemed to be sensible of the delicacy of the captain's situation, and therefore assured him, that, in an affair of this kind, he should consider himself as a mere agent, without seeking any profit for himself. The skins being laid before this merchant, he examined them over and over again with particular attention; and at last informed Captain King, that he could not think of offering more than 300 dollars for them. As the captain knew he had not offered one half of their value, he, therefore, in his turn, demanded 1000 dollars; the Chinese merchant then advanced to five, and, at length to 700 dollars; upon which the captain lowered his demands to 900. Here, each of them declaring that he would not recede, they parted; but the Chinese speedily returned, and proposed finally, that they should divide the difference, which the captain agreed to, and received 800 dollars. The subsequent remarks, relative to Canton, were collected by Captain King, from the intelligence which he received from several English gentlemen, who had resided a long time near that city.

Canton, containing the old and new town, with the suburbs, is about 10 miles in circumference. The number of its inhabitants, as near as can be computed, may be from 100 to 150,000. Exclusive of whom there are 40,000 who reside constantly in Borges, called Sampares, or floating-houses upon the river. They are moored in rows close to each other,

other, with a narrow passage, at intervals, for the boats to pass up and down the river.

The streets of this city are long, narrow, and destitute of uniformity. They are well paved with large stones, and, in general, kept extremely clean. The houses are built of brick, and are only one story high. They have, for the most part, two or three courts backwards, in which are erected the warehouses for the reception of merchandize; and, in the houses within the city, are the apartments for the females. Some of the meaner sort of people, though very few, have their habitations composed of wood.

Those that belong to the European factors, are built on a fine quay, having a regular facade of two stories towards the river. They are constructed, with respect to the inside, partly after the Chinese, and partly after the European mode. Adjoining to them are a considerable number of houses which belong to the Chinese; and are let out by them to the commanders of vessels, and to merchants, who make only an occasional stay. As no European is permitted to take his wife with him to Canton, the English supercargoes live together at one common table, which is maintained by the Company, and each of them has also an apartment appropriated to himself, consisting of three or four rooms. The period of their residence rarely exceeds eight months in a year; and as, during that time, they are almost constantly employed in the service of the Company, they may submit, with the less uneasiness, to the restrictions under which they live. They seldom make any visits within the walls of Canton, except on public occasions. Nothing contributed more to give Captain King an unfavourable opinion of the Chinese, than his finding that several of them who had resided in that country for near 15 successive years, had never formed any social connection or friendship. When the last ship departs from Wampu, they are all under the necessity of

retiring

retiring to Macao; but they leave behind them all the money they possess in specie, which, Mr. King was informed, sometimes amounts to 100,000l. sterling, and for which they have no other security than the seals of the Viceroy, the Mandarines, and the merchants of the Hong: a striking proof of the excellent police maintained in China.

During our continuance at Canton, Mr. King accompanied one of the English gentlemen on a visit to a person of the first distinction in the place. They were received in a long room or gallery, at the further end of which a table was placed, with a large chair behind it, and a row of chairs extending from it, on both sides, down the room. The captain having been previously instructed, that the point of politeness consisted in remaining unseated as long as possible, readily submitted to this piece of etiquette; after which he and his friend were treated with tea, and some fresh and preserved fruits. Their entertainer was very corpulent, had a dull heavy countenance, and displayed great gravity in his deportment. He had learned to speak a little broken English and Portugueze. After his two guests had taken their refreshment, he conducted them about his house and garden; and when he had shewn them all the improvements he was making, they took their leave.

The captain being desirous of avoiding the trouble and delay that might attend an application for passports, as well as of saving the unnecessary expence of hiring a sampane, which he was informed amounted at least to 12 pounds sterling, had hitherto designed to go along with the supplies to Macao, in the country merchant's ship we mentioned before: but receiving an invitation from two English gentlemen, who had found means to procure passports for four, he accepted, together with Mr. Phillips, their offer of places in a Chinese boat, and intrusted Mr. Lannyon with the superintendance of the men and stores, which were to sail the following day.

On

On Sunday, the 26th, in the evening, Captain King took his leave of the supercargoes, after having returned them thanks for their many favours; among which must be mentioned a present of a considerable quantity of tea, for the use of the companies of both ships, and a copious collection of English periodical publications. The latter proved a valuable acquisition to us, as they not only served to beguile our impatience, in the prosecution of our tedious voyage homewards, but also enabled us to return not wholly unacquainted with what had been transacting in our native country during our absence. On the 27th, at one o'clock in the morning, Messrs. King and Phillips, and the two English gentlemen, quitted Canton, and, about the same hour of the succeeding day, arrived at Macao, having passed down a channel situated to the west of that by which we had come up.

In the absence of our party from Macao, a brisk traffic had been carrying on with the Chinese for our sea-otter-skins, the value of which had augmented every day. One of our sailors disposed of his stock, alone, for 800 dollars; and a few of the best skins, which were clean, and had been carefully preserved, produced 120 dollars each. The total amount of the value, in goods and cash, that was obtained for the furs of both our vessels, we are confident was not less than 2,000l. sterling; and it was the general opinion, that at least two-thirds of the quantity we had originally procured from the Americans, were by this time spoiled and worn out, or had been bestowed as presents, and otherwise disposed of in Kamtschatka. If, in addition to these facts, we consider, that we at first collected the furs without having just ideas of their real value; that most of them had been worn by the savages from whom we purchased them; that little regard was afterwards shewn to their preservation; that they were frequently made use of as bed-clothes, and likewise for other purposes, during our cruise to the northward;

ward; and that, in all probability, we never received the full value for them in China; the benefits that might accrue from a voyage to that part of the American coast where we obtained them, undertaken with commercial views, will certainly appear of sufficient importance to claim the public attention. So great was the rage which our seamen were possessed to return to Cook's River, and there procure another cargo of skins, by which they might be enabled to make their fortunes, that, at one time, they were almost on the point of proceeding to a mutiny. And Captain King acknowledges, that he could not refrain from indulging himself in a project, which was first suggested to him by the disappointment we had met with in being compelled to leave the Japanese Archipelago, as well as the northern coast of China, unexplored; and he is of opinion, that this object may still be happily attained, by means of our East-India Company, not only with trifling expence, but even with the prospect of very beneficial consequences. The state of affairs at home, or perhaps greater difficulties in the accomplishment of his plan than he had foreseen, have hitherto prevented its being carried into execution; but, as the scheme seems to be well contrived, the reader will not be displeased with our inserting it here.

In the first place, Captain King proposes, that the East-India Company's China ships should, each, carry an additional number of men, making 100 in the whole. Two vessels, one of 200 tons, and the other of 150, might with proper notice, (as Mr. King was informed) be purchased at Canton; and, as victualling is as cheap there as in Europe, he has calculated that they might be completely equipped for sea, with one year's provisions and pay, for the sum of 6,000l. including the purchase. The expence of the requisite articles for barter is very inconsiderable.

Captain King particularly recommends that each
of

of the ships should have a forge, five tons of unwrought iron, and a skilful smith, with an apprentice and journeyman, who might occasionally make such tools, as the Indians should appear to have the greatest inclination for possessing. For, though half a dozen of the finest skins, obtained by us, were purchased with twelve large green glass beads, yet it is very certain, that the fancy of these people, for ornamental articles, is extremely capricious and variable; and that the only sure commodity for their market is iron. To this might be added several bales of coarse woollen cloth, two or three barrels of glass and copper trinkets, and a few gross of large pointed case-knives. He then proposes, that two vessels, not only for the greater security of the voyage, but because single ships ought never, in his opinion, to be sent out for the purpose of discovery. For where risques are frequently to be run, and uncertain and dangerous experiments tried, it can by no means be expected that single ships should venture so far, as where some security is provided against an unfortunate accident. When the ships are prepared for sea, they will sail with the first S. W. monsoon, which usually sets in about the commencement of the month of April. They will steer a northward course, with this wind, along the Chinese coast, beginning to make a more accurate survey from the mouth of the Nankin river, or the river Kyana, in the 30th degree of latitude, which is supposed to be the remotest limit of this coast hitherto visited by European vessels. The extent of the great gulph called Whang Hay, or the Yellow Sea, being at present unknown, it may be left to the commander's discretion, to proceed up it as far as he may think proper: he must be cautious, however, not to entangle himself in it too far, lest he should not have sufficient time left for the prosecution of the remainder of his voyage. The same discretion may be used, when he has reached the straits of Tessoi, with regard to the islands of

Jeso,

Jeso, which, if the wind and weather should be favourable, he must not neglect to explore. Having arrived in the latitude of 51 deg. 40 min. where he will make the most southerly point of the Isle of Sagaleen, beyond which we have a considerable knowledge of the sea of Okotsk, he will steer towards the S. probably about the beginning of June, and exert his endeavours to fall in with the most southern of the Kurile Islands. If the accounts of the Russians may be depended on, Ooroop, or Nadeschda, will furnish the ships with a commodious harbour, where they may recruit their wood and water, and provide themselves with such refreshments as the place may afford. Near the end of June the commander will direct his course to the Shummagins, whence he will proceed to Cook's River, purchasing, in his progress, as many skins as possible, without losing too much time, since he ought to sail again to the southward, and trace the coast with the utmost accuracy between the 56th and 50th degrees of latitude, the space where contrary winds drove us out of sight of land. We think it proper to observe here, that Captain King considers the purchase of skins, in this expedition, as a secondary concern, for defraying the expence; and, from our experience in the present voyage, there is no reason to doubt that 250 skins, each worth 100 dollars, may be obtained without loss of time; particularly as they will, in all probability, be met with along the coast of the S. of Cook's River.

The commander of this expedition, after having continued about three months on the American coast, will set out on his return to China in the former part of October, taking care, in his route, to avoid, as much as possible the tracks of preceding navigators. All that remains to be added on this subject, is, that if the fur trade should become an established object of Indian commerce, many opportunities will occur of completing whatever
may

may have been left unfinished, in the voyage of which the outlines are here delineated.

During our absence, a very ludicrous alteration took place in the dress of all our crew, in consequence of the barter which the Chinese had carried on with us for our sea-otter skins. On our arrival in the Typa, not only the sailors, but likewise the younger officers, were extremely ragged in their apparel; for, as the voyage had now exceeded, almost by a year, the time it was at first supposed we should continue at sea, the far greater part of our original stock of European clothes had been long ago worn out, or repaired and patched up with skins, and the different manufactures we had met with in the course of the expedition. These were now mixed and eked out with the gayest silks and cottons that China could produce.

On the 30th, being Friday, Mr. Lannyon arrived with the stores and provisions, which, without delay, were stowed in due proportion on board both the ships. While in the Typa, Captain King was shewn, in the garden of an English gentleman, at Macao, the rock, under which, according to traditional accounts, Camoens, the celebrated Portuguese poet, was accustomed to sit and compose his Lusiad. It is an arch of considerable height consisting of one solid stone, and forming the entrance of a grotto dug out of the elevated ground behind it. Large spreading trees overshadow the rock, which commands a beautiful and extensive prospect of the sea, and the islands dispersed about it. During our continuance in the Typa, we heard nothing with respect to the measurement of the ships; we may therefore reasonably conclude, that the point so strongly contested, in Commodore Anson's time, by the Chinese, has, in consequence of his firmness and resolution, never since been insisted on. By the observations made while our vessels lay here, the harbour of Macao is situated in the lat. of 22 deg.

deg. 12 min. N. and the long. of 113 deg. 47 min. E. our anchoring place, in the Typa, in lat. 22 deg. 9 min. 20 sec. long. 113 deg. 48 min. 34 sec. E. It was high water in the Typa, on the full and change days, at a quarter after five o'clock; and in the harbour of Macao, at 50 minutes past five: the greatest rise was six feet one inch. We shall conclude these remarks, and this chapter, with the prices of labour, and a few articles of provisions in China.

PRICES of LABOUR and PROVISIONS at CANTON.

	£.	S.	D.	
A Coolee, or Porter, - -	0	0	8	Per Day
A Taylor. - - - - - - -	0	0	5	and rice
A Handicraftsman - - - -	0	0	8	ditto

A common Labourer from 3d. to 5d. per day.
A Woman's labour considerably cheaper.

	£.	S.	D.	
Butter - - - - - - - - -	0	2	4 4/5	Per Catty
Beef - - - - - - - - - -	0	0	2 1/4	or 18 oz.
Calf - - - - - - - - - - -	1	6	9 1/5	each
Ducks - - - - - - - - - -	0	0	5 1/2	Per Catty
Ditto, wild - - - - - - -	0	1	0 4/5	each
Eggs - - - - - - - - - -	0	2	0	Per 100
Frogs - - - - - - - - - -	0	0	6 2/5	Per Catty
Fowls, Capons, &c. - - - -	0	0	7 2/5	ditto
Geese - - - - - - - - - -	0	0	6 2/5	ditto
Ham - - - - - - - - - -	0	1	2 3/5	ditto
Hog, alive - - - - - - - -	0	0	4 1/4	ditto
Kid, ditto - - - - - - - -	0	0	4 1/4	ditto
Milk - - - - - - - - - -	0	0	1 1/4	ditto
Pork - - - - - - - - - -	0	0	7 1/5	ditto
Pig - - - - - - - - - - -	0	0	5 3/5	ditto
Pheasants - - - - - - - -	0	5	4	each
Partridges - - - - - - - -	0	0	9 3/5	ditto
Pigeons - - - - - - - - -	0	0	5 1/5	ditto
Rabbits - - - - - - - - -	0	1	4	ditto
Sheep - - - - - - - - - -	3	6	8	ditto

Spices

Spices	0 16	8	Per Catty
Soy	0 0	1¼	ditto
Samfui ditto	0 0	2¼	ditto
Turtle	0 0	9¾	ditto

CHAP. XXI.

A. D. 1780. ON Tuesday, the 11th of January, two sailors, John Cave quartermaster, and Robert Spencer belonging to the Resolution, went off with a six-oared cutter; and though the most diligent search was made, both this and the following morning, we could not gain any intelligence of them. It was imagined, that these seamen had been seduced by the hopes of acquiring a fortune, if they should return to the fur islands. On the 12th, at noon, we unmoored, and scaled the guns, which, on board the Discovery, amounted at this time to ten; so that her people by means of four additional ports, could fight seven on a side. In the Resolution likewise, the number of guns had been augmented from 12 to 16; and, in each of the ships, all other precautions were taken to give our inconsiderable force a respectable appearance. We considered it as our duty to furnish ourselves with these means of defence, though there was some reason to believe, that they had in a great measure been rendered superfluous by the generosity of our enemies; for we were informed, by the public prints, which Captain King had brought with him from Canton, of instructions having been found on board all the French ships of war, that had been taken in Europe, importing, that their commanders, if they should happen to fall in with the Resolution and Discovery, were to suffer them to proceed unmolested on their voyage. It was also reported, that the American Congress had given similar orders to the vessels employed in their service. This intelligence being further confirmed by the private letters of some of the super-cargoes, Captain King deemed it incumbent on him, in return for the liberal exceptions which our enemies had made in our favour, to refrain from embracing any opportunities of capture, and to maintain the strictest neutrality during the whole of our voyage. Having got under sail about two o'clock, P. M. we passed the fort of Macao, and saluted the garrison with eleven four-pounders, which they answered with an equal number. We were under the necessity of warping out into the entrance of the Typa, which we gained by eight o'clock in the evening of the 13th; and lay there till nine o'clock the following morning, when we stood, with a fresh easterly breeze, to the S. between Wungboo and Potoe. At four in the afternoon, the Ladrone was about two leagues distant in an eastern direction. On Saturday, the 15th, at noon, we observed in lat. 18 deg. 57 min. long. 114 deg. 13 min. On the 16th, we struck soundings over Macclesfield Bank, and found the depth of water to be 50 fathoms, over a bottom consisting of white sand and shells. We computed this part of the bank to be situated in lat. 15 deg. 51 min. and in long. 114 deg. 20 min. Thursday, the 19th, at four o'clock, P. M. we had in view Pulo Sapatra, bearing N. W. by W. and distant about four leagues. Having passed this island, we stood to the westward; and on the 20th made the little group of islands known by the name of Pulo Condore, at one of which we anchored in six fathoms water. The harbour where we now moored, has its entrance from the N. W. and affords the best shelter during the N. E. monsoon. Its entrance bore W. N. W. quarter W. and N. by W. the opening at the upper end bore S. E. by E. three quarters E. and we were about two furlongs distant from the shore. On the 21st, early in the morning, parties were sent out to cut wood,

wood, the commodore's principal motive for touching at this island being to supply the ships with that article. None of the natives having as yet made their appearance, notwithstanding two guns had been fired at different times, Captain Gore thought it adviseable to land, and go in search of them. Accordingly, on Sunday, the 22nd, he desired Captain King to attend him. They proceeded in their boats along shore for the space of two miles, when perceiving a road that led into a wood, they landed. Here Captain King left the commodore, and, attended by a midshipman, and four armed sailors, pursued the path, which appeared to point directly across the island. They proceeded through a thick wood up a steep hill, to the distance of a mile, when after descending, they arrived at some huts. Captain King ordered the party to stay without, lest the sight of armed men should terrify the inhabitants, while he entered and reconnoitred alone. He found, in one of the huts, an elderly man, who was in a great fright, and preparing to make off with the most valuable effects. However a few signs, particularly that most significant one of holding out a handful of dollars, and then pointing to a herd of buffaloes, and the fowls that were running about the huts in great numbers, left him without any doubts as to the objects of their visit. He pointed towards a place where the town stood, and made them comprehend, that by going thither, all their wants would be supplied. On their first coming out of the wood, a herd of buffaloes, to the number of 20 at least, came running towards them, tossing up their heads, snuffing the air, and roaring in a hideous manner. They had followed them to the huts, and now stood drawn up in a body, at a little distance; and the old man made them understand, that it would be exceeding dangerous to move, till they were driven into the woods; but so enraged were the animals grown, at the sight of them,

them, that this was not effected without a good deal of time and difficulty. The men not being able to accomplish it, they called to their assistance a few little boys, who soon drove them out of sight. Afterward they had an opportunity of observing, that in driving these animals, and securing them, which is done by putting a rope through a hole made in their nostrils, little boys were always employed, who could stroke and handle them with impunity at times, when the men durst not approach them. Having got rid of the buffaloes, they were conducted to the town, which consists of between 20 and 30 houses, built close together; besides 6 or 7 others that are scattered about the beach. The roof, the two ends, and the side fronting the country, are neatly constructed of reeds; the opposite side, facing the sea, is entirely open; but, by means of a kind of bamboo screens, they can exclude or let in as much of the sun and air as they please. They were conducted to the largest house, where the chief, or captain, as they called him, resided, but he was absent, or would not be seen; therefore no purchases could, as they said, be made. At two o'clock, in the afternoon, they returned to the ships; as did likewise several of our shooting parties from the woods, about the same time. At five o'clock, six men in a proa, rowed up to the ships, from the upper-end of the harbour; and one of them, who was a person of decent appearance, introduced himself to Captain Gore, with an ease and politeness which indicated that he had been accustomed to pass his time in other company than what Condore afforded. He brought with him a sort of certificate, written in the French language, of which the following is a translation.

"Peter George, Bishop of Adran, Apostolic Vicar of Cochin-China, &c. The little Mandarin, who is the bearer hereof, is the real Envoy of the Court to Pulo Condore, to attend there for the reception of all European vessels, whose destination is to approach that place, &c.

"A Sai-Gon, 10 August, 1779."

He gave us to understand, that he was the Mandarin mentioned in it; and produced another paper, which was a letter sealed up, and addressed to the captains of any European ships that may touch at Condore. From this letter, and the whole of Luco's conversation, the Mandarin, we had little doubt, that the vessel he expected was a French one. We found, at the same time, that he was desirous of not losing his errand, and was not unwilling to become our pilot. We could not discover from him the precise business which the ship he was waiting for designed to prosecute in Cochin-China. We shall only add, that he acquainted us, that the French vessels might perhaps have touched at Tirnon, and from thence sail to Cochin-China; and as no intelligence had been received, he imagined that this was most likely to have been the case. Captain Gore afterwards enquired, what supplies could be procured from this island. Luco replied, he had two buffaloes belonging to him, which were at our service, and that considerable numbers of those animals might be purchased for four or five dollars each. We had purchased eight of these animals; and on the 23d, early in the morning, the launches of both ships were dispatched to the town to bring them away, but our people were much at a loss to bring them on board. After consulting with the Mandarin, it was determined, that they should be driven through the wood, and over the hill, down to the bay, where our two captains had landed. This plan was accordingly executed; but the untractableness, and amazing strength of the animals, rendered it a slow and difficult operation. The mode of conducting them was, by putting ropes through their nostrils, and round their horns; but when they were once enraged at the sight of our people,

they

they became so furious, that they sometimes tore asunder the cartilage of the nostril, through which the ropes passed, and set themselves at liberty; at other times they broke the trees, to which it was found necessary to fasten them. On such occasions, all the endeavours of our men, for the recovery of them, would have been unsuccessful, without the aid of some little boys, whom the buffaloes would suffer to approach, and by whose puerile managements their rage was quickly appeased; and when brought down to the beach, it was by their assistance, in twisting ropes about their legs, in the manner they were directed, that our people were enabled to throw them down, and, by that means, to get them into the boats; and, a circumstance very singular, they had not been a whole day on board, before they were as tame as possible. Captain King kept a male and a female for a considerable time, which became great favourites with the seamen. Thinking a breed of these animals, some of which weighed, when dressed, 700 pounds, would be an acquisition of some value, he intended to have brought them with him to England; but that design was frustrated by an incurable hurt which one of them received at sea. Besides the buffaloes, of which there are several large herds in this island, we purchased from the natives some remarkably fine fat hogs, of the Chinese breed. We procured three or four of the wild sort; several of whose tracks were seen in the woods; which also abound with monkeys and squirrels, but so shy, that it was difficult to shoot them. Here we found the cabbage-tree, and other succulent greens, with which our people made very free without asking questions. Two wells of excellent water had been discovered, in consequence of which part of the companies of both ships had been employed in providing a competent supply of it. Our numerous subscribers will be pleased to recollect, that in our history of Captain Cook's

Cook's first and second voyages, we have given a concise, though comprehensive account of Pulo Condore, Celebes, Sumatra, Java, the Philippine, Ladrones, and, in short, all the principal islands in the Indian Sea; it therefore only now remains, during the remainder of our passage home, with a view of establishing the credit and reputation of this work, and of rendering it the most complete undertaking of the kind extant, to mention a few particulars that came under our own observation, and which may be reckoned as improvements since the labours of former compilers, or the expeditions of prior navigators.

Pulo Condore signifies the Island of Calabashes, its name being derived from two Malay words, Pulo, implying an island, and Condore, a Calabash, great quantities of which fruit are produced here. Among the vegetable improvements of this island, may be reckoned the fields of rice that we observed; also cocoa-nuts, pomegranates, oranges, shaddocks, and various sorts of pompions. We continued at this harbour till the 28th, when the little Mandarin took leave of us; at which time the commodore gave him, at his request, a letter of recommendation to the commanders of any other vessels that might put in here. He also bestowed on him a handsome present, and gave him a letter for the bishop of Adrian, together with a telescope, which he desired might be presented to him as a compliment for the favours we had received, through his means, at Pulo Condore. The latitude of the harbour is 8 deg. 40 min. N. and its longitude, deduced from many lunar observations, 106 deg. 18 min. 46 sec. E. At full and change of the moon it was high water at 4 h. 15 m. apparent time; after which the water continued for 12 hours, without any perceptible alteration. The transition from ebbing to flowing was very quick, being in less than five

five minutes. The water rose and fell seven feet four inches perpendicular.

On Friday, the 28th, we unmoored, and cleared the harbour. On the 30th, at one o'clock, P. M. we had sight of Pulo Timoan, and at five, Pulo Puiflang was seen in the direction of S. by E. three quarters E. At nine o'clock, we had, from the effect of some current, out-run our reckoning, and found ourselves close upon Pulo Aor, in the lat. of 2 deg. 46 min. N. long. 104 deg. 37 min. E. in consequence of which we hauled the wind to the E. S. E. This course we prosecuted till midnight, and then steered S. S. E. for the straits of Banca.

On Tuesday, the 1st of February, we observed in lat. 1 deg. 20 min. N. and our long. by a number of lunar observations, we found to be 105 deg. E. Towards sun-set, we had a view of Pulo Panjang; at which time our lat. was 53 min. N. On the 2d, we passed the Straits of Sunda; and, at noon, we came in sight of the small islands known by the name of Dominis, lying off the eastern part of Lingen. At one o'clock, P. M. Pulo Taya made its appearance in the direction of S. W. by W. distant 7 leagues. On the 3d, at day-break, we had sight of the three islands; and, not long afterwards, saw Monopin Hill, in the island of Banca. Having got to the W. of the shoal, named Frederic Endric, we entered the Straits of Banca, and bore away towards the S. On the 4th, in the morning, we proceeded down the straits with the tide; and, at noon, the tide beginning to make against us, we cast anchor, at the distance of about one league from what is denominated the Third Point, on the Sumatra shore; Monopin Hill bearing N. 54 deg. W. and our lat. being 2 deg. 22 min. S. long. 105 deg. 38 min. E. At three in the afternoon we weighed, and continued our course through the straits with a gentle breeze. In passing these straits, ships may make a nearer approach to the coast of Sumatra than to that

that of Banca. On Sunday, the 6th, in the morning, we passed to the W. of Lusepara; and at five o'clock, P. M. we descried the Sisters, in the direction of S. by W. half W. At seven we cast anchor three leagues to the northward of those islands. On the 7th, at five o'clock, A. M. we weighed, and in three hours afterwards we were in sight of the Sisters. These are two islands of very small extent, plentifully stocked with wood, and situated in 50 deg. S. lat. and in long. 106 deg. 12 min. They lie nearly N. and S. from each other, encompassed by a reef of coral rocks. At noon, we had sight of the Island of Java; and about four in the afternoon, we perceived two vessels in the Straits of Sunda; one of which lay at anchor near the mid-channel island, the other nearer the shore of Java. On the 8th, about eight o'clock in the morning, we weighed, and proceeded through the Straits of Sunda. On Wednesday the 9th, between ten and eleven, Captain King was ordered by the commodore to make sail towards a Dutch vessel, that now came in sight to the southward, which we imagined was from Europe; and, according to the nature of the information that might be obtained from her, either join him at Cracatoa, or to proceed to the south-eastern extremity of Prince's Island, and there provide a supply of water, and wait for him. In compliance with these instructions Captain King bore down towards the Dutchman; and on the 10th, in the morning, Mr. Williamson went on board her; where he was informed, that she had been seven months from Europe, and three from the Cape of Good Hope; that, before her departure, the kings of France and Spain had declared war against his Britannic Majesty; and that she had left Sir Edward Hughes at the Cape with a squadron of men of war, and also a fleet of East-India ships. On the return of Mr. Williamson, Captain King took the advantage of a fair breeze, and made sail towards the island of Cracatoa, where he soon after perceived the Resolution at anchor, and immediately dispatched a boat to communicate to Captain Gore the intelligence procured by Mr. Williamson. When we saw our consort preparing, at the distance of near two leagues, to come to, we fired our guns, and displayed the signal for leading a-head, by hoisting an English jack at the ensign staff. This was intended to prevent the Discovery's anchoring, on account of the foul ground, which the maps on board our ship placed in this situation. However, as Captain King met with none, but, on the contrary, found a muddy bottom, and good anchoring ground, at the depth of 60 fathoms, he remained fast till the return of the boat, which brought him orders to proceed to Prince's Island the ensuing morning.

Cracatoa is the southernmost of a cluster of islands lying in the entrance of the Straits of Sunda. It has a lofty peaked hill at its southern extremity, situated in lat. 6 deg. 9 min. S. and in long. 105 deg. 15 min. E. The whole circumference of the island does not exceed nine miles. The Island of Sambouricou, or Tamarin, which stands 12 miles to the northward of Cracatoa, may easily be mistaken for the latter, since it has a hill of nearly the same figure and dimensions, situate likewise near its south end. The lat. of the road where we cast anchor is 8 deg. 6 min. S. long. by observation, 105 deg. 36 min. E. It is high water on the full and change days, at seven o'clock in the morning; and the water rises three feet two inches perpendicular.

On Friday, the 11th, at three o'clock, A. M. the Discovery weighed anchor, and steered for Prince's Island; and, at noon, she came to, and moored off its eastern extremity. On Monday, the 14th, at day break, we descried our consort, and, at two o'clock, P. M. we anchored close by her. By the 16th, both ships started their casks, and had replenished

nished them with fresh water. In the evening the decks were cleared, and we prepared for sea. On Saturday, the 19th, being favoured with a westerly breeze, we broke ground, to our extreme satisfaction, for the last time in the Straits of Sunda; and on the 20th, we had totally lost sight of Prince's Island. If Mr. Lannyon had not been with us, we should probably have met with some difficulty in finding the watering place: it may, therefore, not be improper to give a particular description of its situation, for the benefit of subsequent navigators. The peaked hill on the island bears N. W. by N. from it. A remarkable tree, which grows on a coral reef, and is entirely detached from the adjacent shrubs, stands just to the north of it; and a small plot of reedy grass, may be seen close by it. These marks will indicate the place where the pool discharges itself into the sea; but the water here, as well as that which is in the pool, being in general salt, the casks must be filled about 50 yards higher up; where, in dry seasons, the fresh water which descends from the hills, is in great measure lost among the leaves, and must therefore be searched for by clearing them away. The lat. of the anchoring-place at Prince's Island, is 6 deg. 36 min. 15 sec. S. and its long. 105 deg. 17 min. 30 sec. E.

On Friday, the 25th, we were attacked with a violent storm, attended with thunder, lightning, and heavy rain. From the 26th to the 28th of March, we had a regular trade wind from the S. E. to E. by S. accompanied with fine weather; and as we sailed in an old beaten track, no incident worthy of notice occurred. It had hitherto been Captain Gore's intention to proceed directly to St. Helena, without stopping at the Cape, but our rudder having been for some time complaining, and on being examined, reported to be in a dangerous state, he resolved to steer directly for the Cape, as the most eligible place, both for the recovery of the sick, and for procuring a new main piece for the rudder.

Monday,

Monday, the 10th of April, a snow was seen bearing down, which proved to be an English East-India packet, that had left Table Bay three days before, and was cruizing with orders for the China fleet, and other India ships. She told us, that, about three weeks before, Monf. Trongollar's squadron, confisting of six ships, had failed from the Cape, and was gone to cruize off St. Helena, for the English East Indiamen. The next morning we stood into Simon's Bay. At eight o'clock we came to anchor, at the distance of one third of a mile from the nearest shore; the S. E. point of the bay bearing S. by E. and Table Mountain N. E. half N. The Nassau and Southampton East Indiamen were here, in expectation of a convoy from Europe. We saluted the fort with eleven guns, and were complimented with an equal number in return. As soon as we had cast anchor, Mr. Brandt, the governor of this place, favoured us with a visit. This gentleman had the highest regard for Captain Cook, who had been his constant guest, whenever he had touched at the Cape; and though he had, some time before, received intelligence of his untimely fate, he was extremely affected at the sight of our vessels returning without their old commander. He was greatly surprised at seeing most of our people in so healthy a state, as the Dutch ship which had quitted Macao, at the time of our arrival there, and had afterwards stopped at the Cape, reported, that we were in a most wretched condition, there being only 15 hands left on board the Resolution, and seven in the Discovery. It is difficult to conceive what could have induced these people to propagate so infamous a falsehood.

On Saturday, the 15th, Captain King accompanied our Commodore to Cape Town; and the next day, in the morning, they waited on Baron Plettenberg, the governor, who received them with every possible indication of civility and politeness.

He entertained a great personal esteem for Captain Cook, and professed the highest admiration of his character, and on hearing the recital of his affecting catastrophe, broke forth into many expressions of unaffected sorrow. In one of the principal apartments of the Baron's house, he shewed our gentlemen two pictures, one of De Ruyter, the other of Van Tromp, with a vacant space left between them, which, he said, he intended to fill up with the portrait of Captain Cook; and for this purpose he requested that they would endeavour to procure one for him, on their arrival in Great Britain, at any price. During our continuance at the Cape, we met with the most friendly treatment, not only from the governor, but also from the other principal persons of the place, as well Africans as Europeans.

False Bay lies to the eastward of the Cape; and at the distance of about 12 miles from the latter, on the western side is Simon's Bay, the only commodious station for shipping to lie in. To the N. N. eastward of this bay, there are some others, from which, however, it may with ease be distinguished, by a remarkable sandy way to the N. of the town, which forms a conspicuous object. The anchoring place in Simon's Bay, is situated in the lat. of 34 deg. 20 min. S. and its long. is 18 deg. 29 min. E. In steering for the harbour, along the western shore, there is a small flat rock, known by the name of Noah's Ark; and about a mile to the N. eastward of it, are others, denominated the Roman Rocks. These are a mile and a half distant from the anchoring place; and either to the northward of them, or between them, there is a safe passage into the bay. When the N. westerly gales are set in, the navigator, by the following bearings, will be directed to a secure and convenient station: Noah's Ark S. 51 deg. E. and the center of the hospital S. 53 deg. W. in 7 fathoms water. But if the S. easterly winds

winds should not have ceased blowing, it is more adviseable to remain farther out in 8 or 9 fathoms water. The bottom consists of sand, and the anchors, before they get hold, settle considerably. About two leagues to the eastward of Noah's Ark, stands Seal Island, whose southern part is said to be dangerous, and not to be approached, with safety, nearer than in 22 fathoms water.

On Tuesday, the 9th of May, signal was made for unmooring, and, about noon, we took our departure from Simon's Bay. We had now provisions, live stock, water, and naval stores, aboard in great plenty: also healthy crews, in high spirits, wishing for nothing but a fair wind to shorten our passage home. On the 14th, we got into the S. E. trade wind, and stood to the W. of the islands of Ascension and St. Helena. Wednesday, the 31st, we were in lat. 12 deg. 48 min. S. long. 15 deg. 40 min. W. On Saturday, the 10th of June, the Discovery's boat brought us word, that, in exercising her great guns, the carpenter's mate had his arm shattered in a shocking manner, by part of the wadding being left in after a former discharge; another man was slightly wounded at the same time. On the 12th, it began to blow very hard; and continued so till the next day, when we crossed the line to the northward, for the fourth time during our voyage, in the long. of 26 deg. 16 min. W.

On Saturday, the 12th of August, we descried the western coast of Ireland, and endeavoured in vain to get into Port Galway, but were compelled by violent southerly winds, to stand to the N. The wind continuing in the same quarter, we made the island of Lewis.

On Tuesday, the 22nd, about eleven o'clock, A. M. both ships came to anchor at Stromness in Scotland: from whence the commodore sent Captain King to inform the Lords of the Admiralty of our arrival.

On

On the 30th, we arrived off Yarmouth, in company with his Majesty's sloops of war the Fly and Alderney. Our boats were immediately sent on shore for provisions, and for a spare cable for our small bower, that we had being nearly worn out.

On the 4th of October, 1780, the Resolution and Discovery reached the Nore in safety; and, on the 6th, dropped anchors at Deptford; having been absent four years, three months, and two days.

It is very extraordinary, that in so long and hazardous a voyage, the two ships never lost sight of each other for a day together except twice; the first time, owing to an accident that happened to the Discovery off the coast of Owhyhee; the second, to the fogs they met with at the entrance of Awatska Bay; a striking proof of the skill and vigilance of the subaltern officers. Another circumstance, no less remarkable, is, the uncommon healthiness of the companies of both ships. When Captain King quitted the Discovery at Stromness, he had the satisfaction of leaving the whole crew in perfect health; and, at the same time, the number of sick persons on board the Resolution did not exceed two or three, only one of whom was incapable of service. In the whole course of the voyage, the Resolution lost no more than five men by sickness; the Discovery not one. A strict attention to the excellent regulations established by Captain Cook, with which our readers have been made acquainted, and the use of that excellent medicine, Peruvian bark, may justly be deemed the chief causes, under the blessing of an all-directing Providence, of this extraordinary success.

F I N I S.

CONTENTS of this WORK.

*** This PUBLICATION having *exceeded* the *Quantity proposed*, our *Subscribers* will observe, that we have (agreeable to our *promise* in our *proposals*) delivered the *Overplus* (several sheets) GRATIS, altho' it has occasioned an extraordinary and very heavy expence to the Publisher.

	Page
PREFACE - - -	3
Captain Cook's First Voyage	9
Captain Cook's Second Voyage	373
Captain Cook's Third and Last Voyage - - - -	1185
Byron's Voyage - - -	793
Wallis's Voyage - - -	941
Carteret's Voyage - - -	1029
Directions to the Binder -	2243

N. B. In writing the Histories of the above very valuable and celebrated Voyages round the World, &c. the Editor has not only carefully incorporated all the important Discoveries made by other Voyagers and Circumnavigators, such as Mulgrave, Anson, Parkinson, Lutwidge, Ives, &c. &c. but has also related the Substance of the most remarkable Travels and Journeys to different Parts of the World, particularly those of Hanway, Hamilton, Carver, Dalrymple, and many others.

The great and increasing Sale of this universally approved Work having already occasioned a fresh Impression of the beginning Numbers, on new Types, &c. the Whole is now re-publishing with all the elegant Copper-plates, in only 80 Sixpenny Numbers: one or more to be had at a Time, at the Option of Purchasers - or the Whole complete handsomely bound and lettered, in Six Volumes, Price only £. 2 8 0

DIRECTIONS

DIRECTIONS to the BINDER,

For placing the COPPER PLATES to

COOK's VOYAGES, &c.

IN SIX VOLUMES, Octavo.

*Those marked with a * are folding Plates.*

☞ Divide the Work into Six Volumes in the following Manner:

The First Volume to Page 372.
The Second Volume Page 373, to Page 792.
The Third Volume Page 793, to Page 1184.
The Fourth Volume Page 1185, to Page 1546.
The Fifth Volume Page 1547, to Page 1939.
The Sixth Volume Page 1940, to the End.

	No.	Page
CAPTAIN Cook to face Title, Vol. I.	1	1
Hawkesworth	66	9
General Chart	26	ib.
*Town in the Island of Terra del Fueggo	35	37
Indians of ditto	12	38
View of Horn Island	27	42
* Chart of Island near Otahatie	29	48
View of the Island of ditto	2	ib.
Military Gorget	11	ib.
Mr. Banks receiving a Visit	46	51
Musician, &c.	5	55
A Corps on Toupapow	39	ib.
A Man of Otahatie in Mourning Dress	4	73
* Chart of Island Otahatie	48	89
A Fly Flap	10	ib.
Tattowing Instruments	55	92
Island of Huaheine	9	107
Dance in Otahatie	16	112
Arched Rock	6	129
Inside of a Hippah	80	159
Family in Dusky Bay	67	163
Chart of Cook's Straits	36	165
Man of New Zealand	64	170
A War Canoe	28	174
Endeavor River	5	205
Animal, called Kinguroo	4	207
Tyger, Lion, &c.	77	342
Tynai-mū Frontispiece, Vol. II.	26	
Various Fish, &c.	25	462
Fortifield Town	1	467
Matavia Bay	3	481

DIRECTIONS TO THE BINDER.

	No.	Page
North East View, Otahatie	42	481
* Chart of Matavia Bay	49	ib.
Otai, &c.	5	489
Landing of Captain Cook	72	498
Otago, &c.	39	502
Man of Easter Island	59	526
Monuments in ditto	23	527
A Man of St. Christina, &c.	67	529
A Chief of ditto	65	530
Resolution Bay	40	531
Captain Cook landing Mallicolo	42	599
Man, &c. ditto	61	ib.
Landing Captain Cook at Erramanga	68	601
Captain Cook landing Tanna	76	605
View of the Island of Tanna	64	610
Man of Tanna, &c.	36	621
View of the Island of New Caledonia	75	639
A Man of ditto, &c.	53	648
View of Island of Pines	54	655
Woman, &c. of Christmas Sound	51	675
View of Christmas Sound	45	676
*Plan, Success Bay, &c.	41	679
The Ice Islands	52	704
Possession Bay, Vol. III. Frontispiece,	74	
Sea Lion	17	812
Interview with Commodore Byron	58	820
View of the Lawn, &c.	57	874
Distress of the Success	44	916
View of the Great Cascade	24	948
Crested Falcon	78	960
Natives of Otahatie, &c.	28	986
Oberea of ditto	40	992
Queen of Otahatie taking Leave	31	998
Bread-Fruit-Tree	44	1041
* North Side of Queen Charlotte Islands	60	1055
* Queen Charlotte Islands	58	1066
* Chart of New Britain, &c.	47	1068
* Island of St. John, &c.	45	1071
* Draught of Bonthain Bay	35	1135
Woman, &c. Van Diemen's Land, Frontispiece, Vol. IV.	10	
Captain James King	61	1185
Sir Francis Drake, &c.	21	1187
View, Race Horse, &c.	7	1195
* Map of Kerguelen's Land	18	1267

Perforated

DIRECTIONS TO THE BINDER.

	No.	Page
Perforated Rock	8	1268
Christmas Harbour	18	1271
* Chart, Van Diemens Land	17	1281
Man and Boy of Otahatie	6	1285
* View and Plan of Adventure Bay	32	1289
Opposiiam, &c.	23	1291
Head of Zelander	3	1324
Chest of Zealand	19	1327
Bludgeons, &c. of ditto	48	ib.
Zealand Warriors, &c.	19	1329
Ditto, in proper drefs	37	1330
Man of Mangea, &c.	14	1342
* Mangea Islands, &c.	56	ib.
View at Anamooko	22	1372
Captain Cook at Hapaee	73	1387
Boxing Match	71	1389
A Dance by Women	30	1394
Ditto, by Men	69	1396
Island in Rotterdam	43	1407
King of Friendly Islands	66	1410
An Afi-too-ca	43	1437
A Fiatooka	13	ib.
* Tongataboo Harbour	53	1445
Natchi, &c.	63	1451
* Friendly Islands	15	1472
Boats of ditto	32	1485
Dance in Ulietea	34	1489
Omai, &c.	50	1508
Tupapow in Otahatie	2	1515
Human Sacrifice	65	1535
View of Huaheine, Frontispiece, Vol. V.	72	
Young Woman of Otahatie, &c.	72	1552
Body of Ice	16	1554
Fleet of Otahatie	47	1560
Habit of Priest	8	1566
Island of Ulietea	38	1607
A Morai, &c.	41	1645
* Chart, Society Isles	50	1656
* Christmas-Islands	57	1696
A Morai in Atooi	69	1706
* Chart of Sandwich Isles	20	1718
Inside of House, &c.	11	1720
Man, &c. Sandwich Islands	68	1724
Canoe of ditto	78	1735
* Noetka Sound	55	1757

Man

DIRECTIONS TO THE BINDER.

	No.	Page
Man of Nootka Sound	29	1762
Infide of a Houfe in ditto	79	1767
Habitations in ditto	21	ib.
Inftruments, &c.	46	1771
Californian Women	56	1774
Indian ditto	33	ib.
Snug Corner	25	1793
Woman, &c. in Prince William Sound	15	1796
* Chart of Cook's River	52	1815
Natives of Onalafhka	70	1828
Tfchuktfchi	14	1849
Sea Horfes	80	1856
* North Weft Coaft of America	13	1866
Inhabitants of North Sound	31	1878
* Chart of Norton Sound	7	1881
* Harbour Samganooda	54	1886
A Sea Ottor	74	1899
A Man of Onalafhka	76	1900
Houfe in ditto	79	1902
Canoes of ditto	63	1904
Whale Fifhery	37	1910
Summer, &c. Habitations, Frontifpiece, Vol. VI.	20	
Karakakooa	33	1930
An Offering, &c.	30	1936
King of Owhyhee, &c.	75	1942
* Death of Captain Cook	27	1969
View in Atooi	24	2031
Man, &c. Sandwich Iflands	70	2049
* Bay of Awatfka	51	2076
Man of Kamtfchatka	34	2087
View, Bolcherebzkoi	62	2096
View of Ice Berg	60	2130
White Bear	12	2168
Town of St. Peter, &c.	71	2175
Man of Kamtfchatka	62	2178
Winter Habitations in ditto	77	2194
* Coaft of Japan, &c.	59	2210
* Sulphur Ifland	22	2213
* Sketch of Typa	38	2215
The Vari	49	2236

www.ingramcontent.com/pod-product-compliance
Lightning Source LLC
Chambersburg PA
CBHW021149230426
43667CB00006B/319